THE FORBIDDEN SECRETS OF HYPNOTIC PERSUASION

HOW-TO PERSUADE ANYONE HYPNOTICALLY AND ALWAYS GET WHAT YOU WANT

BRYAN WESTRA

Indirect Knowledge Limited
MURRAY, KENTUCKY

Copyright © 2014 by Bryan James Westra.

All rights reserved. No part of this publication may be reproduced, distributed or transmitted in any form or by any means, including photocopying, recording, or other electronic or mechanical methods, without the prior written permission of the publisher, except in the case of brief quotations embodied in critical reviews and certain other noncommercial uses permitted by copyright law. For permission requests, write to the publisher, addressed "Attention: Permissions Coordinator," at the address below.

Bryan Westra/Indirect Knowledge Limited
2317 University Station
Murray, Kentucky/42071
www.indirectknowledge.com

Book Layout ©2014 indirectknowledge.com

Ordering Information:
Quantity sales. Special discounts are available on quantity purchases by corporations, associations, and others. For details, contact the "Special Sales Department" at the address above.

The Forbidden Secrets of Hypnotic Persuasion: How-To Persuade Anyone Hypnotically And Always Get What You Want
Bryan Westra. —1st ed.
ISBN-10: 0990513254
ISBN-13: 978-0-9905132-5-4

DISCLAIMER

This document is geared towards providing exact and reliable information in regards to the topic and issue covered. The publication is sold with the idea that the publisher is not required to render accounting, officially permitted, or otherwise, qualified services. If advice is necessary, legal or professional, a practiced individual in the profession should be ordered.

- From a Declaration of Principles which was accepted and approved equally by a Committee of the American Bar Association and a Committee of Publishers and Associations.

In no way is it legal to reproduce, duplicate, or transmit any part of this document in either electronic means or in printed format. Recording of this publication is strictly prohibited and any storage of this document is not allowed unless with written permission from the publisher. All rights reserved.

The information provided herein is stated to be truthful and consistent, in that any liability, in terms of inattention or otherwise, by any usage or abuse of any policies, processes, or directions contained within is the solitary and utter responsibility of the recipient reader. Under no circumstances will any legal responsibility or blame be held against the publisher for any reparation, damages, or monetary loss due to the information herein, either directly or indirectly.

Respective authors own all copyrights not held by the publisher.

The information herein is offered for informational purposes solely, and is universal as so. The presentation of the information is without contract or any type of guarantee assurance.

The trademarks that are used are without any consent, and the publication of the trademark is without permission or backing by the trademark owner. All trademarks and brands within this book are for clarifying purposes only and are owned by the owners themselves, not affiliated with this document.

THE TABLE OF CONTENTS

SUSPENDING DISBELIEF AND DOUBT 1

Why Do You Need To Know How-To Suspend Someone's Disbelief And Doubt 3

What You Need To Understand First Before You Learn To Suspend Someone's Disbelief And Doubts 4

How Do We Change Someone's Mind By Asking Them To Suspend Their Disbelief And Doubt 7

How Else Might You Apply Your New Found Knowledge Concerning Doubt And Disbelief To Benefit You In Other Ways As Well 10

Final Purport 11

Take Action Now 13

AN INTRODUCTION TO HYPNOTIC ARCHETYPAL TRIGGERS 17

Why You Want To Know About Hypnotic Archetypal Triggers 19

What You Need To Understand About Hypnotic Archetypal Triggers 22

How Might You Take This Information Concerning Hypnotic Archetypal Triggers And Use It To Hypnotize People To Do What You Want Them To Do 25

How Else Might This Information Be Useful In Other Types Of Contexts 32

Final Purport 34

Take Action Now 37

AFFINITY TO OTHER 41

Why You Need To Understand Affinity To Other To Be Able To Persuade And Influence People Hypnotically 44

What Do You Need To Know In Order To Hypnotically Persuade Others Using Affinity To Other 47

How Do You Hypnotically Influence Someone To Believe Your Persuasions Using Affinity To Other 47

How Else Might This Hypnotic Archetypal Trigger Known As Affinity To Other Be Useful For Helping You Hypnotically Influence And Persuade People To Your Way Of Thinking 49

Final Purport 51

Take Action Now 53

MYSTERY 57

Why Do You Need To Understand The Hypnotic Archetypal Trigger Mystery To Be A More Effective Conversational Hypnotist 58

What Do You Need To Do To Prepare Yourself To Position Yourself And Your Products As Mysterious .. 60

How Do You Use Mystery To Hypnotize People Into Believing Your Persuasions 61

How Else Might You Use Mystery To Hypnotize People To Achieve All The Other Results Besides Indoctrinating Them 63

Final Purport 65

Take Action Now 66

EXCITEMENT 71
- Why You Need To Understand The Hypnotic Archetypal Trigger Known As Excitement To Be Able To Hypnotize People Into Believing Your Persuasions 72
- What You Need To Know About Hypnotic Archetypal Triggers Specifically Pertaining To Excitement 75
- How Do You Persuade Someone By Using The Hypnotic Archetypal Trigger Known As Excitement To Achieve Your Desired Outcomes 77
- How Else Can You Use Excitement And Benefit 78
- Final Purport 80
- Take Action Now 82

EXCLUSIVE 87
- Why You Need To Understand The Principles Of Exclusivity 89
- What You Need To Know Before You Can Position Yourself As Being Exclusive 90

How Can You Position Yourself And Products As Exclusive In Your Marketplace 91

How Else Might You Use Exclusivity To Influence And Persuade Your Hypnotic Subjects 94

Final Purport 96

Take Action Now 97

FORBIDDEN 101

Why You Should Understand The Hypnotic Archetypal Trigger Forbidden 104

What You Need To Understand About The Hypnotic Archetypal Trigger Forbidden So That You Can Hypnotize Your Subjects Into Complying With Your Every Request 107

How To Use The Hypnotic Archetypal Trigger Forbidden To Position Yourself, Your Brand, And Your Products In Such A Way Most People Want Them 109

What Other Ways Can You Use The Hypnotic Archetypal Trigger Forbidden To Change People's Minds About Anything 111

Final Purport 113

Take Action Now 115

ORIGNAL 119

Why Would You Want To Position Your Product Or Service Using The Hypnotic Archetypal Trigger Known As Originality 121

What You Need To Understand In Order To Advertise Someone Using The Hypnotic Archetypal Trigger Originality 123

How Can You Brand Yourself As Original, And Magnetize People To Products And Ideas 124

What Else You Need To Do And Understand In Order To Hypnotize Your Subject Utilizing The Hypnotic Archetypal Trigger Known As Originality 127

Final Purport 129

Take Action Now 130

RARE 135

    Why You Might Want To Know About Rarity In Order To Utilize This Hypnotic Archetypal Trigger To Influence People To Take The Actions That You Want Them To Take 137

    What Do You Need To Understand First And Foremost About Rarity, Before You Implement In Whatever Application You Have Planned For It 138

    How Can You Use The Hypnotic Archetypal Trigger Known As Rarity To Hypnotize People Into Paying The Price You Want In Changing Their Minds 139

    How Else Might You Use Rarity To Change Minds And Get What You Want 142

    Final Purport 143

    Take Action Now 144

POPULAR 149

    Why Do You Need Understand The Hypnotic Archetypal Trigger Called Popularity 151

What Do You Need Understand To Create A Value Proposition Utilizing The Hypnotic Archetypal Trigger Known As Popularity.. 153

How Do You Create Intrinsic Value Utilizing The Hypnotic Archetypal Trigger Known As Popularity.. 153

How-Else You Can Harness The Hypnotic Power Of Popularity To Get What You Want 155

Final Purport... 157

Take Action Now 158

CONTRARY 163

Why Do You Need To Understand This Hypnotic Archetypal Trigger Known As Contrary 167

What You Need To Understand In Order To Apply The Hypnotic Archetypal Trigger Known As Contrast 173

How Do You Use The Hypnotic Archetypal Trigger Contrary In Order To Persuade People Hypnotically 177

What Other Contexts Can Contrary Be Applied In Order To Hypnotically Persuade Other People To Do What You Tell Them To... 179

Final Purport 181

Take Action Now... 181

DIFFERENCE... 185

What You Need To Know In Order To Persuade People Hypnotically Utilizing The Hypnotic Archetypal Trigger Known As Difference................... 186

How To Hypnotize Someone Utilizing The Hypnotic Archetypal Trigger Known As Difference................... 187

How Else Can You Apply Difference To Captivate People's Attention.. 190

Final Purport 192

Take Action Now... 193

HYPNOSIS... 197

Why Do You Need Understand Hypnotism, Before You Understand Conversational Hypnotism 201

Ultradian Rhythms 205

What You Need To Understand In Order To Be Able To Hypnotize Someone 209

How-To Hypnotize Someone 211

What Other Applications Can You Use Hypnosis To Help People...213

Final Purport 214

Take Action Now 217

MILTON ERICKSON'S INDIRECT, COVERT, CONVERSATIONAL HYPNOSIS, AND NLP MODEL OF PERSUASION 221

Advantages Of Conversational Hypnosis 222

Conversational Hypnosis Suggestions 223

A Conversational Induction 240

Fundamental Procedure For Analogical And Tonal Marking 241

Step By Step Instructions To Marking Embedded Commands 243

Creating NLP Anchors 245

NLP Anchoring: Directions To Make NLP Anchors . 248

Respondent Conditioning/Anchoring V. Shaping Behavior 255

Hypnotic Words Create Post Hypnotic Anchors 257

Trancelike words for Post Hypnotic Suggestions 259

Final Purport 260

Take Action Now 261

HYPNOTIC PERSUASION PATTERNS 265

Take Action Now 283

NARRATIVE TRANSPORTATION THEORY: A PERSUASION MODEL FOR HYPNOTIC STORYTELLING 287

Why You Need To Understand The Pure Fundamental Nature Of Narrative Transportation Theory As A Hypnotic Persuasion Model 298

What You Need To Know In Order To Put Into Action This Narrative Transportation Persuasion Model 300

How-To Actually Integrate Narrative Transportation Theory 'Simply' Into Every Hypnotic Story You'll Ever

Tell To Increase The Intensity Of Impact These Stories Have On Your Hypnotic Subjects..................... 303

How Else Narrative Transportation Theory Might Be Applied Successfully To Other Hypnotic Persuasion Contexts 307

Final Purport.. 309

Take Action Now 310

HYPNOTIC STORYTELLING 315

Why You Must Learn Hypnotic Storytelling To Help You Hypnotically Persuade Anyone.............................. 316

What You Should Know About Hypnotic Storytelling 318

How-To Tell Hypnotic Stories To Affectively Move People To Take Action, Change Their Minds, And Give You What You Want.. 323

Basic Transformational Story.. 324

Hypnotic Hero's Journey... 331

Nested Loop Hypnotic Stories....................................... 343

Layering In Hypnotic Elements 348

Trance Signs 349

Final Purport 350

Take Action Now... 351

HOW CULTS MANAGE TO RECRUIT, INDOCTRINATE, DECEIVE, MANIPULATE, CONTROL, HYPNOTIZE, AND BRAINWASH PEOPLE.. 355

Why You Need To Know How Cults Recruit, Indoctrinate, Deceive, Manipulate, Control, Hypnotize, And Brainwash People............................... 358

What You Need To Know Upfront Concerning How Cults Recruit, Indoctrinate, Deceive, Manipulate, Control, Hypnotize, And Brainwash People 359

How-To Recruit, Indoctrinate, Deceive, Manipulate, Control, Hypnotize, And Brainwash People Into Joining And Actively Participating In Your Cult........ 369

What If We Take This Knowledge And Apply It Positively To Other Contexts 375

Final Purport 377

Take Action Now 377
THE BIBLIOGRAPHY 385
THE INDEX 391
MORE BOOKS BY THE AUTHOR 413

Dedicated to Jennifer Bonilla

Almost all people are hypnotics. The proper authority saw to it that the proper belief should be induced, and the people believed properly.

—CHARLES HOY FORT

INTRODUCTION

I hope you read this entire book. Most people never read a book cover to cover. I've been guilty of this myself. This book follows a logical order. In chapter one, you'll learn about the power of disbelief and doubt; namely, how to utilize it for the persuasion context you have in your mind—that is, of course, why you bought this book—to learn how to hypnotize people, change minds and peoples' persuasions. If someone doubts you, or has a disbelief in what you will be persuading them about, then, certainly, you have a problem, do you not? Actually, most people believe this to be so; however, the resistance people have toward your rationalities or irrationalities can, and does, help you more easily persuade them. Those familiar with Ericksonian Indirect Hypnosis will perceive this as being Erickson's 'Utilization Principle' and that would be correct. I'll teach you how to use peoples' doubts and disbeliefs to suck them into your persuasion funnel, and make it simply seem like a walk in the park approach.

The next chapter will introduce you to what I have coined 'Hypnotic archetypal triggers'. This introduction will be followed by ten more chapters, which will teach you in depth about ten of the most profound 'Hypnotic archetypal triggers' that you can immediately use in all of your persuasion contexts instantly to secure attention, interest, desire, and get people to take actions willingly, thinking it is their idea. These 'Hypnotic archetypal triggers' create massive goodwill and immense intrinsic value in your influences, and persuasions. Your hypnotic subjects, prospective cult members, potential customers, or anyone else you wish to persuade hypnotically, sell, or convince of something, will be instantly drawn to you and your persuasions like a powerful magnet attracting all types of metals to it. Adopting these 'Hypnotic archetypal triggers' into your conversations, marketing communications, advertisements, words, and so on, will make you more hypnotic than you will ever be able to imagine. However, the book doesn't stop there...

From Chapter 13, onward, you'll learn and master hypnosis and NLP as they are applied to persuasion contexts. You'll learn conversational hypnosis, or what has also been coined permissive hypnosis, or Ericksonian Hypnosis. You'll learn 54 covert indirect hypnotic language patterns. You'll learn to master hypnotic language. You'll learn how to anchor people to experience emotions you want them to experience, simply by performing an innocuous gesture. You'll learn how to do the same thing, only instead of having your hypnotic subject experience an emotion; they'll be anchored to a trigger that makes them uncontrollably do what you want them to do.

The last chapter is on Hypnotic Storytelling. In this final chapter I teach you in depth how to take everything you've learned from the first chapter to this end most chapter and intertwine it inside a seemingly innocent story. Nothing is less innocent than a story. You'll learn advanced master's level hypnotic storytelling techniques that will leave you astonished, imagining how you ever got along before, without this information you'll have learnt.

I'm telling you forthrightly, and boldly, with absolute confidence, this book will get you what you want. For me to say this isn't something to take light. I'm trained in covert indirect Ericksonian hypnosis, NLP, and psychotherapy, as a master's level practitioner, and I happen to be an international trainer's trainer. I'm rarely overly confident with anyone, let alone bold, and much fewer times forthright. For me to be so direct with you, before you have even had a chance to immerse yourself in the content, means you'll be mind-blown and astonished!

I don't know what your true intentions are for wanting to learn what I will be teaching you in this book. I hope it is for the good of humanity and for the betterment of your own self. I know there will be many who will purchase this book for reasons dishonest, manipulative, and mind controlling. I'm not here to judge anyone. My belief is if this information is used for good, good things will happen. If it is used for bad, bad things will happen.

One thing is for sure…

I have kept nothing from you. I have spilled the beans, so to speak, regarding the world's most secret and forbidden hypnotic persuasion practices; the ones the planet's most powerful people don't want anyone knowing. These skills are not taught in public schools, any more than they're taught in public speaking or interpersonal communication courses in colleges. The reason being: They're forbidden knowledge, and for people who know these skills, it would be imaginably difficult to control them. If you cannot control your sheep, your sheep will go aloof. No shepherd wants this. I hope you get my metaphor.

CHAPTER 1

SUSPENDING DISBELIEF AND DOUBT

I will never forget the first time I heard the words, "I doubt it." I was seven or eight years old, and I asked my father if we were going to town at some point in the day. My father's response was very automatic, he said, "I doubt it." If I had heard those words, "I doubt it" before this first remembered occurrence, I must not have ever paid attention, because I instantly asked my father what the word 'doubt' means. My father tried his best to explain that 'doubt' was more or less saying 'probably not', but my father was a man of few words, so for him to articulate to his young son what this phrase meant, was somewhat of a challenge for him. In this chapter, we are going to be exploring this concept of doubt in great detail. Sometimes when someone says, "I doubt it," they are politely telling you "No." Other times, when someone says, "I doubt it," they are unsure of the outcome, of which you're inquiring of them. Doubt can usually be defined in most circumstances as being equal to the phrase 'probably not'. It doesn't mean emphatically 'no', but the chances of something coming to pass are concluded to be doubtful and improbable. Often times in persuasion scenarios people remain unconvinced, one hundred percent, regarding what they want to do. More often than not, conversely, they have some type of idea about what sort of an outcome they want to achieve. However, they are unsure exactly how to achieve it.

I'm going to teach you why understanding about 'doubt', and why when people are more willing to 'suspend their doubts' and 'disbeliefs' can help you to sell your ideas, products, and persuasions. I'm also going to explain to you what you need to understand to get someone to 'suspend their disbelief' and instantly take to your proposition, so that it becomes probabilistically more likely they will agree to whatever actions you insist they take. After we've covered why this is important and what you need to know, I am then going to take you step-by-step through this process to ensure you correctly get people to suspend their disbelief and doubts. When you can master this, your hypnotic subject will blindly follow whatever direction you lead them toward, to achieve the results you want. After I've taught you how to get someone to suspend their disbelief, I am going to ask you to open up your own mind to understanding and conceiving of other 'what if' scenarios, which having learnt this information will serve you purposefully throughout the rest of your life. In other words, how else might you be able to take this information and use it in other persuasive contexts; beyond the contexts, I'll be describing for you. Sidestepping what first comes to mind, can sometimes, and I would even venture to insist more often than not, will lead to helping you achieve notwithstanding more substantial results as you influence and cause people to adopt a certain position, and your persuasions, regardless if those persuasions are true or not.

Why Do You Need To Know How-To Suspend Someone's Disbelief And Doubt

Transitioning, people already have formed opinions about what they believe and what they don't believe to be true. We've often heard it said, "It's hard to teach an old dog, new tricks." This, again, is a conviction we have all been socially conditioned to believe is true. We take this saying to mean: it's difficult to change someone's mind; expressly, someone who is ardently attached to those beliefs. This may seem like common sense to you. Already, you may be fighting me, in your mind, believing I don't know what I'm talking about, or even worse—assuming I'm advocating it is actually easy to change someone's mind. This is not what I'm advocating. I'm advocating you simply need to encourage someone in the right way to suspend their disbelief's and doubts, whenever those doubts and concerns begin to surface in conversation.

This is important, because if you get someone first to suspend their disbelief and doubt regarding what you're denoting and inferring, you stand a better chance of getting them to change their mind and accept your persuasions.

What You Need To Understand First Before You Learn To Suspend Someone's Disbelief And Doubts

What you first need to understand in order to suspend someone's disbelief and doubt, so you can change their mind about whatever it is you want, is all good things happen during the times in people's lives when they intentionally have chosen to suspend their disbelief and doubts. This is a very powerful point you must understand, in order to change minds and effortlessly persuade people hypnotically. The reason, has to do with getting someone to recollect and re-imagine all the times in his or her life, which have been the best times. Once someone has conjured up in their mind these past experiences, they have also mentally and emotionally reconnected to those earlier states, which were 'buying states'. By 'buying states', I only solely mean it is a time when someone has made a decision to move forward with an idea or purchase, as a result of emotionally drawn to do so. In hypnosis, we call this re-vivification, which is merely someone reliving cerebrally an experience or event. We are very strategically achieving our desired result, by methodically and systematically making our subject relive, inwardly; certain key events in their lives that were most memorable, pleasant, and happy. If you can change someone's state of mind first, you can open them up to accept new ideas and beliefs more easily.

What you must understand past this first principle is you're not asking people to agree with you. Had you asked them not to believe what they believe to be true or suspect as being absolute, then you would've stood in front of a resistance barrier that would have prevented you from being able to change their mind at all. By being more indirect, asking someone simply to suspend their doubt for just a moment, you are opening them up to move in a more agreeable direction—one that will assist you later in helping them change their mind, so they will be more receptive to your ideas.

I want to talk to you a moment about exactly what I mean when I ask someone to suspend their disbelief and doubt. When I look back and reflect on all the times in my life, at what times, I have suspended my disbelief and doubt, I realize these to be some of the most happiest and joyous times in my life. For example, if you take the time I followed my heart, and I got on an airplane bound for India, because I wanted to learn firsthand what India was all about, and learn more about Hinduism and Eastern philosophy, I remember at first I was very doubtful this would ever happen. I remember there was a part of me that said, "Stop! This is outside your comfort zone. At this moment, you cannot jump on an airplane, as you have no money, and because you have responsibilities. It's just not feasible for Bryan." This part of me was an overriding aspect, responsible for influencing the doubts inside of me. At once, I dismissed (rejected) the idea it would be possible for me to pick up and leave my life behind. I managed even to talk myself out of wanting to go, telling myself, "It doesn't make sense to go." One night I was reading the Bhagavad-Gita, and something inside me said, "Just have faith." Somehow when I was thinking about faith, I was thinking about all the times in my life when I thought things wouldn't work out; however, no matter how, in some way, they unfailingly managed to. It was consistently through suspending my disbelief the impossible became possible. I get goose bumps thinking about this. Some people might call these goose bumps me having an incorporeal experience, or a spiritual awakening. I'll just label it goose bumps. I eventually decided, even though the cards were stacked against me, I would take a leap of faith, suspend my disbelief and my doubt, and go anyway. That experience being in India, was one of the most spiritually elevating times of my life. Had I at no time suspended my disbelief and doubt, I never would've had that experience. Most people, who truly live their lives and get to experience such memorable happenings, do so as a result of suspending the disbeliefs which hold them back. Most people regret more the chances they never took; rather, than the ones they took.

How Do We Change Someone's Mind By Asking Them To Suspend Their Disbelief And Doubt

Sometimes asking someone to suspend their disbelief is as simple as doing a couple of things. I want to cover those things now with you in this section, to assist you with helping other people suspend their disbeliefs and doubts, so they may have faith and even blind faith, so they suspend resistance and go with the flow, trusting you. When someone trusts you more than they have confidence in themselves, you truly have power over them to the point they will let you control them and take them in any direction you wish them to go. Influencing and persuading them becomes then becomes easy. So what are the steps?

Step one: simply asking someone to have faith, is often times enough reason for them to suspend their doubt and disbelief. The reason for this happening is most people who have faith in a God or a higher power associate faith with the virtue of being religious or spiritual. If you look at most people, in which they rank the most important things in their lives, for some people, and a great majority of people, faith and God rank above just about anything else. The association of God and faith is something so closely linked to doubting and disbelief; it makes it possible and likely most people will opt to decide to suspend their disbeliefs and doubts in lieu of having faith, taking a leap of faith in the direction you wish for them to go, because of their overwhelming inherent regard for their highest principle.

The second step to getting people to suspend their disbelief is by empathizing with them and acknowledging their concerns. This simply stated means you acknowledge openly that they have concerns, and they may or may not agree with you, but that you would simply ask them to choose to hold on just a moment while you continue explaining your rationale. Most people will be kind enough at this point to give you an opportunity to move on to step three.

Step three requires only that you teach people how every time in their lives, they have suspended their disbelief and doubt that good things happened, which produced positive outcomes. This is when you simply tell them the story, like I related you about my trip to India, where I took a leap of faith and decided to go with the flow and the trust there were factors out there I had no control over, which would assist me along my journey. It's very powerful mojo, telling these stories. The reason for this has to do with the fact all our lives we are told stories about someone who was living in a normal reality, that for whatever reasons decided to fight against normalcy, and venture out into an unknown direction, which became a magically liberating journey for them. This character in these novels and movies are the heroines and heroes which are the protagonists we have come to love and grow close to as onlookers. We always take the side of the protagonists, because a protagonist is a metaphor for ourselves and our own reality. We empathize deeply on a level we don't, in spite of everything understand, with this protagonist character (metaphor), and we remain with them on their journey, until which time the movie is over or that book is shut closed. Counter to siding with the protagonist is siding with the secondary and tertiary characters and notwithstanding in some instances the antagonist, or evil being which wishes to hold the protagonist back from realizing their true nature or forgotten nature. Most often the antagonist is someone we despise, and the very nature of this individual is something we wish not to identify with. When you ask someone to suspend their disbelief and hold back their doubts, you're essentially asking them to have faith in the protagonist archetype they have sided with their entire life. For this reason, it is easy for them to agree to sidestep their doubts and disbelief and take that leap of faith, and take the journey with you, into an unknown reality that can oftentimes be scary and frightening—even unbelievable.

How Else Might You Apply Your New Found Knowledge Concerning Doubt And Disbelief To Benefit You In Other Ways As Well

There are many applications where it may be necessary for you to get someone to suspend their doubt and disbelief. Some of these situations might include getting someone to agree to take you somewhere in their automobile, asking someone for a favor, asking and someone to buy your product. Often times when you ask someone to do you a favor, they might right away doubt you'll ever pay them back. They might also instantly believe that what you're asking for is more than they are willing to deliver and give you. For this reason asking them to take a leap of faith and believe that you'll pay them back, giving them both logical and emotional benefits can help your case. I've seen it often times when someone flat out said no, actually come around and do me the favor that I asked them for. Sometimes this was out of guilt, but more often than not this guilt stems from their desire to not be the antagonist in the story, but rather the person who contributed most to help the protagonist. And by the way, the protagonist is always you. When you need someone to do something for you, or need them to change their mind about a certain issue, you must assume the role of the protagonist, in order for them to identify you as the good guy, and the thing or person holding you back as the antagonist or in layman's terms the bad guy. Again, all of this is deeply rooted in our psychologies, brought about by social conditioning.

Final Purport

One of the most persuasive maneuvers is simply to ask someone to suspend their doubts and disbeliefs and to take a leap of faith—enter your story, trust you, buy from you, join you, and so on. In sales, this can be a lead-in to a closing opportunity. In cult recruitment, this can be a means of decreasing fear and trepidation, giving the sense it is okay to let go, surrender, and let one's self be a part of something or some organization that is not completely understood fully, yet, which is larger than one's own reality. It could simply be to trust someone who may know more than you know to make your decision(s) for you. For some, this suspension of doubt and disbelief is easier than making a decision on one's own behalf. Psychologically, people fear making a poor decision. A simple decision like letting-go, and letting 'god' (or someone else) direct your life path and journey is for many easier and less encumbering.

In this chapter, I shared with you why it is important to suspend doubt. The main attribute of doubt is 'not likely', but not 'no'. The advantage of this attribute is it minimizes the probability of someone saying no, providing you can get them to suspend this doubt for a moment, while you explain logically, while at the same time making an emotional appeal, why it is someone should do what you would have them to do. You must at this point sell your ideas, because resistance has been pushed aside for a time. Before this, resistance, comes back to reject your ideas, you must get your hypnotic subject to commit to taking some action in the direction of the outcome/result you desire. The benefit for you in having someone suspend their doubts is it give you a feeling of certainty and inner strength, because the likelihood of you selling your idea(s) increases exponentially, pushing the probabilities in your favor. You can feel good about the odds, that is.

The easiest way to sell someone on suspending their doubts and disbeliefs is to tell a story about how every time in your life you've suspended your own doubts and disbeliefs you've prospered and come up on top of the world. It could be a story about your uncertainty of getting married, due to the high divorce rate. And, by suspending your doubts and disbeliefs about marriages never working out, you've been able to enjoy a fantastic marriage with the perfect person. Perhaps this person completes you, and keeps you from being lonely, and for this reason suspending your trepidations led you to the best possible outcome. The key ingredient in this preliminary persuasion lesson is to understand that anytime someone suspends their disbelief and takes a forward action; they come up on top almost always. A decision or problem simply cannot be solved without first suspending doubt and disbelief and taking a leap of faith, and trusting everything will work out, regardless how.

As human beings, we don't always have the answers or solutions to life's problems. Rarely, do we act without some suspicion, fear, doubt, or disbelief lingering inside our minds. Only when we let go of resistance and allow things to happen and flow naturally and smoothly for us do we realize such answers and solutions. This is really the key ingredient in overcoming any persuasion hurdle one might become faced with. Master this first lesson, and you've acquired more than most of the top negotiators, salesmen, cult leaders, advertising executives, and marketing professionals.

Take Action Now

In order to get any value whatsoever from this book you must take action now on the instructions I'm going to be laying out for you. Do not be like most people—buy a book, half read it, set it aside, forget about it, never take action, never gain the advantages and benefits it has to offer you.

There is a reason you purchased this book. Do not forget that reason. If you attended one of my live training workshops, you would have participated in doing many exercises at the end of each module I taught you. This is because you get considerably more value practicing the techniques in a safe environment, before going out and practicing them in the real-world. Many people do not feel comfortable testing techniques they've just learnt blindly on real-life contexts. Do not be afraid to do these exercises: They are for your own good and self-development. Your personal power will increase when you proactively apply this knowledge to your specific contexts. Part of learning this information (the largest part) is applying it hands-on. Suspend your doubts and disbeliefs that you can do these exercises, because your insights will elevate to a higher level once you do them. You will only learn a fraction of what I teach in this book from reading the book. The great majority of your learning comes when you apply this information in whatever contexts you have been intentioned on learning it.

To prove this point: Think about your first kiss. You may have talked to friends about their first kiss to get some insight. Maybe you read a book on adolescent sexuality, where kissing was covered. You may have watched movies of actors kissing on the big-screen. Until you actually kissed a girl or guy for the first time, you didn't realize all that was involved in kissing, as you hadn't practiced it, and learned from that experience. I bet after you kissed for the first time, regardless how good or bad the kiss was; you felt pretty amazing afterward, and felt much more confident in kissing other people. I'm right, and you know it, so do these exercises! In fact, make a promise to yourself; you will not move on to the next chapter until these action steps have been completed. You'll thank yourself. I promise.

I. Make yourself take out a piece of paper and a pen/pencil and write down exactly how you'll utilize the information found in this chapter to fit your particular persuasion context.

II. Find an opportunity to apply what you learned in this chapter and apply it. After you have taken this initial action, journal your discoveries and results.

III. Take a 3x5 index card and summarize the leading points from this chapter. Let this summary serve as a quick flash card to jog your memory once a day, as you continue reading this book, and doing future exercises. This is important, because this book has a lot of information, and a fast flash card to look at daily will help you not to forget what you have learned. Over time, this knowledge will become imprinted on your hypnotic mind, where you'll take action on this knowledge without thinking about it consciously.

IV. Teach what you have learned in this chapter to a trusted friend whom you think might benefit. Teaching information to others helps you gain greater clarity and insights you'd likely not have gained trying to keep it all in your own mind.

V. Discuss with the friend you've taught this information to and take notes on their thoughts and understanding of the material. This way, you'll gain another person's perspective and likely gain a deeper understanding of the material.

After you have successfully completed each of these exercises, only then, proceed in moving forward to the next chapter. Do not take shortcuts and tell yourself the lie you'll come back and do the exercises later. Statistically speaking the probability is improbable you ever will. Take a leap of faith and do the exercise, please! Trust me; it's worth it, if you want to gain true mastery in hypnotic persuasion.

====================xx==================

CHAPTER 2

AN INTRODUCTION TO HYPNOTIC ARCHETYPAL TRIGGERS

When I was a kid, I went through a series of stages in which I was attracted to different ideas and philosophies that were outside the norm of my childhood existence. I've always found it interesting to learn about things that seemed mysterious, for bid in, rare, and outside my reality. I think this is one reason many people engage in watching television, movies, good books, doing online research about things they have no clue about; namely, because there are definite Hypnotic archetypal triggers that attract our attention, and have the power to affect our psyche, which can even lead to certain behaviors. There is a process formula that individuals go through when deciding to act. Usually this is brought on by some type of stimulus and the outside environment in which we call reality. Take a child, for example, who watches movies about martial arts and ninjitsu, and then sooner rather than later starts to karate chop doors, and brothers and sisters. You might think this is common sense: The child sees the ninja jumping walls and throwing flying stars, all dressed in a mysterious black uniform not to reveal his or her true identity, and the child becomes interested and absorbed in this fantasy world of the ninja. So what does a child do? The child begins to act out in a manner that reflects his or her attachment for wanting to sustain the belief that he/she can also be a ninja. Being a ninja is exciting. Being a ninja insinuates you have special powers, you have total self-confidence, you believe in an honor system and a certain type of value system. All the things inside the child, that may be lacking, are identified with through this archetype, which will simply be named 'ninja'.

Hypnotic archetypal triggers are actually the essence behind the archetype labeled 'ninja'. And, this could be true for any type of archetypal character you could possibly think of. The essences behind these archetypes are what we all find ourselves attracted to, without knowing why, and even wishing and wanting desperately to align our own identities with. To prove this: Have you ever liked something and didn't know why you liked it? Answer: It was the hypnotic archetypal trigger behind what you liked, that was the secret magnetic power causing you to be attracted to it.

Over the next several chapters, I'll be taking you through some of these hypnotic archetypes, which people often find themselves drawn to. It is important to understand these hypnotic archetypes, because they can be used as powerful influence mechanisms to persuade other people in a particular direction, you wish to persuade them. In this, chapter, I'm going briefly to present you with the 10 Hypnotic archetypal triggers that I'll be going into greater detail with throughout the next several chapters of this book. I'm going to explain to you why you need this overview in order to be successful in mastering these Hypnotic archetypal triggers. Then I'm going to walk you through everything you need to know before you start engaging in all the things you'll later learn in this book. I will also teach you how-to study these hypnotic archetypal triggers. And lastly, I will go one step further and bring into your awareness how else you might want to think about applying these hypnotic archetypal triggers in other contexts beyond one-on-one communication with another person.

Why You Want To Know About Hypnotic Archetypal Triggers

As I have mentioned, hypnotic archetypal triggers are the essence behind classic storytelling archetypes. By essence, I simply mean they are the hidden attributes working covertly in the backdrop to create and develop a character's personality. Personality is something that is typically developed through one's environment and cultural upbringing. As children we're conditioned to survive within our environment. Most of this conditioning is indoctrinated to us by our parents, teachers, mentors, and other people whom we communicate with regularly. We are also told stories, allowed to watch television programming, let go to movies, and listen to other people's accounts of things that have happened to them in their pasts. A lot of things, such as the stories we hear, equally important have a profound impact on how we view the world. We learn early on that there is the 'real world', and then there is the land of fantasy, imagination, and so on. We live in a world of rationality and logic, as well, the parallel world of imagination, play, and the things that dreams are made of. Sometimes people gravitate toward the world of logic and reasoning, and common sense, and, then, sometimes, they gravitate toward things in which faith is built upon. Faith is simply believing in something and calling it true, without any substantial proof that it is true. Another way of looking at faith is to say that it is the belief in a lie.

Is something that is said, which isn't necessarily true, something more likely than not false? So you might be thinking I am presenting you with this idea there are things that are right and true, based, in reality, and there are things, which are false and wrong and based outside of what we might call reality. All of this is completely debatable. People find themselves in these types of debates all the time. Much of what determines our beliefs stem from whatever state of mind we happened to be in at a particular time in our lives. Human beings go through evolutionary stages of belief. As children, it's easy for us to believe in make-believe, to play pretend, to immerse ourselves in our own imaginations. We make up fairytales to tell our brothers and sisters. We intentionally daydream about our lives being different than what the actual reality registers. For some children, who grow up in not so nice circumstances, dissociating from reality and associating with a robust pretend reality can mean the difference between survival and happiness. For some, it may make more sense to believe in a higher power protecting, guiding, and loving us unconditionally. For others, such a notion may be perceived as silly rubbish, ridiculousness, craziness, or even poor decision-making. I am not here to debate what is right and wrong. Notwithstanding it is debatable to suggest that what we perceive as reality, i.e. the rational world we live in— where logic, rules, order, and critical thinking dominate— that even this type of constrained reality is a false reality itself.

What we're interested in understanding is the essence of an archetypal character we have defined. You need to know behind every ninja is an essence of mysteriousness, forbidding secrecy, and rarity. Because, things like mystery and forbidden secrecy are qualities that essentially help to attract people to certain realities, where they identify themselves with these realities, and then feel compelled to maintain these identities. Even though this is the essence of what's behind the character traits, these types of essences can be substantially abstract in nature. Let me give you an example: take the word forbidden, and try to define it. Sure you can go to the dictionary, and find the definition there, but what I'm asking you to do is conjure up in your mind what this abstract idea of something being for bidden is really all about. What is the deeper rooted essence of the word for bidden? For example, in some cultures, where Christianity is prevalent as a religion, forbidden goes all the way back to the days of Adam and Eve where the two characters acted against the will of God and ate the forbidden fruit. There's a psychological principle at play here. Human beings want what they can't have. These are the reason children below the age of eighteen will find ways to break the law and purchase cigarettes, and alcoholic beverages. Some adults would say, "Well, kids will be kids!" So, looking at these hypnotic archetypal triggers, which provoke people to act in a certain way, in a manner, defies logic and reason. These triggers can be very motivational, and when understood can be used to influence other people to think, behave, and act in a fashion you want them to.

What You Need To Understand About Hypnotic Archetypal Triggers

To begin with, you must understand these triggers are prevalent in all societies around the world. They form the basis of erratic behavior, and questionable actions. This is the reason marketers are able to get you to buy their products. You also need to understand whenever you're positioning an idea or product in front of a group of people or even an individual these triggers, when used strategically, can activate instant reactions by the members of that group or a single individual. What else you need to understand is we're all susceptible to these hypnotic anchors, and when they're presented to us as a stimulus, we are unconsciously hypnotized to respond unthinkingly. Depending on how well these hypnotic archetypal triggers are anchored in front of us perceptually, will determine the likelihood of the response we give.

Stop for just a moment. Engage in a little thought experiment: I want you to imagine just for a moment that you're the father or mother of a 13-year-old daughter. You have taken care of this child her entire life. You've showered her with love, affection, and protection. You read her bedtime stories when she was a little. You introduced her to your religion and your beliefs in God. And you instilled in her certain values and beliefs that define for her what is a good person. This 13-year-old daughter has always played by the rules, and for the most part, been a loving daughter. Then one day out of the blue your daughter comes to you crying. Instantly, you stop doing everything you were engaged in, and go to her to find out what is the matter. She tells you she's pregnant, and she's going to have a baby. Stop!

Thank you for doing that. What I want to do next is dissect this little story. In the story, we have a couple of archetypes. We have the caring and sheltering parents. We also have a young lady who, for the most part, has always played by the rules and been an affectionate daughter toward her parents. She's just now reaching adolescence, and she is dropping bad news onto her parents. Now I say, "bad news," but what I'm really saying is she's coming to her parents and alerting them something has happened and is more than likely going to have some shock value. When you found out the daughter who was only thirteen years of age was pregnant, I want you to ask yourself how you felt? Where did your mind go to? Were you shocked? Did you have some type of suspicion before the bad news got dropped, that more than not there was going to be some type of climax, and it wasn't distinctly possible it was going to be all that positive? Some people, may have notwithstanding experienced an afterthought in which they questioned what they would actually do in this type of scenario. The daughter is an archetype which represents purity and perhaps global mess, and possibly unvarying weakness. These are attributes we might generally associate with this type of archetype. We are conditioned to believe certain attributes exist whereas a small young girl is concerned. This is proven in we educate our children about right and wrong, so we can protect them from the forces of evil that lurk in the backdrop of darkness. These evil characters, can be a parent's worth worse nightmare. We start to conjure up ideas and thoughts of what this nightmare looks like. We have emotions that surface whenever this archetypal nightmare becomes a thought in our mind. These emotions even though they're directed and connected to a certain thought or idea, can actually cause us to behave in completely neutral circumstances quite differently. These types of thoughts can become bottled up, stored in our minds, and compounded until we become overly protective parents, extremely angry individuals, or start to formulate beliefs that are baseless presuppositions we start buying into in the other areas of our life.

You need to understand all of this, because this is the foundation of where we're going in this book, as we start to identify some of these essential hypnotic archetypal triggers our behaviors have become anchored to.

How Might You Take This Information Concerning Hypnotic Archetypal Triggers And Use It To Hypnotize People To Do What You Want Them To Do

After we go through the next ten chapters, exploring ten powerful hypnotic archetypal triggers, I'm going to teach you conversational hypnosis and how to use language in a way where you can hypnotize people conversationally, without them being aware they're hypnotized. This will be useful, because then you'll be able to use your knowledge of hypnotic archetypal triggers and quickly put people under your hypnotic spell. You will be getting them to do what you want them to do. You will be the puppet master pulling the strings. For now, the steps you need to be concerned with are:

I. First, you need to understand that the effect of each of these Hypnotic archetypal triggers bring to the table of influence and persuasion.

II. Second, you need to be able to decipher intuitively, which Hypnotic archetypal triggers will work best in certain given contexts.

III. Third, you need to understand is how to drop someone into trance using these hypnotic archetypal triggers they're already anchored to.

What you effectively want is to hold a conversation with someone and slowly begin asking them questions—determining what their fears are, what brings them joy, and basically just to find out what makes them tick. Once you achieve this goal, the next thing you want to do is start to test some of the anchors by triggering them with certain hypnotic means. These set-ups can be stories. They can be questions. They can be statements. Once you have triggered one of these anchors, you'll know how deeply rooted that anchor is, based on the response and behavior you obtain from that individual. Going back to the example I adduced using the young girl who tells her parents she's pregnant: Different people reading this book, will have a different response based on that hypnotic archetypal trigger, in which they have been socially conditioned to respond to. For some, they will want angrily to go in search of the boy or individual who got their daughter pregnant. They're angry, and their defenses have now turned to maternal offenses—their needs to be retribution for this act, which has occurred unjustly. The trigger has been set off by the young girl's conversation. This has caused the change in the state of the parent listening to what the daughter has to say. The state that happens, though predictable, can bring about slightly different reactions by the parents. The parents may feel as though their daughter has dishonored them. The parents may wish to disown the daughter in some instances. The parents may become more protective of the daughter. In other circumstances, the parents may even be overjoyed their daughter is having a baby. When we watch television or movies, and see these types of roles play out, we're not only becoming socially conditioned, we're becoming empathetic to the characters on the screen in front of us. Occasionally, we say things we don't mean, and we use the excuse we're not in the right state of mind. Sometimes the change in state causes us to act in ways we normally would never act. You might be thinking if someone had gotten your 13-year-old daughter pregnant, straightaway, you would find this person and kill them. Some people might very well do this. Others may think of killing; although, because of their social conditioning, and believing killing is wrong, these individuals wouldn't actually follow through with the act of killing someone. What underlie the probability of one's behaviors are hypnotic archetypal triggers we've become most empathetic to, and educated and indoctrinated about the deepest.

There is a technique in hypnosis known as repetition. When something is repeated enough times, it becomes true. I want you to think about how many programs on television or in movies where a young girl has had to confront her parents about being pregnant. Think about that... Now, consider what the parental responses have been? Have they mostly been anger and disappointment? The more something is repeated, the more hypnotized we become; yet, the more conditioned we become to believe it is the truth.

Now I want to do another thought experiment with you, so we might transition into how else this information could be useful for you. I want you to think about a few minutes ago when I asked you to imagine your 13-year-old daughter came to you and told you she was pregnant. When you think back to how you felt at that exact moment, were you expecting me to have you consider that type of reality? It was rather random, was it not? Now I want you to think a little further out and ask yourself did you go from an emotional state where you were highly susceptible and erratic in your thought process to quite quickly coming back to your senses—to realize this was only a thought experiment. When you started leaving that state of emotion to circumnavigate back to logic and reason, did you feel a shift start to take place? Stories have the ability to interrupt our lives for a short period of time. The connection we have with stories can feel every bit as real as the connection we have with everyday life. The vivid image of the experience I had you consider for our thought experiment became a trigger access for certain emotions. This image activated, what most television programs you've watched have triggered inside you—an emotional response to a thought. Then what happens is a fading off of that heightened emotional response until conscious awareness and critical-thinking return. This usual logical and rational state of mind, by the way, is where we do most of our critical-thinking. Critical-thinking is important, because it allows us to plan out matters logically—sidestepping our own emotional irrationalities.

When someone is in a highly emotional state of mind logic and reason go out the window, generally. They tend to react without critical thinking. You can present suggestions and ideas to someone in such a highly irrational state, i.e. an emotional state and presented in the right way will act on your instructions thoughtlessly. The way in which we communicate with someone to get them to do what we want them to do is through indirect communication. We will be covering this in much more detail later in the book. First learn the hypnotic archetypal triggers, because they activate the unconscious hypnotic mind thoughtlessly. They invoke automatic attraction to whatever we associate them to. If we're selling a product, and associate them to a product, they make the product instantly more valued and attractive. They create intrinsic value, which can make anything more valuable to someone. You have to be careful though, because they can, if used in the wrong way, make something less valuable than the practical value it actually possesses.

Consider someone who is upset with you. Imagine this scenario in your mind. Where do you tend to have the better outcome: (a) when you communicate with this person using a direct approach without any sensitivity toward their emotional state, or (b) when you take a moment to understand this person is in an erratic state of mind, and you need to be more passive—to bring them back down to earth, so to speak, communicating with them cautiously? I'm going to suggest the latter, i.e. option '(b)' seems more likely the answer. It really is, isn't it? A lot of times when someone is in a relationship with someone, and their partner has done something to displease them; they may go so far as to say, "Don't talk to me," or say, "Just leave me alone. You don't want to go there, right now!" This is because we have become conditioned to know better. We learn early on in life, most of us, that in an emotional state, we will have the tendency to say things and do things that otherwise we would never say or do. People who are able to realize this, i.e. that their mental state could cause them to act in a way not appropriate, or that could cause them to regret later, will probably, through past experiences, pause, and take time to calm down before responding or acting impetuously. For others, they may simply act irresponsibly and irrationally in ways that will be detrimental to the relationships. Later, they might regret their responses and their actions. Some though, chances are, in order to alleviate the dissonance and uneasiness, they're experiencing, will simply rationalize away the situation, after the fact. This is what happens when people go to buy a brand-new car. They might get on the dealership lot, be confronted by a slick energetic salesperson, and the salesperson may activate some of these hypnotic archetypal triggers through mere conversation, and the individual may very well walk off the lot with the automobile, only later to come to learn they were ripped off—charged way too much for the vehicle, and basically took advantage of. For some this may cause cognitive dissonance, which in this case is 'buyer's remorse'. This buyer's remorse may cause them to want to take the car back, or simply decide not to do business with that dealership again. More often than not, however, an individual will start to false-rationalize all the reasons the car purchase was actually a good decision on their part. For example, they might say to themselves, "The car that will assist me in generating even more money, because I'll be saving on gasoline, because now I have a smaller, extra fuel efficient engine." They come up with some logical justification for why it is satisfactory they got taken advantage of. We see this happening in many other contexts as well; not just car buying.

How Else Might This Information Be Useful In Other Types Of Contexts

Knowing hypnotic archetypal triggers exist, make it possible to take advantage of people's emotional states. How this can be achieved is simply by activating the anchored response, which is the trigger. This will, then in turn, cause the individual to enter a certain responsive state. When someone is in a highly elevated emotional state, they become more susceptible to relying on other people's advice, over their own. The reason for this is they no longer trust they are capable of making logical decisions. They rely on other people to make up their mind for them as a safety net. Therefore the thing to keep in mind is being that trusted friend. I know this is a very general answer, hence let me give you an example how to apply it. Let's, for instance, assume your partner in crime, i.e. boyfriend/girlfriend, wife/husband has already indicated to you where they want to eat at for dinner. Maybe you don't want to eat there. Perhaps you're vegetarian, and the restaurant they wish to eat at is a steakhouse. Let's say you want to change their mind about eating there. You might say something like, "My friend was telling me just the other day that restaurant nearly shut down because rats were discovered gnawing into the steaks, and management turned a blind eye and served them to the general public. In fact, I heard several people even got sick from the steaks. We can go there; however, you might want to order something other than the steak you were wanting." This seems like an argument that might get some result. Once this person has entered into a disgusted emotional state, mentally imagining these dirty disease-ridden rats eating the steaks at this restaurant, he or she will likely be up for any other suggestion. The hypnotic archetypal trigger is not the actual rats which have eaten the steaks, rather the essence of what a rat represents. The hypnotic archetypal trigger is the mysterious nature typifying the rat. This mystery can sometimes be intriguing in some circumstances, except in the type of circumstance we're talking about here, with rats eating steaks, as here the mysterious nature of the rat is quite different. This type of mystery is one we want to shy away from and not entertain in our minds. Most of us have been taught rats carry diseases, they are to be avoided at all cost, and if you see one you should perhaps call an exterminator, because you have a problem. We have sayings in our society such as, "You dirty rat." These easily drum-up the colorings of what a rat represents. They are filthy, dreaded creatures. For this reason, the effect this type of anchoring will have on the individual who is very excited one moment to go to this steakhouse, is now thinking about rats, management turning a blind eye, and people getting poisoned. And just as they would avoid any rat; they will also avoid the restaurant as well, which is an anchor to this image in their mind. The restaurant now has an association that is linked to the hypnotic archetypal trigger of fearful mystery, and that is the core essence of the rat archetype. The restaurant is the anchor that triggers this deep emotion, which, by the way, is much stronger a reaction than the thought of eating steak. The hypnotic archetypal trigger is stronger than the desire of eating steak. The decision not to go to the restaurant ever again is made. We will talk more about NLP anchors in a future chapter, to clarify this point better.

Final Purport

Throughout this chapter we talked in depth about the hypnotic archetypal triggers in the general sense.

I shared why you need to understand them; telling you, people can be emotionally triggered by these already predominant hypnotic anchors. These anchors are usually brought about more so by our social conditioning, than brought about by actual experiences. Because of repetition and constantly hearing stories in the media that some things are favorable, while other things are less favorable, we naturally have hot wired into our brains an automatic reaction to these hypnotic archetypal triggers. I then took you into an explanation of what you needed to understand before you could digress further into this book. I told you what you need to understand on a fundamental level are hypnotic triggers aren't the actual archetypes themselves, but the deeper meaning rooted at the essence of an archetype. What we associate on a value scale makes us more or less attracted to the things we're attracted to. Remember the thought experiment, to contrast how emotions have a tendency to become deactivated. This means we may find ourselves immediately emotional whenever one of these hypnotic archetypal triggers is activated due to the imprinting of these triggers in our brains. Once we're emotionally susceptible, logic and reason go out the window, until some time has passed, and we slowly start coming back to having common sense, which is our logical and rational state of mind.

As we continue venturing through this book, I want you to understand I'm going to be using some terminology for these two metaphoric minds. Some people call the logical mind the 'conscious mind', and call the emotional mind the 'subconscious mind' or 'unconscious mind'. In this book, my preference is to call the logical mind simply the 'mind', and to call the emotional mind the 'hypnotic mind'. The reason I prefer the hypnotic mind to the subconscious mind or unconscious mind, is because, for one, the hypnotic mind is consistently active seeing things and experiencing things we're not experiencing invariably at a conscious level. We are still experiencing it though, that is, we're experiencing it through our emotions, and outside the limitations of consciousness. When we're not in the state of consciousness, and yet we're not actually asleep, we're in the main hypnotized. For this reason when you activate someone's emotional mind, you are activating their hypnotic mind. In other words, life is happening, but because they are emotionally directed and focused very narrowly in one direction, the rest of them loses sight of all other conscious activities. In this state of mind, it is very easy to slip in covert suggestions and instructions, that later, after the person has become less emotional, will start to identify with rationally. They might even assume your ideas are their ideas, and for such reasons desire very much to act on those considerations.

Trust me, we're just barely scratching the surface of everything you're going to be learning in this book, and yet you're already so much further ahead than many people who have studied influence and persuasion most of their lives. I'm talking about sales professionals, expert negotiators, teachers, partners, and just about anyone really, because in the scheme of things, we're all trying on some level to reinforce our own beliefs—trying to get other people to believe our personal persuasions. We are all influencing other people; we are all being influenced by other people.

Take Action Now

In order to get any value whatsoever from this book you must take action now on the instructions I'm going to be laying out for you. Do not be like most people—buy a book, half read it, set it aside, forget about it, never take action, never gain the advantages and benefits it has to offer you.

There is a reason you purchased this book. Do not forget that reason. If you attended one of my live training workshops, you would have participated in doing many exercises at the end of each module I taught you. This is because you get considerably more value practicing the techniques in a safe environment, before going out and practicing them in the real-world. Many people do not feel comfortable testing techniques they've just learnt blindly on real-life contexts. Do not be afraid to do these exercises: They are for your own good and self-development. Your personal power will increase when you proactively apply this knowledge to your specific contexts. Part of learning this information (the largest part) is applying it hands-on. Suspend your doubts and disbeliefs that you can do these exercises, because your insights will elevate to a higher level once you do them. You will only learn a fraction of what I teach in this book from reading the book. The great majority of your learning comes when you apply this information in whatever contexts you have been intentioned on learning it.

To prove this point: Think about your first kiss. You may have talked to friends about their first kiss to get some insight. Maybe you read a book on adolescent sexuality, where kissing was covered. You may have watched movies of actors kissing on the big-screen. Until you actually kissed a girl or guy for the first time, you didn't realize all that was involved in kissing, as you hadn't practiced it, and learned from that experience. I bet after you kissed for the first time, regardless how good or bad the kiss was; you felt pretty amazing afterward, and felt much more confident in kissing other people. I'm right, and you know it, so do these exercises! In fact, make a promise to yourself; you will not move on to the next chapter until these action steps have been completed. You'll thank yourself. I promise.

I. Make yourself take out a piece of paper and a pen/pencil and write down exactly how you'll utilize the information found in this chapter to fit your particular persuasion context.

II. Find an opportunity to apply what you learned in this chapter and apply it. After you have taken this initial action, journal your discoveries and results.

III. Take a 3x5 index card and summarize the leading points from this chapter. Let this summary serve as a quick flash card to jog your memory once a day, as you continue

reading this book, and doing future exercises. This is important, because this book has a lot of information, and a fast flash card to look at daily will help you not to forget what you have learned. Over time, this knowledge will become imprinted on your hypnotic mind, where you'll take action on this knowledge without thinking about it consciously.

IV. Teach what you have learned in this chapter to a trusted friend whom you think might benefit. Teaching information to others helps you gain greater clarity and insights you'd likely not have gained trying to keep it all in your own mind.

V. Discuss with the friend you've taught this information to and take notes on their thoughts and understanding of the material. This way, you'll gain another person's perspective and likely gain a deeper understanding of the material.

After you have successfully completed each of these exercises, only then, proceed in moving forward to the next chapter. Do not take shortcuts and tell yourself the lie you'll come back and do the exercises later. Statistically speaking the probability is improbable you ever will. Take a leap of faith and do the exercise, please! Trust me;

it's worth it, if you want to gain true mastery in hypnotic persuasion.

====================xx==================

CHAPTER 3

AFFINITY TO OTHER

I want you to imagine for the moment a young teenage girl texting on her smart phone to her best friend. Now imagine an older gentleman with graying hair wearing a suit. Have you got those images in your mind? There is not a lot of similarity between the older man wearing a suit and the young teenage girl texting on her mobile device. For this reason, there is a 'disconnect'. Provided that the young girl and the aged gentleman sat down across from each other in a coffeehouse one can only envisage what the conversation would consist of. Let's suppose the older gentleman is a sales representative trying to sell the juvenile girl a new home. Straightaway it doesn't seem conceivable the young girl would want to buy a new home from him, does it? Now there are exceptions to every rule, but generally, young girls don't invest in real estate. And to be fair about this, we don't know anything about the young girl any more than we know anything about the older gentleman selling the house. All we know is what we're presented with on the surface. I want you to imagine again this young girl texting on her mobile device. I want you also to imagine a teenage boy roughly her same age sitting on a picnic table at a local park. Do you have that mental image in your mind? Good! At the present time I want you to imagine the youthful girl holding her cell phone, sitting across from the teenage boy sitting at the picnic table bench in the park. Imagine now the teenage boy is trying to talk the adolescent girl into having sex with him.

Okay, sorry about that graphic, nonetheless, I assure you I'm going somewhere with all this. I want you now to imagine instead of the teenage boy sitting across from the girl, trying to convince her to have sex with him, instead is the older gentleman trying to convince the young girl to have sex with him. Again, I'm sorry about the graphic. Now, I want you to imagine the teenage boy and the teenage girl sitting in the coffeehouse, and the adolescent boy trying to sell her a piece of real estate he owns.

Now that we have played out all four of these imaginative pretend scenarios, I want you to think about what determines the likely outcome of each. Do you think the youthful girl ended up buying the house from the older gentleman? Do you think the adolescent girl ended up having sex with a teenage boy her own age? Do you think that the young girl ended up having sex with the older gentleman who was generations apart in age? Lastly, do you think the teenage girl bought the piece of property from the teenage boy? Out of these four scenarios, the one scenario which seems to be the most believable, and likely, is the scenario where the young girl is sitting across the picnic table from the juvenile boy, who's trying to influence her into having sex with him. Why do you think this is?

The answer to this is what we'll be studying in this chapter. There is a hypnotic archetypal trigger called *affinity to other*. Affinity to other in layman's terms means "You and I are alike." There is a similarity between the youthful girl and teenage boy. They are both roughly the same age, and they almost certainly have a lot of common interests. Being teenagers, both children are in all likelihood to a certain extent hormonal, and a little bit inexperienced if not completely inexperienced with sexual intercourse. The act of having sex to these teenagers may be perceived as forbidden, mysterious, and even rare. Perhaps, there aren't always that many opportunities for young people, who generally live with their parents, to escape the banes of everyday routine to engage in activities with members of the opposite sex. Hypnotic archetypal triggers such as mystery, forbidden, and rarity, are not what I want to talk about in this chapter. What I want to talk about in this chapter is a similarity between the teenage boy and girl.

Throughout this chapter I'm going to be teaching you why you need to know this particular hypnotic archetypal trigger; to be exact, 'affinity to other'. I'm also going to give you the information you need to know in order to be able to use this hypnotic archetypal trigger to influence and persuade other people in certain contexts. I finally am going to show you exactly how you can use affinity to other to position yourself in front of other people so they embrace you, buy from you, and are more likely believe your persuasions. After we cover all of this material, I will take part with you in thinking of other ways you might apply affinity to other to benefit you as well.

Why You Need To Understand Affinity To Other To Be Able To Persuade And Influence People Hypnotically

In neuro linguistic programming or NLP, there is a rapport principle, which suggests people like people like themselves. If you're a sales professional, and you're walking in on a sales call, introducing yourself for the first time to potential customer, you only have a few brief period of time to engage them and build rapport with them, drastically to increase your chances of being able to do business with that individual. This can be done by pointing out objects in that prospective customer's office that may have some type of significance or meaning to them on a personal level. For instance, say you see your prospective customer has a fish mounted up on their office wall, with a name tag that reads the same as the name tag on that potential customer's desk. You might start to draw the conclusion this person is interested in fishing. If you happen to know anything about fishing, or enjoy fishing whatsoever, you may wish to comment on that fishing trophy, to get more clarity and insight into the thinking and belief structures of that potential customer. This can be a segue into introducing your product later. So let's pretend this scenario actually happened. Let's assume you know a little about fishing. And, let's also assume this potential customer is a professional fisherman, when he's not running his mechanic's shop. So we start the conversation off by simply inquiring about the trophy. After that the potential customer starts to share the story behind the trophy, explaining to you how he came to earn it. You subsequently start asking more questions about fishing, only to learn this gentleman spends most of his free time out on the lake engaging in his best-loved activity, fishing. Because, you are a fisherman, outside your day-to-day sales job, you start telling him where some of your favored fishing holes are, and before you know it the conversation moves in the direction of fishing, and further and further away from your intention for being there in the first place, which is to sell him some type of advertising, let's say. After a few minutes, and several fishing stories later, you're both laughing, and really enjoying each other's company. As a result, when you start to present your sales pitch to this individual, because you have built rapport with this person, it increases your opportunity to make a sale. Why? The answer is very simple: you made the sale, because you and he are alike. You have equivalent interests. And because you like the same things, the prospective customer feels relaxed around you, and believes on a deeper level, a level (one that he or she is unaware of unaware of) you have their best interest at heart. They feel easy around you, and people like to do business with people they feel comfortable with, and people they trust. We tend naturally to trust people who are like ourselves. Because we know ourselves so well inwardly, we like other people like ourselves, and as a result we do business with them.

If we revisit the scenario between the teenage boy and the teenage girl, we see a common thread; that is to say, they have common interests, and as such the adolescent girl more closely aligns herself with the juvenile boy. The aged gentleman, on the other hand, may be more representative of a fatherly figure to the girl, and because this person represents authority over her, there is a 'disconnect' between the two of them, and so the young girl withdraws herself from doing business with the older gentleman. The closer we are aligned to other people, i.e. like them; the more we increase our chances of persuading them to do what we want them to do.

What Do You Need To Know In Order To Hypnotically Persuade Others Using Affinity To Other

You first must know that you are not always going to be equally aligned with someone in age. This is not necessarily that important. It does help though. Going back to our example of the salesman and the mechanic, we established commonality through a shared activity—fishing. This was all it took to create camaraderie between the two of them. So what you need to know first with affinity to other is it doesn't always matter that the commonality is age; rather, the most important thing to know is there should be an interpersonal link that connects personalities in such a dynamic way both individuals sense intuitive similarity. The more closely aligned you are with the person you want to hypnotically persuade, the more you increase your chances of being able to win them over to your side of an argument, or get them to accept a belief you want them to have.

How Do You Hypnotically Influence Someone To Believe Your Persuasions Using Affinity To Other

The first step to creating commonality is to harness the power of this hypnotic archetypal trigger known as 'affinity to other'. This commonality can take the form of interests, personality, likes and dislikes, and even socioeconomic background. Next up is to identify yourself as an archetype that most closely resembles the archetype the person you're wishing to hypnotically persuade is exhibiting to you. This means matching and mirroring the same representation that is being reflected from them to you. Matching and mirroring are NLP terms. Matching someone's behavior is done by covertly replicating the behavior they are presenting to you. For example, if someone you're trying to influence keeps scratching their head with their right hand, you might suddenly do the same and scratch your head with your right hand. Mirroring is very closely the same; the only difference would be instead of scratching your head with the same hand that person scratched their head with, you would instead scratch your head with your left hand, which would be the mirror reflection of the activity they were doing. You want to be extremely careful when you're matching and mirroring, because if the individual senses you are intentionally mocking them, or trying to pull the wool of their eyes, they may quickly lose rapport with you, and you will be blocked by a wall of resistance you will not be able to permeate. Next up is to reframe the conversation in the direction of commonality. This means if you have found in step one this individual is interested in fishing, you redirect away from selling them something, and instead redirect the conversation in the direction of fishing.

The last step, after you have built rapport with the individual through dialogue, is to bring the conversation back to the reason you're there. Often times in a negotiation or a sales scenario the individual will like you so much, their decision to buy from you increases, and the likelihood you make a sale is nearly automatic.

How Else Might This Hypnotic Archetypal Trigger Known As Affinity To Other Be Useful For Helping You Hypnotically Influence And Persuade People To Your Way Of Thinking

The key thing to remember with affinity to other is, people like people like themselves. It's easier to negotiate and to do business with someone if they're closely aligned with your principles and values, your beliefs, interests, and way of carrying yourself conversationally. One way to accomplish this is to align yourself with the individual so they are put at ease, and start believing certain things about you, that don't necessarily have to be true. By congruently aligning yourself with their value system, you increase your opportunity to persuade them later in whatever direction you wish to. It might mean trying to recruit them into an organization you're affiliated with. When I was in college, I was friends with eight or nine guys my own age. We all worked together at the same restaurant. We hung out a lot together, talked about girls together, and were very closely aligned in age. However, I didn't know these friends of mine were all members of a fraternity where I went to college. Now, just for the record, I always told myself I would never join a college fraternity. When it came time for rush week, and many of the other freshman were joining fraternities, I had told myself I was not going to rush. At work one afternoon a few of the guys I worked with asked me if I was in a fraternity. I told them I wasn't, and made it clear I had no interest in joining one. They all then started to encourage me at least to come by the house, and at least engage in some of the activities they were all going to be a part of that week. You probably already know how this story ends, and if you guessed I ended up joining the fraternity, you would be right. Why did I join the fraternity? I joined because of the hypnotic archetypal trigger known as affinity to other. These guys were my friends. They all did the same things together. It only made sense I would join the fraternity, because I wanted to be also associated with the same common interests; not left out in the cold. I didn't want to be perceived as an outsider looking in. I wanted to be an insider experiencing the same type of happenings my friends were experiencing. These were my peers, and they were my equals. They were just like me.

Now of course everybody is distinctive. We all have unlike backgrounds. We all have distinct religions. We all have unusual world views. We all have different political persuasions. When you actually stop to think about it, there are very few people in the world who are really all that closely aligned with one another. We're all very different. Nevertheless, it is because of perception we're like other people, and other people are like us. This is how it is possible for us to be influenced by people who are actually quite different than ourselves.

Final Purport

Affinity to other is a hypnotic archetypal trigger which corresponds to our innate nature to associate ourselves with things and people who match our individual profile. This is why people with common interests share those interests in groups. There are groups who meet on any interest you can think up. The key thing to keep in mind is people like people like themselves. The reason for this is comfort and understanding. We want to do business with people who understand our needs. Naturally, we believe persons, who share things in common with us, understand us better than those who don't. It may seem like common sense; however, you'd be surprised how many persuaders out there forget this critical point.

We are hard wired to group together in groups we're most closely aligned with. This is why people of various skin colors tend to group together into social groups. It is why women have their 'girl's night out' away from the guys. It is why on college campuses international students tend to stick to social groups made up of other people of their cultural background. Differences tend to repel people. Even professional groups tend to cluster together socially. The marketing department doesn't usually mix with the sales department. People are friends with people in their same professional class. All of this has to do with the deep hypnotic archetypal trigger 'affinity to other'.

In this chapter we covered why affinity to other is important to understand; what you needed to know to apply it effectively in your persuasion messages; how-to make it work applicably to you particular persuasion contexts; and, how else it can be applied to persuade other's to take to your persuasions more smoothly. The main take away from this chapter is learning how to be more likeable, so other people feel more comfortable around you. You can be more charismatic when you are linked as an equal to the people you are persuading. We went in great depth about hypnotic rapport using NLP's matching and mirroring techniques, and how to more effectively master communication through applying affinity to other in your persuasive messages. Keep in mind, affinity to other, is a deeply rooted anchor embedded into everybody's psyche as a result of evolution.

Take Action Now

In order to get any value whatsoever from this book you must take action now on the instructions I'm going to be laying out for you. Do not be like most people—buy a book, half read it, set it aside, forget about it, never take action, never gain the advantages and benefits it has to offer you.

There is a reason you purchased this book. Do not forget that reason. If you attended one of my live training workshops, you would have participated in doing many exercises at the end of each module I taught you. This is because you get considerably more value practicing the techniques in a safe environment, before going out and practicing them in the real-world. Many people do not feel comfortable testing techniques they've just learnt blindly on real-life contexts. Do not be afraid to do these exercises: They are for your own good and self-development. Your personal power will increase when you proactively apply this knowledge to your specific contexts. Part of learning this information (the largest part) is applying it hands-on. Suspend your doubts and disbeliefs that you can do these exercises, because your insights will elevate to a higher level once you do them. You will only learn a fraction of what I teach in this book from reading the book. The great majority of your learning comes when you apply this information in whatever contexts you have been intentioned on learning it.

To prove this point: Think about your first kiss. You may have talked to friends about their first kiss to get some insight. Maybe you read a book on adolescent sexuality, where kissing was covered. You may have watched movies of actors kissing on the big-screen. Until you actually kissed a girl or guy for the first time, you didn't realize all that was involved in kissing, as you hadn't practiced it, and learned from that experience. I bet after you kissed for the first time, regardless how good or bad the kiss was; you felt pretty amazing afterward, and felt much more confident in kissing other people. I'm right, and you know it, so do these exercises! In fact, make a promise to yourself; you will not move on to the next chapter until these action steps have been completed. You'll thank yourself. I promise.

I. Make yourself take out a piece of paper and a pen/pencil and write down exactly how you'll utilize the information found in this chapter to fit your particular persuasion context.

II. Find an opportunity to apply what you learned in this chapter and apply it. After you have taken this initial action, journal your discoveries and results.

III. Take a 3x5 index card and summarize the leading points from this chapter. Let this summary serve as a quick flash card to jog your memory once a day, as you continue

reading this book, and doing future exercises. This is important, because this book has a lot of information, and a fast flash card to look at daily will help you not to forget what you have learned. Over time, this knowledge will become imprinted on your hypnotic mind, where you'll take action on this knowledge without thinking about it consciously.

IV. Teach what you have learned in this chapter to a trusted friend whom you think might benefit. Teaching information to others helps you gain greater clarity and insights you'd likely not have gained trying to keep it all in your own mind.

V. Discuss with the friend you've taught this information to and take notes on their thoughts and understanding of the material. This way, you'll gain another person's perspective and likely gain a deeper understanding of the material.

After you have successfully completed each of these exercises, only then, proceed in moving forward to the next chapter. Do not take shortcuts and tell yourself the lie you'll come back and do the exercises later. Statistically speaking the probability is improbable you ever will. Take a leap of faith and do the exercise, please! Trust me;

it's worth it, if you want to gain true mastery in hypnotic persuasion.

====================xx==================

CHAPTER 4

MYSTERY

The next hypnotic archetypal trigger is known as mystery. Human beings are drawn to things that are mysterious in nature. Something that is mystifying is intriguing and alluring and causes us to want to learn more about it. This is a psychological archetype that is behind many people's personalities. Something that is mysterious is generally something that can captivate our attention. When we're hypnotizing people, one of the underlying principles is we must captivate someone's attention and focus it narrowly. I will be sharing more about this in later chapters in this book. When you think of a mysterious villain in a movie, there is an instant attraction to this character, which begs us to want to uncover more of this person to find out who they are on a deeper level. I remember when I was in high school, there was a boy who used to dress in dark clothing, and wear a trench coat. He painted his nails black, and was imaged as the stereotypical Goth. This individual was very mysterious. He often attracted naive young girls to him, because they were captivated by his demeanor. The girls wanted to uncover the layers of mystery, so that they could figure him out. They were attracted to him for this reason.

We also think of mysteries like Sherlock Holmes. He was the great detective who could somehow see the clues other people couldn't. As we watch these types of episodes on TV and in the movies, we find ourselves sucked into trying to decipher the ending well before it finishes. We love movies that are mysterious, and can't figure out. It keeps us guessing, always wanting to know more about what's to come next. Mystery and intrigue are very powerful hypnotic archetypal triggers, because so often in order to figure something out that is mysterious we must buy into the positioning of the character or product being represented in this fashion.

Why Do You Need To Understand The Hypnotic Archetypal Trigger Mystery To Be A More Effective Conversational Hypnotist

When reflecting on the history of hypnosis, often time's people are attracted to it because of its mysterious origins. We want to figure out how the hypnotist on stage can say a few words and instantly control the people they hypnotize. We're captivated. We wish to decode this mysterious reality, which is the world of the hypnotist. We wonder why people are so drawn to people who are mysterious. It has to do with our social conditioning. From an early age, we are immersed in normalcy so much so that whenever something out of the ordinary or mysterious enters our reality, our boredom quickly dissipates. We're taken off to holy realities, which beg to be explored. You can present yourself with an air of mystery. You can set yourself up to draw in the interest of other people who wish to figure you out. In some types of situations, you may find yourself in, simply adapting adopting an enigmatic nature, can attract people to you. Sometimes you will want to present your offer as being somewhat inexplicable. This has the same effect. If you look at the title of this book, for example, you'll notice there's an air of mystery and an obscure vibe that causes people who stumble upon this title to feel intrigued. Mystery has a twin sister named forbidden. Of course on the title of this book is the word forbidden, which itself has a same effect in many ways as does mystery. Sometimes it is difficult for people to tell the difference between something that is forbidden and something that is mysterious. Sometimes we think of things that are mysterious as being forbidden and off-limits. Sometimes we think of something that is forbidden as being kept from us, and therefore, being somewhat on the border of mystery. We want to figure things out. We want to know the hidden truth behind mysteries. We can't help it. We are conditioned socially this way.

What Do You Need To Do To Prepare Yourself To Position Yourself And Your Products As Mysterious

Mainly, what you want to know is how other people are going to think about your product when you presented as mysterious. You also want to know and have an idea of how people are going to respond to you if they perceive you as mysterious. This can work both ways for you. In one sense, mystery can be captivating and attractive, yet on the other end of the spectrum mystery can be scary and perhaps something we don't want necessarily to uncover. If you think of Pandora's box, for example, here is a box that we don't know what's in it. It's mysterious and unknown to us. We have a sense that whatever is in the box needs to stay in the box and never be let out, but on the other hand, there's a part of us that's dying to see what's inside. Unfortunately, if we open that box, there's a good chance that we will die as a result. Mystery and intrigue can work either for or against you in persuasion. There are different levels of mysteriousness, you see. Something can be on the lighter end just mysterious enough it creates a desire for people to want to find out more about something. On the other end of the spectrum, there are the mysteries most of us don't want to know. Instead, we prefer to keep Pandora's Box closed. So, what you may want to consider is how intense a conveyance did you want regarding whatever context you have in mind for employing mystery—your personality, the products you sell, and even your individual persuasions; namely, the ones you intend indoctrinating others into believing. However, you also need to understand often times when people join cults. They join because of an element of mystery; conversely, only enough mystery to keep followers engaged and wanting to learn more. What individuals quickly learn is the mystery that seemed somewhat delicate starts gradually to become deeper and deeper. The more intense the mystery becomes the more an individual becomes consumed by the mystery itself. So if you're a cult leader, and you're trying to recruit people into your cult, one thing you need to know is you want to create only enough mystery, to lure people in, and then continue to evolve the mystery until which time you have new converts intrigued to the extent, they become lifelong loyal followers.

How Do You Use Mystery To Hypnotize People Into Believing Your Persuasions

As I have indicated, mystery in small doses can be used to lure people into wanting to know more about a product, a religious organization or cult, and even an individual. Now we're going to reflect on the steps necessary to use mystery in the direction of hypnotizing people into believing our persuasions.

I. The first step to hypnotizing people using the hypnotic archetypal trigger known as mystery, is to create a subtle mystery around the belief we want them to believe. How to do this is simply by taking some mysterious elements that are the common thread that runs through all things mysterious, and start to build a story around something you want people to believe. For example, if you want to attract people into your cult, for the purpose of indoctrinating them with many varied beliefs, the first thing you must do is take some mysterious elements, such as a story never figured out, or develop an air of mystery around a particular ideology or belief system, and then position it in front of the subject you wish to hypnotize. Whenever someone becomes drawn to the mystery, it binds them into further exploring the belief system in which you wished to indoctrinate them into. Since you have created the mystery, you hold the keys to the doorway into that mystery. For this reason, our hypnotic subject will start to think only about the mystery. The hypnotized subject starts asking us more and more questions, becoming more and more interested and hypnotized to the ideas and ideology only we hold the keys to. For this reason, they must rely on us to uncover the truth.

II. The second step, since we hold the truth to the mystery, and the only way, our hypnotic subject can gain entry into that mystery is through us; we can use psychology to control their level of interest by withholding the mystery from them, which can have a psychological impact of them wanting to know even more about the mystery. They will beg us to let them into the kingdom where the mystery is resolved.

III. Step three requires us never to reveal the mystery to them. The hypnotic subject can at no time learn of the great mystery, because once it stops being a mystery, the hypnotic subject will lose all interest in the ideology itself.

IV. Step four requires you sometimes to build on the mystery, in order to keep our hypnotic subjects continually engaged in the ideology.

How Else Might You Use Mystery To Hypnotize People To Achieve All The Other Results Besides Indoctrinating Them

If you're in sales, you may apply mystery to the product you are selling to create more desire for it. This is especially useful whenever the product is less known, and not so well marketed. Lesser-known products without mystery may be perceived as boring or generic and inconsequential for potential buyers. This can actually inhibit a sale from being made. When you position a product as having an element or an air of mystery to it, it creates a different effect mentally in the mind of your hypnotic subject. Instead of them finding your product boring or inconsequential, because of its poor marketing strategy, they start instead to think that your product may be to a lesser degree known, because it has been intentioned that it be less known. They start to wonder in their minds what's so special about this product, that the company doesn't want everybody knowing about it. There is an influence principle known as scarcity, and in this way of making your product less known, because you've positioned it using the hypnotic archetypal trigger mystery, it tends to create in the mind of your potential customer this idea of scarcity. In other words, they begin to believe if they don't purchase your product now, that they will not get a second chance ever. In this way, they can quickly find themselves needing to decide for or against your product. When positioning your product as mysterious, with the potential really to help consumers fulfill a need or solve a problem, this alone can cause shoppers to fall off the fence and take action and buy your product. There are many other applications in which mystery can be applied; however, I do caution you to be careful with this hypnotic archetypal trigger, because used in the wrong way, as I have indicated earlier, it can actually have a reverse effect on the psyche of the consumer or hypnotic subject. The essence of mystery itself is very hypnotic. When something is mysterious, it captivates our attention, and causes us to enter a journey that is unknown and exciting.

Final Purport

In this chapter, I covered with you the hypnotic archetypal trigger known as mystery. I took you into why you need to understand mystery; namely, given its hypnotic disposition. I also told you what you needed to know before hand in order to hypnotize people using hypnotic positioning and mystery, specifically. I then took you through the vital steps you can immediately take to hypnotize your hypnotic subjects and potential customers to achieve the outcomes and results you desire. I also covered the bases in terms of other applications— sales, for example—so you can begin to get your gears churning in order so you can utilize mystery and intrigue in the future when you need to. There truthfully are so many different applications in which you can use mystery to hypnotize individuals, so they become spellbound and attracted to you and your persuasions, but then again, also your products and anything else for that matter.

Take Action Now

In order to get any value whatsoever from this book you must take action now on the instructions I'm going to be laying out for you. Do not be like most people—buy a book, half read it, set it aside, forget about it, never take action, never gain the advantages and benefits it has to offer you.

There is a reason you purchased this book. Do not forget that reason. If you attended one of my live training workshops, you would have participated in doing many exercises at the end of each module I taught you. This is because you get considerably more value practicing the techniques in a safe environment, before going out and practicing them in the real-world. Many people do not feel comfortable testing techniques they've just learnt blindly on real-life contexts. Do not be afraid to do these exercises: They are for your own good and self-development. Your personal power will increase when you proactively apply this knowledge to your specific contexts. Part of learning this information (the largest part) is applying it hands-on. Suspend your doubts and disbeliefs that you can do these exercises, because your insights will elevate to a higher level once you do them. You will only learn a fraction of what I teach in this book from reading the book. The great majority of your learning comes when you apply this information in whatever contexts you have been intentioned on learning it.

To prove this point: Think about your first kiss. You may have talked to friends about their first kiss to get some insight. Maybe you read a book on adolescent sexuality, where kissing was covered. You may have watched movies of actors kissing on the big-screen. Until you actually kissed a girl or guy for the first time, you didn't realize all that was involved in kissing, as you hadn't practiced it, and learned from that experience. I bet after you kissed for the first time, regardless how good or bad the kiss was; you felt pretty amazing afterward, and felt much more confident in kissing other people. I'm right, and you know it, so do these exercises! In fact, make a promise to yourself; you will not move on to the next chapter until these action steps have been completed. You'll thank yourself. I promise.

I. Make yourself take out a piece of paper and a pen/pencil and write down exactly how you'll utilize the information found in this chapter to fit your particular persuasion context.

II. Find an opportunity to apply what you learned in this chapter and apply it. After you have taken this initial action, journal your discoveries and results.

III. Take a 3x5 index card and summarize the leading points from this chapter. Let this summary serve as a quick flash card to jog your memory once a day, as you continue

reading this book, and doing future exercises. This is important, because this book has a lot of information, and a fast flash card to look at daily will help you not to forget what you have learned. Over time, this knowledge will become imprinted on your hypnotic mind, where you'll take action on this knowledge without thinking about it consciously.

IV. Teach what you have learned in this chapter to a trusted friend whom you think might benefit. Teaching information to others helps you gain greater clarity and insights you'd likely not have gained trying to keep it all in your own mind.

V. Discuss with the friend you've taught this information to and take notes on their thoughts and understanding of the material. This way, you'll gain another person's perspective and likely gain a deeper understanding of the material.

After you have successfully completed each of these exercises, only then, proceed in moving forward to the next chapter. Do not take shortcuts and tell yourself the lie you'll come back and do the exercises later. Statistically speaking the probability is improbable you ever will. Take a leap of faith and do the exercise, please! Trust me;

it's worth it, if you want to gain true mastery in hypnotic persuasion.

=====================xx==================

CHAPTER 5

EXCITEMENT

The next hypnotic archetypal trigger we will cover is excitement. People are drawn to things that excite them. If you don't believe me think of any event that draws a crowd of people (e.g., ball games, concerts, pep rallies, fairs, etc.). Take, for example, a theme park. Perhaps this theme park has fast-moving roller coasters and water rides, etc.. These rides are sometimes referred to as 'thrill rides'. When something is thrilling it is exciting. Excitement draws people in, and hypnotizes them to want to experience sensations that parallel the excited state. In this chapter, I'm going to take you through all you need to understand about the hypnotic nature of the hypnotic archetypal trigger known as excitement. I'm going also to take you by the hand and teach you what you must know in order to create an atmosphere of excitement around yourself and the product or service you happen to be selling, assuming you are selling anything. Next, I'm going to give you step-by-step instructions on how exactly you can hypnotize and persuade people to buy your ideas using this hypnotic archetypal trigger known as excitement. Finally, will explore some other outlets where excitement may be useful and beneficial to you.

Why You Need To Understand The Hypnotic Archetypal Trigger Known As Excitement To Be Able To Hypnotize People Into Believing Your Persuasions

Excitement has been called a buying state. This means when people are excited, they are more prone to making a purchase than if they aren't excited. When people are excited there on fire, ready and willing to engage in any type of purchasing activity. I remember when I used to sell Yellow Pages advertising, and I would enter a sales call in a very excited state myself. Perhaps I had just earned a huge commission from a sale I had gathered on the previous sales call, and I was still elated from having made that sale. That excitement would carry over into the next sales call, and as a result it would, in fact, the potential customer whom I was talking to at that time. Often times what resulted, and I didn't truly understand this principle at the time, but because I could excite the potential customer at that next sales call, they somehow seem to instantly be more interested, and excited purchase my product.

If you look at a stereotypical myth or story, you find straightaway that the protagonist character tends to be living out at first in ordinary existence, which to most of us would seem quite boring. The protagonist may be engaged in every-day laborers, in order to keep a roof over his or her head, and to remain in that existence. There are expectations on us from society at large, that keep us on that level, to where we live our lives based on this concept of normalcy. If we start to venture out past the social construct known as normalcy, we start instantly to find ourselves being criticized, or facing sometime of resistance, meant to keep us down, and motivated in the other direction. Sometimes a protagonist makes the hard decision to continue moving forward in the story, and follow his or her heart into the great unknown that becomes a great journey. When this happens many things happen along the lock the way; such as, incidents which are construed as being excited. These ups and downs throughout the narrative continue to engage the reader or the onlooker, if say it happens to be a movie, and this back-and-forth of conflict creates an internal excitement within us. We also become empathetic to the character, to the extent where we find ourselves imagining that we are, in fact, that character, having that experience. Disengaging from normalcy means entering into a new thrilling world. At what time a customer makes a purchase from you, and you've positioned your product in such a way it takes them out of normalcy, and has them entering the holy grail of reality, which is 'excitement', is one in which they believe by purchasing your product; they are going to either solve a problem, experience the thrill of buying something, or be feeling the thrill of owning something brand new—an exciting proposition in itself.

If the customer doesn't make a purchase, it simply means that they have decided to remain in the state of normalcy, in which they feel comfortable, and okay with. There may still be some guilt and discomfort after the salesperson is gone that they didn't actually make a purchase. When they don't buy something it is almost as though they experience a sort of loss. When you do make a purchase, you are actually gaining something, that could be more valuable than the money you spent to make the purchase. When you position your product as being exciting, part of that loss stems from your experience of not gaining that excitement for yourself. It's like you give it up. So excitement is something you really need to understand, especially if you happen to be selling products or services, because it truly is perhaps the greatest state for your potential customer to be in to make them want to buy your product. If you're feeling excited, one thing you're not experiencing is boredom. This, in and of itself, is a compelling enough reason to want to experience excitement. If the cost of excitement is making a purchase, people find that making a purchase makes perfect sense to them.

What You Need To Know About Hypnotic Archetypal Triggers Specifically Pertaining To Excitement

What you need to understand about excitement is it can happen any time and anywhere. This is important to understand because as you're exciting your hypnotic subject, just know that you can get them excited at any time. When people are excited they experience exuberance and elation. They become emotional in the stirred sense, and sometimes to the extent that they can almost hardly contain their exhilaration.

I remember when I was a kid nine or 10 years old, and my parents were about to take me and my brother and sister to the local County fair. At the fair, there was rides, food, and most always people we knew from school, i.e. our schoolmates The fair only came around once a year, in the summertime, and just before school was to begin again in August for another term. Because of this rarity factor whenever the fair came to town, my brother and sister and I would become filled with excitement. My parents could have asked me to clean my room, do the dishes, take out the trash, and weed the garden, and I would have done it without twice thinking about it. Nothing mattered, except getting to the fair, because it was the one time of the year me and my classmates and siblings could enjoy time outside, when school was not in session. We always had a blast.

The reason I tell a story is because I want you to imagine and be transported into that reality for just a moment so you can fathom the type of excitement I'm talking about here. It doesn't take a lot necessarily to excite a child. Surprisingly, though it doesn't take much usually to excite and an adult either. For adults, it is sometimes the simple things, which get them excited. Having an extra off from work, for example, can really insight the emotions of excitement. You also need to understand that when people become excited, they often enter a different world, in which their defenses go down and their susceptibility level to other people's ideas increases. In the story, I told you about going to the fair as a child, I mentioned to you my parents could have asked me to do anything, anything at all actually, and I would have done it without questioning it. The reason for this wasn't because I was being threatened that if I didn't do what they asked me to do I couldn't go to the fair, but because I was in such a state of excitement, I didn't mind doing anything I normally might would have objected doing. The excitement won out over the chore or task which was, more or less, undesirable to a small child. You really need to understand this point, because it is this point alone they can have you easily achieving the outcomes you desire as it pertains to influencing other people to accept your persuasions as the truth.

How Do You Persuade Someone By Using The Hypnotic Archetypal Trigger Known As Excitement To Achieve Your Desired Outcomes

In order to hypnotize someone using excitement as a trigger for trance, you simply need to follow a couple of steps, which I will outline for you now:

Step one: become excited yourself. This cannot be underscored enough, and the same goes for any type of state you want someone else to enter. By assuming the state of mind first, it overpowers other people's frames, and induces them to enter the same state. This is one reason why psychotherapists will advise their patients not to associate with negative influences. Whenever you associate with someone who is in a depressed state, or state of weakness, it is easy for yourself to become infected by these emotional diseases. It is best to associate yourself with people who are positive and uplifting, and people who will make you a better you. When you associate with excellence, you become excellent yourself.

Step two: in this step, you intentionally transfer your excitement onto other people. And you begin to watch your hypnotic subject begin to become infected themselves with that state of Jolly excitement. It's hard not to get excited, when other people are excited. Even if you just excited for them, you still are excited. So the idea with this step is to encourage people to follow suit as you lead them into a state of excitement.

Step three: in step three simply watch for some subtle trend signs happening, such as the dilated pupils, less resistance present, and a willingness in the individual to want to comply with your requests. During this phase of the process you are calibrating, your hypnotic subject to determine how hypnotized and excited they truly are. Whenever you notice that they are not excited enough or as compliant as you would like for them to be you simply step back to stage two and begin transferring more of your excitement onto them. Then of course you come back to step three and continue testing until which time the individual is absolutely yielding to your requests. When you finally reach the point where your subject is entirely obliging this is when you begin to slip in your hypnotic suggestions, as well as your direct requests, because the stage your spellbound subject is in is a buying state, and they will buy whatever it is you're selling—even ideas.

How Else Can You Use Excitement And Benefit

Besides just hypnotizing someone and getting them to comply with your requests directly and indirectly, you may also use excitement to build were poor with an individual, or even anchor the state of hypnosis and excitement with some type of NLP anchor. To build rapport with someone, using excitement you can simply watch them grin at you, as you beamed brightly at them. The more excited you become, the more excited they become too. When two people are excited and laughing and having a good time, friendships have a habit of developing. If you want to set an NLP anchor so you can get your hypnotic subject excited there are lots you can do with a simple gesture, First you must decide what unique gesture it is you want to set as the trigger for that anchored response. The way you accomplish this is by beginning to get someone stimulated, and just before they reach the pinnacle of their highest elevated state of excitement slip in that innocuous gesture without them knowingly understanding what it is you're doing. Your hypnotic subject will be tremendously excited, that this gesture will completely bypass the resistance radar. So, for example, let's pretend that you're in a sales call with a possible client. And you want this potential customer to become excited anytime you give two thumbs-up to them. What you do is wait until just before their excitement climax happens, and then give them two thumbs-up while they're actually climaxing and next as they become less excited be sure that your thumbs are down or to your side, otherwise the anchor will not stick, and you will not be able to trigger that response using NLP anchoring technique.

We have covered quite a bit in this chapter on excitement. Excitement can position you in a number of ways, we've said. Excitement can position you as someone who can be the life of the party; as someone who is charismatic and always fun to be around; and as someone who doesn't take himself or herself too seriously to where others become concerned they only have their best interest at heart. We've also mentioned when people are excited, they will do just about anything you ask of them. Excitement is a buying state, we've said. We've also talked about how else you can use excitement, such as using it to set NLP anchors, as well as to build hypnotic rapport and charisma with the person you're hypnotizing. By inducing excitement into your hypnotic subject, you open the floodgate to allowing your hypnotic suggestions to bypass their critical resistance quickly, and to slip into their hypnotic mind to be carried out later.

Final Purport

I this chapter we've explored the hypnotic archetypal trigger 'excitement' to learn it is a 'buying trance' that opens doors to selling products and persuading people, with much less effort than other persuasion modalities. Excitement is imprinted on our hypnotic mind. It leads people to more enjoyable, more talked about, experiences that other internal states just cannot reach by comparison.

I have taken you through why you need to understand this hypnotic archetypal trigger; elaborating on the attributes that comprise 'excitement'. I also expanded this by relaying to you the logical advantages, like using excitement to drop people into hypnosis by over stimulating their minds. I also went one step further by forecasting potential benefits that can come about from using excitement to persuade your hypnotic subjects. These are benefits like feeling excited yourself, and sharing a positive emotional connection with your hypnotic subject. Also, achieving higher levels of self-confidence knowing you'll be making more sales, changing minds, and negotiating more positive outcomes.

I also explained to you what you needed to know up front before you start using excitement to persuade people to believe your persuasions. This delved into a deeper understanding of what other people generally experience when they're induced into a state of excitement. You learned people are more willing to do things they usually wouldn't do under normal circumstances. You also learned people are likely to let down their guard and be persuaded.

The steps to persuading people hypnotically using the hypnotic archetypal trigger 'excitement' we covered next. This was the sequential order of steps you can take to hypnotically persuade others using the hypnotic archetypal trigger 'excitement'. These steps were simply: (a) get excited, (b) transfer your excitement, and (c) watch for others to become likewise excited.

The last thing we covered in this chapter were other ways you can use 'excitement' to hypnotize people into doing your bidding. These applications are many. It is key to note that not always will it be appropriate to be overly-excited. A business meeting, where the tone is more business-serious, will be one such context where excitement may not always be helpful. However, there are a number of other contexts like a family vacation, spending time with loved ones, persuading people to join your cult, and group activity contexts, where persuading people using 'excitement' would be helpful. The main thing excitement does is help you create a better internal experience. People will often remark how time flies, when they are in an excited state and conversing with other excited people. The reason for this is because they feel good about their interactions with others.

Take Action Now

In order to get any value whatsoever from this book you must take action now on the instructions I'm going to be laying out for you. Do not be like most people—buy a book, half read it, set it aside, forget about it, never take action, never gain the advantages and benefits it has to offer you.

There is a reason you purchased this book. Do not forget that reason. If you attended one of my live training workshops, you would have participated in doing many exercises at the end of each module I taught you. This is because you get considerably more value practicing the techniques in a safe environment, before going out and practicing them in the real-world. Many people do not feel comfortable testing techniques they've just learnt blindly on real-life contexts. Do not be afraid to do these exercises: They are for your own good and self-development. Your personal power will increase when you proactively apply this knowledge to your specific contexts. Part of learning this information (the largest part) is applying it hands-on. Suspend your doubts and disbeliefs that you can do these exercises, because your insights will elevate to a higher level once you do them. You will only learn a fraction of what I teach in this book from reading the book. The great majority of your learning comes when you apply this information in whatever contexts you have been intentioned on learning it.

To prove this point: Think about your first kiss. You may have talked to friends about their first kiss to get some insight. Maybe you read a book on adolescent sexuality, where kissing was covered. You may have watched movies of actors kissing on the big-screen. Until you actually kissed a girl or guy for the first time, you didn't realize all that was involved in kissing, as you hadn't practiced it, and learned from that experience. I bet after you kissed for the first time, regardless how

good or bad the kiss was; you felt pretty amazing afterward, and felt much more confident in kissing other people. I'm right, and you know it, so do these exercises! In fact, make a promise to yourself; you will not move on to the next chapter until these action steps have been completed. You'll thank yourself. I promise.

I. Make yourself take out a piece of paper and a pen/pencil and write down exactly how you'll utilize the information found in this chapter to fit your particular persuasion context.

II. Find an opportunity to apply what you learned in this chapter and apply it. After you have taken this initial action, journal your discoveries and results.

III. Take a 3x5 index card and summarize the leading points from this chapter. Let this summary serve as a quick flash card to jog your memory once a day, as you continue reading this book, and doing future exercises. This is important, because this book has a lot of information, and a fast flash card to look at daily will help you not to forget what you have learned. Over time, this knowledge will become imprinted on your hypnotic mind, where you'll take action on this knowledge without thinking about it consciously.

IV. Teach what you have learned in this chapter to a trusted friend whom you think might benefit. Teaching information to others helps you gain greater clarity and insights you'd likely not have gained trying to keep it all in your own mind.

V. Discuss with the friend you've taught this information to and take notes on their thoughts and understanding of the material. This way, you'll gain another person's perspective and likely gain a deeper understanding of the material.

After you have successfully completed each of these exercises, only then, proceed in moving forward to the next chapter. Do not take shortcuts and tell yourself the lie you'll come back and do the exercises later. Statistically speaking the probability is improbable you ever will. Take a leap of faith and do the exercise, please! Trust me; it's worth it, if you want to gain true mastery in hypnotic persuasion.

====================xx==================

CHAPTER 6

EXCLUSIVE

"Exclusive! Exclusive! Read all about it!..." These were the words often shouted on busy streets, newspaper boys, back during the days when newspapers were the only major source for connecting the world with news and information. What an incredible way to get someone's attention, right?

Not everything is able to be bought. Some things are so restricted, that only the wealthiest of the wealthy can even afford to buy them. These things which are extremely exclusive, have so much intrinsic value; yet, oftentimes they're impractical in terms of functionality. In this chapter, we're going to look at the hypnotic archetypal trigger known as 'exclusivity'. Exclusivity breeds the feeling of significance when we know that we can have something that other people cannot. Whenever someone is presented with an opportunity to receive something that most people cannot receive, there is an intrinsic value that is perceived by that individual, whereas whatever it is they're being offered becomes all that much more valuable. Then here's a secret: not everything that is exclusive has practical value; notwithstanding, it will have intrinsic value. Intrinsic value often times is more important than the practical value something has. This is the reason why an automobile that has less practical value in terms of saving people money at the gas pump, or being able to haul around a family, can be 100 times more expensive than a minivan that has four cylinders, and can transport a family of six rather easily. The minivan has practical value, because it's relatively good on gas, and can haul a considerable amount of people, as well as other items for transport. A Corvette, on the other hand, has less practical value, because it is unable to carry around a large family, and a Corvette costs an unfathomable amount of money to most people who earn an average income. However, because the car is exclusive, it has so much intrinsic value, that the automobile manufacturer can raise the sticker price, and it actually makes the car more valuable in the mind of the consumer. Sometimes people have this idea that the more expensive something is, the better it must be. This isn't always true, but people still believe it.

In this chapter will you be looking at why you need to understand the principles of exclusivity. We're also going to discuss what you need to know in order to position yourself as being exclusive, as well as exclusively positioning your offers to potential customers. We are then going to cover exactly how you can make all this happen;

namely, by going step-by-step through the instructions that I will be giving you. And lastly, we will look at how else you might want to use exclusivity to get people to do what you want them to.

Why You Need To Understand The Principles Of Exclusivity

When something is exclusive, we want it more. This is psychological, because most of the time we want things, we can't always have. A lot of this stems from childhood, where someone may have grown up in a family where resources were scarce, and children didn't regularly get what they wanted. When my mother was a little girl, she lived on an island, where her father, my grandfather, was a commercial fisherman. Her mother didn't work, and there were five children to feed. My mother used to tell me how she didn't always have nice clothes to wear to school, which was way out on the mainland. She tells me how she wished for the day she could earn her own money and be able to buy the clothes she wanted and other things. She promised herself as a child that she would never be poor. When my mother grew up, she got a job that paid well, and would go to shopping malls and by clothes at designer stores, and walk out wearing them. She wanted clothes that most other people couldn't afford to buy. She achieved that goal. As we all know markups in designer stores are quite pricy. A shirt that costs $100 may be just as functional as a shirt that cost $20. If you look at the economics, you might even say that my mother could have afforded five shirts at $20 apiece, over purchasing one shirt at $100. My mother wanted the shirt that most people wouldn't and couldn't buy, because she wanted what she perceived of as the best. So the best is determined by how exclusive it is in the marketplace. This is why some stores can charge a considerable amount more for their merchandise, as they have positioned their brand and their products in alignment with the principles of exclusivity. You need to understand that by positioning yourself, and whatever product you happen to be selling, as being completely exclusive, you stand a chance that people will be willing to pay a premium for that item or your services. When we think of someone who has celebrity authority status, we understand this individual to be a mover and a shaker in their industry. If we think of real estate, we might think of Donald Trump. If we think of the stock market and investing in securities, we might think of worn buffet. These gentlemen are exclusive in their own right in the industry that they have positioned themselves in.

What You Need To Know Before You Can Position Yourself As Being Exclusive

If you're in going into business for yourself, or your selling products for a company, there are ways you can position yourself so when you deal with other people, they perceive you as having a high value. The way to do this is by demonstrating higher value to your clients and prospects. This can be applied to nearly any field, and if done right you position yourself as an authority, but over time, you become a celebrity authority, which is the highest exclusive place to be in your industry. What you need to understand first are that the specific actions which can propel you in the direction of celebrity authority status. However, there are also actions that demonstrate a lower value, which can decelerate your positioning as being exclusive to the marketplace. You must understand everything you do is being judged as either having a higher value or having a low value. In a sense, there is a social ranking, or pecking order, in which everyone in a particular marketplace is trying to outdo each other. Why some people fail is because they have failed to understand the difference between a high-value action and a low-value action.

How Can You Position Yourself And Products As Exclusive In Your Marketplace

We have already talked about this concept of demonstrating high-value versus demonstrating lower value actions. A higher-value action is one where you take authority over other people in terms of your leadership in the way you express yourself in the marketplace. A demonstration of lower value is when you do anything to make someone think less of you, or perceive you as, less competent. Let's observe the sequential steps you can take to achieve exclusivity in your niche.

I. Step one: the first step to position yourself and products as being exclusive in your marketplace is to acquire the mentality known as "act as if...." Even though you may not be an authority, let alone a celebrity authority in your industry, you still have the ability to act as if you are. This means having massive self-confidence and yourself and belief in your product.

II. Step two: the next up in the process of positioning yourself and products as being exclusive to the marketplace is, you must constantly be demonstrating higher value that everyone you come in contact with. This means every piece of communication you engage in you must act as if you know what you're talking about, and have the self-confidence and surety whatever you suggest someone else do they will, in fact, do that activity. Make a compelling argument that is direct and confident, oftentimes people look for this type of behavior before they make a buying decision. If they sense you don't know what you're talking about, or you aren't absolutely sure what you're offering them is what they need, chances are they will refuse to do business with you and do business with your competition instead. Demonstrating exclusivity to your market or your hypnotic subject must constantly be demonstrating higher value to them; even if it means acting as if you know what you're talking about, when in fact you don't, until which time you actually do. You always want to stay 10 steps in front of your hypnotic subject or the person who happens to be your potential customer. Staying ahead, means also educating yourself about your industry, and everything that is needed in order for you to get the outcome you want, and to be able to persuade people to believe your persuasions.

III. Step three: step three requires that you take stock of every interaction that you engage in communications wise. You must also always be critiquing yourself mentally, and asking yourself if you are displaying a high-value, or low-value to your hypnotic subject.

How Else Might You Use Exclusivity To Influence And Persuade Your Hypnotic Subjects

Whenever someone sees something that we can afford, there's a part of them that internalizes the need to have the means through which to afford what it is they cannot have. As human beings, we like to think that we have the power to create for ourselves whatever lifestyle we desire. Whenever something is presented to us as being exclusive, and out of reach, psychologically it tells us that where an inferior person; that is to say, we don't have as much value as what we would like to have. When we understand products have more value than what we have, there is an inner jealousy that occurs, which makes us want to prove our self-worth to ourselves and other people. One way you can take advantage of this psychological phenomenon is to use a tiered advantage by letting your hypnotic subject believe and think you can increase their own self-worth and value. If you can take someone who feels inferior to others, and present them with an argument stressing how you can help them be more successful; achieve more what they want out of life; and, gain self-confidence and financial stability, then you are playing into this psychological principle, where they don't believe it's possible, yet they wish it were. If you can persuade someone to follow your lead, by presenting and demonstrating high-value propositions to them, they will perceive you as having high-value, and will want to associate with you, because they believe by associating with you, they too will achieve a higher value themselves. This has a lot to do with the pack mentality. In early human history, human beings discovered if they gathered together into groups of about 50 people or so, that they could work jointly to increase their chances of survival and replication. When these tribes formed it became survival of the fittest. This means the member of the tribe who had the highest value, which normally took the form of physical force, then this person would lead the tribe. This individual was also typically a male and for that reason, we have labeled this archetype as the 'alpha male' character. The alpha male dominated the tribe, and gave the orders. Whatever this individual decided; other people had to follow his instructions, or else be kicked out of the tribe, or worst, killed! Getting kicked out of the tribe also meant lessening your chances of survival and replication, and increasing the chances your family lineage would be weeded out from all of existance. Survival meant you had to follow the leader. In cults, there has to be a leader, who gives the orders, and more or less runs everything as a central figurehead. This member typically has an exclusive value, which is created through rare appearances, mythological stories about this individual, and the social proof, in which everybody loves the leader, and is constantly talking about how great the leader is. It's a same type of activity we observe with early human groupings, where the leader was the alpha male member of the pack or tribe. The person on top is the celebrity authority, the person that everyone wants to be like, in which everyone respects. In order to influence and persuade other people you must demonstrate a higher value to a group in order to position yourself as the leader of that group. You must also never demonstrate a lower value if you can help it. Demonstrating lower value, or weakness, subtracts your exclusive value.

Final Purport

In this chapter, we covered the hypnotic archetypal trigger 'exclusivity'. We determined in order to rise above the noise and clutter in a marketplace one way we can do this is through demonstrating higher value to the people we do business with, and the people we interact with. By doing this it elevates you and adds to the persona of you having not only higher perceived value, but also exclusivity over other people in that marketplace. This simply stated means you become the person everyone else wants to become, and ironically enough the person no one else can become. As I mention in the beginning of this chapter---exclusivity is this idea we want things we cannot have. I told you the story about my mother who would walk into a shopping mall and walk out wearing the new clothes she just purchased, and clothes most people couldn't afford to buy. I talked about the psychology behind why people are attracted to this idea of exclusive goods and personal branding. I taught you what you needed to know about exclusivity; particularly, you must be able to demonstrate a higher value to people while lessening a lower-value perception. Finally, I showed you exactly how to do this: You act as if you are exclusive. You demonstrate higher value by your actions and communication. You calibrate your interpersonal communications with others to determine if you are demonstrating higher value or lower value to them. You master self-confidence so people perceive you as the leader of your tribe. And, you position yourself in such a way people want to associate themselves with you, even though they normally cannot. This combination creates an exclusive shell around you and the products you sell, which most people don't believe they can afford or are worthy enough to own or associate with. You can use this to your advantage when you actually do decide to do business with them, and still come out on top, because they already perceive you as having high intrinsic worth. When they do pay the premium, they will gladly do so, because they believe they're getting something other people can't.

Take Action Now

In order to get any value whatsoever from this book you must take action now on the instructions I'm going to be laying out for you. Do not be like most people—buy a book, half read it, set it aside, forget about it, never take action, never gain the advantages and benefits it has to offer you.

There is a reason you purchased this book. Do not forget that reason. If you attended one of my live training workshops, you would have participated in doing many exercises at the end of each module I taught you. This is because you get considerably more value practicing the techniques in a safe environment, before going out and practicing them in the real-world. Many people do not feel comfortable testing techniques they've just learnt blindly on real-life contexts. Do not be afraid to do these exercises: They are for your own good and self-development. Your personal power will increase when you proactively apply this knowledge to your specific contexts. Part of learning this information (the largest part) is applying it hands-on. Suspend your doubts and disbeliefs that you can do these exercises, because your insights will elevate to a higher level once you do them. You will only learn a fraction of what I teach in this book from reading the book. The great majority of your learning comes when you apply this information in whatever contexts you have been intentioned on learning it.

To prove this point: Think about your first kiss. You may have talked to friends about their first kiss to get some insight. Maybe you read a book on adolescent sexuality, where kissing was covered. You may have watched movies of actors kissing on the big-screen. Until you actually kissed a girl or guy for the first time, you didn't realize all that was involved in kissing, as you hadn't practiced it, and learned from that experience. I bet after you kissed for the first time, regardless how good or bad the kiss was; you felt pretty amazing afterward, and felt much more confident in kissing other people. I'm right, and you know it, so do these exercises! In fact, make a promise to yourself; you will not move on to the next chapter until these action steps have been completed. You'll thank yourself. I promise.

I. Make yourself take out a piece of paper and a pen/pencil and write down exactly how you'll utilize the information found in this chapter to fit your particular persuasion context.

II. Find an opportunity to apply what you learned in this chapter and apply it. After you have taken this initial action, journal your discoveries and results.

III. Take a 3x5 index card and summarize the leading points from this chapter. Let this summary serve as a quick flash card to jog your memory once a day, as you continue reading this book, and doing future exercises. This is important, because this book has a lot of information, and a fast flash card to look at daily will help you not to forget what you have learned. Over time, this knowledge will become imprinted on your hypnotic mind, where you'll take action on this knowledge without thinking about it consciously.

IV. Teach what you have learned in this chapter to a trusted friend whom you think might benefit. Teaching information to others helps you gain greater clarity and insights you'd likely not have gained trying to keep it all in your own mind.

V. Discuss with the friend you've taught this information to and take notes on their thoughts and understanding of the material. This way, you'll gain another person's perspective and likely gain a deeper understanding of the material.

After you have successfully completed each of these exercises, only then, proceed in moving forward to the next chapter. Do not take shortcuts and tell yourself the lie you'll come back and do the exercises later. Statistically speaking the probability is improbable you ever will. Take a leap of faith and do the exercise, please! Trust me; it's worth it, if you want to gain true mastery in hypnotic persuasion.

====================XX==================

CHAPTER 7

FORBIDDEN

When something is forbidden it is off-limits. It means you don't have access to it. When you're not privy to knowing something, owning something, or having access to something, which only select few people have access to, there is a psychological principle at play that makes you want it all that much more. This is a reason people fight for their rights. Gun owners, for example, are constantly fighting for the right to own guns, even though not everybody can own a gun due to regulations and perhaps past crimes committed. When someone gets out of prison, and are told they're not allowed to own a gun, often times they wind back up in prison because they were found in possession of having a gun. If you tell me, "You can't do something," I want to be able to do it so I can prove you wrong. My father was born in 1931 just after the Great Depression. He actually lived through the tail end of it, but he told me the story once, and I'll happily share it with you here, because it really drives home the point I want to make when it comes to the psychological principle behind something being forbidden. My father's father, so my grandfather, was a truck driver. One day, he was stopped in at a truck stop, sitting at the local diner, where a group of guys were having this conversation. One of the guys in the group declared his cargo was so locked up nobody would be able ever to take it. My grandfather listening to this conversation slipped out of the man's mouth, and proceeded to step back outside. He returned about 45 minutes later. The guys were still sitting there having the same conversation talking about all the different ways they can protect their cargo, and boasting about what great truck drivers they were. They were boasting about always getting the loads there on time. They were boasting about how many hours they could stay awake while driving. They were doing what a lot of truck drivers do; namely, having truck driver discussions about how great they are as truck drivers. It really is humorous, if you ever find yourself sitting in on one of these types of conversations. My father was also a truck driver, so I have set in on some of these types of conversations in my past. Let me tell you they are quite interesting. So my grandfather finished his coffee and went back out to his truck and took off. He told my father years later, who eventually shared this story with me, that what he did was go outside when those guys were bragging, and he cut a hole in the floor of that guy's trailer floor, at the back end, where it was unlikely, any cargo would be placed at (cargo is loaded in front-end first). Once he cut the hole he simply found the cargo he wanted and slipped it through the hole in the bottom of the trailer. The guy was hauling food products, so I guess my grandfather ate well for about a month.

So why exactly did my grandfather steal this man's cargo? The answer is he was told nobody could steal it. He wanted what he couldn't have. The cargo was the forbidden fruit, so to speak. It's the same reason Adam and Eve, if you believe the Bible to be historically accurate, eight of the fruit of the tree of good and evil. That forbidden fruit they ate was eaten because they were told it was off-limits, and they were forbade from eating it. We always want we can't have. It is psychological and is deeply imprinted in our psyche. For this reason, the hypnotic archetypal trigger forbidden is one you need to commit to memory. In this chapter I will be walking you through why you need to be able to present yourself as off-limits to others as well as your products if you happen to be in sales. I will also be explaining why this specific hypnotic archetypal trigger is so hypnotic in nature. Then I'm going to walk you through what you need to know to create positioning so you achieve your desired outcomes. After which, I will teach you exactly how to position yourself as hypnotic using the hypnotic archetypal trigger 'forbidden'. After we cover all of this, we will have a discussion about how else this hypnotic archetypal trigger may be useful in other contexts as well.

Why You Should Understand The Hypnotic Archetypal Trigger Forbidden

If you take away people's rights, they rebel. We see this all throughout history. If you restrict someone from being able to do something, it makes them want to do it all that much more. Tell someone they cannot join your group; they will desire more strongly to join it. Tell someone they don't qualify for a particular credit card, they will be sure to keep applying. Because of this psychological phenomenon, we can predict behavior. If I were to tell you, "You cannot buy my next book," showing there were at most going to be a limited number printed, and I had those reserved for a select group of people. It would probably, and this could very well be an unconscious understanding, but chances are you probably would want one of those books. It is psychological. You want what you cannot have. You want what's forbidden. If something is off-limits, without a good enough reason, you can't stop thinking about wanting it, and therefore, are willing to pay whatever price you have to, in order to get it.

I really like this specific hypnotic archetypal trigger, because it parallels the influence principle of scarcity. When resources are scarce demand increases, and higher intrinsic value is created. If I told you, only ten copies of my next book would be available for sell, it would create a buying frenzy of people wanting to own the book, and demand for the book would increase. This is basic economics. It is basic supply and demand principles at play. Even if you don't want something, if you're told you can't have it, psychologically a light switch gets turned on, and all of a sudden you and everybody else in the marketplace, want it.

Often times, at least was a case in my situation, I was invited to come to a friend's house after school and stay the night. My mother, however, never liked having company at our house, so she didn't think it was fair I should be staying the night at other friend's homes. She knew she wasn't going to reciprocate and allow that parent's child to come stay the night at our house. My mother had three kids, and sometimes my nephew and stepbrothers would come and stay, so she was sort of burnt out on company most of my childhood. When I was told I was told I couldn't stay the night at my friend's homes, I thought it was the greatest injustice in the world. It made me want to stay the night all that much more. Often times when I became a little older, I disobeyed my parents, and I wouldn't say the night at friend's house anyway. I wanted what I couldn't have. Interestingly, later, when my parents allowed me to stay the night at my friend's home, my interest diminished to the point where I preferred staying at my own home instead. I was allowed now to do it, and therefore, I cared less about doing it. We always want what we can't have. For this reason, you really need to get your mind wrapped around this hypnotic archetypal trigger 'forbidden'. It uncontrollably compels people to do things they shouldn't do. You can position your ideas as being forbidden, and see new results in your sales calls (if you're in sales). You can tell people they shouldn't do something, citinge it's off-limits and forbidden, and you'll quickly find them doing it. You can use this hypnotic archetypal trigger to your advantage. So you might ask yourself "Why exactly do people do things they shouldn't do?" or "Why do they do thing forbidden of them?" You'll probably come up with the answer, "It's because they're hypnotized by things which are forbidden." A different part of their brain fires and their consciousness subsides while their hypnotic mind kicks in and they automatically behave accordingly to the psychological principle.

When my brother and I were teenagers, my brother started smoking cigarettes. There was a convenience store a few blocks away. One afternoon my brother asked my mom if he could borrow the car to drive down to the convenience store, so he could buy a pack of cigarettes. My mother told him no. She said she forbid him from using her automobile to support his bad habit, which she didn't approve of. In other words, she didn't want to enable him to buy cigarettes. I remember walking up my parent's driveway, as, I had just been visiting a friend at a park across the street, and my brother driving my mother station wagon into the driveway. I remember this, because my father was hiding behind a tree. The second my brother got out of the car my dad went up to my brother punch him, and threw him into the air, and said, "your mother told you not to take the car, but you took it anyway. And for that, you get what you deserve." I can't get the picture out of my head of my brother flying through the air like Superman. My father's adrenaline was pumped allowing him to do a superhuman feat right before my eyes. And when I say fly, I mean my brother literally flew about twenty feet in the air, and it was a spectacle to watch, let me tell you. Why did my brother take the car? You know the answer to this now. It was because he was forbidden from taking it, he took it anyway.

What You Need To Understand About The Hypnotic Archetypal Trigger Forbidden So That You Can Hypnotize Your Subjects Into Complying With Your Every Request

The first thing you need to understand about the hypnotic archetypal trigger forbidden is different people will respond to this trigger differently. Some people are conditioned enough they will simply comply and not break the rules. For a great many of the other people, they will break the rules in order to do what is forbidden. For this reason, you need to understand the personality of the person you're dealing with. If you're dealing with someone, who is submissive, who always complies with everything they're told to do, and who is more of a beta personality, then this hypnotic archetypal trigger may not have the same impact it would on someone else. If you're dealing with someone who is an alpha personality, who is used to getting their way, and who charts their own course, so to speak; then chances are this individual will not respond well when forbidden from doing something. This individual will go to great lengths to have and do whatever it is they are forbidden from having or doing. The second thing you need to understand about this hypnotic archetypal trigger is it almost a subliminal trigger. It can be used to achieve outcomes you desire. When something is forbidden, it's almost like saying, "You can't do this," and there're some secrets behind why. People want to know other people's secrets. They don't want to be left in the dark. The natural detective in an individual starts to come out whenever they suspect the reason something is forbidden is because it is being used to cover up a secret. If you go back to the title of this book, you'll notice I used the hypnotic archetypal trigger forbidden in the cover title. I did this intentionally, because I wanted to sell a lot of copies of this book. I don't apologize for that. I wanted to sell a lot of copies, because I knew this book would benefit a lot of people; namely: people in sales, people in marketing, cult leaders, and anyone who wishes to persuade someone else to believe their persuasions. I also chose to use the word forbidden in the title because sometimes people think of hypnosis as being a forbidden art form, so to speak. Many people think the hypnotist has control over their subject, and for this reason, there is an air of mystery, which begets curiosity. To create a book title that infers the information in it is forbidden from other people knowing about, while associating it with the mysterious world of hypnosis, triggers psychologically the parts of the brain responsible for desiring something and people will stop at no cost to get it. By the way, I'm glad you bought the book. As you're beginning now to understand there are a lot of forbidden aspects relative to the information I'm revealing to you. I hope you'll use it wisely and ethically.

How To Use The Hypnotic Archetypal Trigger Forbidden To Position Yourself, Your Brand, And Your Products In Such A Way Most People Want Them

Conspiracies are built on the foundation of things forbidden. There is knowledge that particular people don't want being exposed to the whole of society. Only a select group of people are privy to that information. There's a veil that stands in the way of someone having access to something they badly want, but cannot access. The mind starts to process ways in which it might be possible to drop the veil and find out what's been undisclosed. The same thing holds true with how you brand yourself. It also holds real with how you brand your product and your company. If you make it so certain things are forbidden that other people learn of, other people will go to great lengths to find them out. Nobody likes someone who keeps secrets. And it is very hard often for most people to keep secrets. Whenever we find something out we shouldn't know, were quick to disseminate that information to other people. There are a couple of steps you can take to use the hypnotic archetypal trigger forbidden to influence people to buy your products.

I. Step one: The first step is to build a mystery around your product that people can buy into.

II. Step two: The second step is to forbid people from trying to figure out your mystery. Incidentally, the mystery doesn't really exist, whatsoever.

III. Step three: The last step is to be indirect in how you associate your product with said mystery. You want to be understated because you want it to be as though it's almost a common truth everybody knows about already. You also want to be subtle because you don't want people thinking you're a kook. Yes, be subtle because when you leave the interaction, after subtly presenting the product, the person, you can bet, will be buying your product before sunset. If they don't the mystery and forbidden quality of that product will continue looming in their mind, until which time they free themselves by actually making a purchase. When you use the word forbidden without giving a rational explanation as to why something is off limits or should be kept hidden, you invoke the hypnotic state, which causes people to want to learn more, to the extent that they're willing to do what they shouldn't in order to discover and have what they want. The old adage: "curiosity killed the cat; satisfaction brought him back." In our case, the curiosity caused the consumer to discover what was forbidden from being known. As a result we gain the satisfaction of knowing that individual bought our product. The same mysterious essence that 'forbidden' possesses can be applied to other scenarios as well. It can be applied to helping you brand yourself personally, but it can also be applied in the same way to help you brand your company as well.

What Other Ways Can You Use The Hypnotic Archetypal Trigger Forbidden To Change People's Minds About Anything

I remember an incident once where a friend of mine backed out of going with me on a three-hour long trip. I wanted this person to come along for company, but also to help me with the driving. Last-minute they call me up on the phone and tell me some excuses to why they can't make it. This is what I told them: "I completely understand, and if I were you, I would probably be scared about the haunted town anyway. Everybody says that outsiders are forbidden from going there. So I completely understand and if you can't make it, you can't make it." My friend started asking me questions about the reported hauntings in the town and why outsiders were forbidden from going through the town. I was completely vague and simply explained I did not know too much about it. And, that I just knew people were not supposed to go there who were outsiders. As I was packing my belongings up, after having gotten off the phone with my friend, it wasn't two minutes later my friend called me back up and told me an excuse why now he could come with me. I had changed his mind simply utilizing this hypnotic archetypal trigger known as 'forbidden'. He wanted to do something he was forbidden from being able to do, because his curiosity had gotten the better of him. Forbidden is psychologically imprinted in our minds; we must do things we're forbidden from doing in order to preserve our rights to be able to do the things we want to do. There are so many different examples that I could give you where presenting something as being forbidden and off-limits, has actually helped me win a client over to buying a product or service I was selling.

There're been situations when I wanted my significant other to eat at the restaurants I wanted to eat at. I simply said, "Yeah, I hear the owner of the place doesn't really allow women to eat there, and he only does so because he is required by law." Let's just say my better-half made it a priority to make sure we ate at that restaurant that night. In fact, after eating there that night we ended up eating there many nights since then. She wants to assert a right to be able to eat wherever she wants; regardless of whether the person who owns a restaurant wants her there or not. I hope she's not reading this book!

Final Purport

When you employ the hypnotic archetypal trigger 'forbidden' into your persuasive messages it draws people to whatever they're forbidden from doing. When I was a child, I was forbid from doing many things, by my mum and dad. I often complied, but every once in a while I couldn't resist the temptation of breaking-the-law, so to speak, and disobeying them. My brother used to cross forbidden boundaries more often than I. I tell you this, because everybody is different. Some people will be attracted to things 'forbidden' and near always take action and do what they shouldn't. Others will heed its message, and obey; while, lesser consequence should impact their lives.

In this chapter you learned why knowing what, how-to, and how else the hypnotic archetypal trigger 'forbidden' can be applied successfully to hypnotically persuade others is so important. You learned behavior is predictable, and when you put something 'forbidden' and 'off-limits' in front of someone how they likely will respond. I shared with you a story of a friend, backing out of going with me on a trip, and how I used 'forbiddances' to change his mind, and persuade him to go indirectly. I taught you the three step formula for applying 'forbiddance' to your persuasion scenarios; namely: (a) build a mystery, (b) forbid your hypnotic subject from uncovering the mystery, and (c) associate your desired outcome into the mystery, indirectly.

The key take-a-way is this: people don't want to be told they cannot do something. When people are forbidden from doing something, psychologically something deep inside them gets triggered, and they are driven to do it anyway. Sometimes other emotions like fear get in the way of this hypnotic archetypal trigger, so you have to position this effectively in your persuasion messages. You don't want a stronger feeling like 'fear' to overpower what's forbidden. If you use this hypnotic archetypal trigger effectively, you can use reverse-psychology to get people to do what you want—for example, if you don't want your teenage boy hanging out around your house on Friday night, you might say, "I don't want you going to the movies with your friends this Friday night. I forbid you from doing that." You may not be surprised to discover your teenager goes to the movies with their friends.

Take Action Now

In order to get any value whatsoever from this book you must take action now on the instructions I'm going to be laying out for you. Do not be like most people—buy a book, half read it, set it aside, forget about it, never take action, never gain the advantages and benefits it has to offer you.

There is a reason you purchased this book. Do not forget that reason. If you attended one of my live training workshops, you would have participated in doing many exercises at the end of each module I taught you. This is because you get considerably more value practicing the techniques in a safe environment, before going out and practicing them in the real-world. Many people do not feel comfortable testing techniques they've just learnt blindly on real-life contexts. Do not be afraid to do these exercises: They are for your own good and self-development. Your personal power will increase when you proactively apply this knowledge to your specific contexts. Part of learning this information (the largest part) is applying it hands-on. Suspend your doubts and disbeliefs that you can do these exercises, because your insights will elevate to a higher level once you do them. You will only learn a fraction of what I teach in this book from reading the book. The great majority of your learning comes when you apply this information in whatever contexts you have been intentioned on learning it.

To prove this point: Think about your first kiss. You may have talked to friends about their first kiss to get some insight. Maybe you read a book on adolescent sexuality, where kissing was covered. You may have watched movies of actors kissing on the big-screen. Until you actually kissed a girl or guy for the first time, you didn't realize all that was involved in kissing, as you hadn't practiced it, and learned from that experience. I bet after you kissed for the first time, regardless how good or bad the kiss was; you felt pretty amazing afterward, and felt much more confident in kissing other people. I'm right, and you know it, so do these exercises! In fact, make a promise to yourself; you will not move on to the next chapter until these action steps have been completed. You'll thank yourself. I promise.

I. Make yourself take out a piece of paper and a pen/pencil and write down exactly how you'll utilize the information found in this chapter to fit your particular persuasion context.

II. Find an opportunity to apply what you learned in this chapter and apply it. After you have taken this initial action, journal your discoveries and results.

III. Take a 3x5 index card and summarize the leading points from this chapter. Let this summary serve as a quick flash card to jog your memory once a day, as you continue reading this book, and doing future exercises. This is important, because this book has a lot of information, and a fast flash card to look at daily will help you not to forget what you have learned. Over time, this knowledge will become imprinted on your hypnotic mind, where you'll take action on this knowledge without thinking about it consciously.

IV. Teach what you have learned in this chapter to a trusted friend whom you think might benefit. Teaching information to others helps you gain greater clarity and insights you'd likely not have gained trying to keep it all in your own mind.

V. Discuss with the friend you've taught this information to and take notes on their thoughts and understanding of the material. This way, you'll gain another person's perspective and likely gain a deeper understanding of the material.

After you have successfully completed each of these exercises, only then, proceed in moving forward to the next chapter. Do not take shortcuts and tell yourself the lie you'll come back and do the exercises later. Statistically speaking the probability is improbable you ever will. Take a leap of faith and do the exercise, please! Trust me; it's worth it, if you want to gain true mastery in hypnotic persuasion.

=====================xx==================

CHAPTER 8

ORIGNAL

I have developed a lot of systems in my time. Most of what I do professionally is create information products people want to buy. When I first got started publishing information on the Internet, many years ago, I didn't have the skill set and knowledge I do today to make the process of developing products easier on myself. I was looking for inventive ways to make my life simple, and in so doing; I create many systems to make what I'm doing much easier. Most of my work is independent of other people. Just the act of writing a book, for example, for someone that has never written a book before, or read any books on how to write books, the task can be quite daunting. I never thought it would happen, but I've written so many books, I don't actually know what number I'm on, in terms of how many I have written. I never thought I would get to this point in my writing career. A lot of the things I've created have been courses online people take, as well as live workshops I teach around the world. In order to be able to construct a workshop, there are many variables, which have to be considered, and the content has to be ordered in such a way the student attending will grasp easily, and see the value of what it is I'm teaching to them. I create systems to help people achieve what it is they want to achieve. The system in itself has value, because of its originality. Whenever you create something that is original, that has never been done before, there is intrinsic value in that and you can position your system or product as being original, and in so doing you will trigger the hypnotic archetypal trigger known as originality. I operate in a couple of niches. Whenever new product comes out that his original and different than anything else I've studied, attended by it. If someone else's hard work and laborers can make my life easier by me purchasing their knowledge I believe I've gotten a pretty good deal. It's also a win-win situation for them, because other people like myself probably feel the same way and as a result the individually came up with the original product or system will profit long into the future as other people see the intrinsic value and make a purchase as well. Have all wanted something that we perceived as valuable due to its originality. In this chapter will investigate the hypnotic archetypal trigger known as originality to exploit it for our purposes of hypnotizing people to make them want to buy our products, do business with us, and change the minds about other things. Were you look at why it's important understand this hypnotic archetypal trigger – originality. Organized for what you need to know in order to position your product or service so that it is perceived as original and therefore perceived of as having intrinsic value to the potential buyer. Or go look at how to systematically rollout this plan of originality, and finally we look at how originality can be is another context beyond just sales and product positioning.

Why Would You Want To Position Your Product Or Service Using The Hypnotic Archetypal Trigger Known As Originality

There are lots of reasons you might want to take advantage of the hypnotic archetypal trigger 'originality'. For the most part, when you develop a system or new product, you want to build intrinsic value by utilizing the hypnotic archetypal trigger known as 'originality' positioning your product, self, or system as uniquely original. You want to do this because when people perceive your product as being different and completely original from everything else out there they realize the only way to go learn the information or enjoy the features, advantages, and benefits of that product are to purchase the product. The only time this doesn't work so sell is with replicated systems. Some people do a fantastic job with this, but the truth remains the replications still have less value than the original product. If you take neurolinguistic programming, for example, which was invented by Dr's.

Richard Bandler and John grander back during the 70s, there are tons of books detailing how to use NLP for self-excellence, personal and professional development, and to do rapid change work in therapeutic contexts. Bandler and Grinder were the original founders of NLP, however; for this reason, these two men have intrinsic value in this specific niche. There have been many people that have come along since the 1970s to contribute and add to the field of neurolinguistic programming, but whenever someone new discovers NLP, one of the first things, they do is buy these earlier books by the original founders. They do this because in their mind, they believe in order fully to understand NLP, they must rely on the original instructions given by Bandler and grinder. Another reason for this has to do with communicating with others about NLP. If you want to seem intelligent, then it is recommended that you look at the original literature, which was produced by the original founders. If someone asked you a question about something that was uncovered in one of these earlier books by Bandler and Grinder, if you haven't read those books, then, instantly it demonstrates a lower value to the person you're communicating with. Originality is different than mere difference. Originality has value because it came first. In order to gain recognition and to position yourself as an authority in a particular field or niche, you really have to create something that is truly unique and original to that niche. You must understand this underlying principle.

What You Need To Understand In Order To Advertise Someone Using The Hypnotic Archetypal Trigger Originality

What you need to understand in order to hypnotize someone using originality as a trigger for trance, is that people are hypnotically attracted to new ideas and concepts, which are truly unique and original. Culturally, we are socially conditioned to want to be known for something. Something that sets us apart from everything else out there. This is why inventors stay motivated, because they know if they create the right invention, people will be hypnotically drawn to it and as a side effect, the inventor, will become well-known and well-respected. Artists want to create a famous masterpiece that will be remembered long after they've left the earth. Writers all want to write the Great American novel; to leave a legacy behind, and set a new bar for writers everywhere to compete with. People in every field want to leave a mark. We start by asking ourselves a question: "What do I want to be remembered for?" Just by asking this question we start to set in motion our minds so we conceptualize and theorize some ideas. We start thinking instead of just having thoughts, about original thinking. This thinking then translates into bright ideas, that lead us to take action to accomplish our life's work. People who have achieved such mastery, have created products and works of art people perceive as having intrinsic value, and earn a name for themselves. We want to be successful, and there is a secret aspect of our inner self who imagines one day being famous for something original. So, what you must first understand upfront is everybody is drawn to products, ideas, and all things created, that have an original component to them. Those values and originality are beyond mere practical value.

How Can You Brand Yourself As Original, And Magnetize People To Products And Ideas

There are some steps involved in positioning yourself or your product so originality is conveyed. Incidentally, you can still create a product based off of someone else's product, and at the same time position it so it is perceived as having an original value. Sometimes when you're sitting in a meeting, listening to someone speak, something they say may trigger an innovative idea that you can capitalize on and make your own. In the section I will cover what the steps are you need to understand in order to position yourself as 'original'; to hypnotically magnetize people to want to do business with you, accepting your ideas and persuasions.

    I.   Step one: first, you must be able to find a spin that is original to whatever it is you're marketing or selling. This means branching off of everything else out there, and formatting and developing it in a way other people who buy your product or listen to your message will perceive it as being totally unique and original.

II. Step two: the next step to creating an aura of originality around a product or yourself, is to present what you have created in such a way people perceive it as being original. By this, I mean you must create some hype around your product using social proof as the means to do so. To do this you will need to get other people on your side, and have other people review your product or your idea and give comments or reviews and shed light on how original and ingenious your idea, product, or self happens to be. At this stage you'll use these reviews and as social proof your product or idea is original, making other people believe the same.

III. Step three: the last step is to spread the word, to bring more fame and notoriety to the product or service you've created. Now that you have your testimonials; have created an atmosphere which positions your product, service, self or ideas as being truly unique and original; it's now time to create momentum behind your launch. The more people who buy the product or your idea mentally or through financial means, the more momentum you will be creating, and more sales you'll make. Some people take the approach of giving their product away for free until which time they gained enough momentum to raise the price for that product. When everybody wants something, the product's intrinsic value gets raised. You must be careful in taking this approach, however, because the idea is to create enough intrinsic value through the presentation of originality, that everyone in a marketplace feels left behind, if they don't own your product or buy into your idea. One year, back during the 90s they came out with a popular toy, all the children (even some adults) wanted, and they sold out, and people were paying exorbitant amounts of money, and doing same very dangerous things to make sure their child received on from Santa. My point is: People died!

What Else You Need To Do And Understand In Order To Hypnotize Your Subject Utilizing The Hypnotic Archetypal Trigger Known As Originality

There are so many ways in which you can sell people on the idea that something is original, but it requires a little thought on your end. If you're a sales professional, and you're walking into a sales call (selling a particular product) you can position it as having original appeal. You simply do this through suggesting it is an original product. You then present your product to your customer as being innovative and really sought after. Products that are original have intrinsic value and are greatly sought after. When people perceive other people are seeking out and wanting your product, it increases the likelihood, they will purchase your product. Another context, which you may want to use this hypnotic archetypal trigger 'originality', is to influence your children or other people you work with to come up with original ideas. You can do this by simply encouraging and inspiring them with your own ideas. This creates a brain-storming effect, and when it rains down one idea, it storms down many more. These should be ideas that will help set you, your company, and the workforce apart from competition. When this happens, people in society will grab hold of your brand, and become loyal and devout. They will want to do business with your company. They will see it as different, however; in the context of originality.

I remember some years ago, though I forget exactly how many years it has actually been, but the car company Saturn gained the attention of the US consumer. Saturn had created an original positioning in which they utilized the friendliness, ideas, and innovations of their workers, (the people who mass-produce and manufacture their car), as a company that was completely unique from the way that other auto manufacturers were doing business. Saturn became the 'go to workplace' setting the stage for other company's repositioning efforts to emerge. Other companies, like Google have followed suit by creating original atmospheres, for their employees to work within. They've created workplaces, which include rooms only for allowing their employees to think and come up with ideas. They have created spaces in their office complexes to allow employees to take naps and to rest when they feel fatigued. They have provided in-house cafeterias so workers can take time to enjoy a meal, without having to drive across town in busy traffic. Google understood if they could keep their employees from being stressed out, this solved a lot of company problems. As a result of these efforts these employees became better employees and have further advanced the company. This type of 'original', outside the box thinking, has led to huge strides in the way businesses productively do business. This is all been done through creating an atmosphere of originality, which is unexpected compared to the way that most other companies do business. Because of this, these companies get tens of thousands of resumes from qualified workers all over the world, who want nothing more than to work at these innovative companies. This has also created devout and loyal followers for these companies and their brands. All of this has equaled more sales, and further advancement of these companies. When you position something as original you set a new standard; one that has never been reached before. There are so many different contexts you can apply this principle to; it only requires a little thinking on your part in order to enact it.

Final Purport

In this chapter, we've covered quite a bit of material. This material is directly related to the hypnotic archetypal trigger known as originality. You have learned originality can be quite hypnotic in attracting people to products and services—even companies. The attraction comes as a result of the differentiation positioned as unique, innovative, and original. People like originality. For this reason, I highly recommend you understand this hypnotic archetypal trigger, as everything ever created fresh and new has come from an original idea someone or some company has developed and come up with.

I walked you through why 'originality' is important. I taught you what you needed to know upfront before implementing this hypnotic archetypal trigger into your hypnotic messages. I then took you through the sequential steps necessary to successfully implement this strategy of 'originality'. Finally, I took you through how else you can take 'originality' to position yourself apart from other people, while encouraging other people to join together and do the same.

Take Action Now

In order to get any value whatsoever from this book you must take action now on the instructions I'm going to be laying out for you. Do not be like most people—buy a book, half read it, set it aside, forget about it, never take action, never gain the advantages and benefits it has to offer you.

There is a reason you purchased this book. Do not forget that reason. If you attended one of my live training workshops, you would have participated in doing many exercises at the end of each module I taught you. This is because you get considerably more value practicing the techniques in a safe environment, before going out and practicing them in the real-world. Many people do not feel comfortable testing techniques they've just learnt blindly on real-life contexts. Do not be afraid to do these exercises: They are for your own good and self-development. Your personal power will increase when you proactively apply this knowledge to your specific contexts. Part of learning this information (the largest part) is applying it hands-on. Suspend your doubts and disbeliefs that you can do these exercises, because your insights will elevate to a higher level once you do them. You will only learn a fraction of what I teach in this book from reading the book. The great majority of your learning comes when you apply this information in whatever contexts you have been intentioned on learning it.

To prove this point: Think about your first kiss. You may have talked to friends about their first kiss to get some insight. Maybe you read a book on adolescent sexuality, where kissing was covered. You may have watched movies of actors kissing on the big-screen. Until you actually kissed a girl or guy for the first time, you didn't realize all that was involved in kissing, as you hadn't practiced it, and learned from that experience. I bet after you kissed for the first time, regardless how good or bad the kiss was; you felt pretty amazing afterward, and felt much more confident in kissing other people. I'm right, and you know it, so do these exercises! In fact, make a promise to yourself; you will not move on to the next chapter until these action steps have been completed. You'll thank yourself. I promise.

I. Make yourself take out a piece of paper and a pen/pencil and write down exactly how you'll utilize the information found in this chapter to fit your particular persuasion context.

II. Find an opportunity to apply what you learned in this chapter and apply it. After you have taken this initial action, journal your discoveries and results.

III. Take a 3x5 index card and summarize the leading points from this chapter. Let this summary serve as a quick flash card to jog your memory once a day, as you continue reading this book, and doing future exercises. This is important, because this book has a lot of information, and a fast flash card to look at daily will help you not to forget what you have learned. Over time, this knowledge will become imprinted on your hypnotic mind, where you'll take action on this knowledge without thinking about it consciously.

IV. Teach what you have learned in this chapter to a trusted friend whom you think might benefit. Teaching information to others helps you gain greater clarity and insights you'd likely not have gained trying to keep it all in your own mind.

V. Discuss with the friend you've taught this information to and take notes on their thoughts and understanding of the material. This way, you'll gain another person's perspective and likely gain a deeper understanding of the material.

After you have successfully completed each of these exercises, only then, proceed in moving forward to the next chapter. Do not take shortcuts and tell yourself the lie you'll come back and do the exercises later. Statistically speaking the probability is improbable you ever will. Take a leap of faith and do the exercise, please! Trust me; it's worth it, if you want to gain true mastery in hypnotic persuasion.

====================xx=================

CHAPTER 9

RARE

When something is rare it's in short supply usually. For this reason, it is automatically catapulted to a level of having intrinsic value. When you think of rare coins, or think of rare art, these are things we might observe in someone's private collection, or be allowed to observe in a museum. People visit museums more often than not so they can experience something they don't experience anywhere else. There's sort of a magnetic draw causing people to want to see things that they can't see anywhere else in the world. The travel industry capitalizes on this 'rare' factor quite a lot. They position trips and idea of experiences of visiting another country as something, which might only happen once or twice in someone's lifetime. For this reason travel can get, quite costly, and people still don't mind paying for expensive airline tickets and hotel stays, because of the intrinsic value built into traveling abroad by the travel industry. There's always this sense in the back of your mind telling you if we don't spend the money, and take the time to travel and see all the spectacular things the world has to offer, then chances are you probably never will. We can spend the money and lose it, and still earn more money, but if we don't take the trip to gain the experience, we can never get that back. So most often when someone takes a trip abroad and has an incredible life experience, whether good, bad, or indifferent, it still is an experience, and so there's intrinsic value that surpasses the practical value. The idea of 'rarity' is a hypnotic archetypal trigger causing people to take actions they may not otherwise take, simply because rarity positions the experience beyond the practical value. Something that is said to be a once-in-a-lifetime opportunity, cannot be ignored. In this chapter you'll be looking at rarity and how you can position yourself and products, and even your communication so you influence and persuade people over to your persuasions, and also to take actions that you want them to take. You will also be covering the details in terms of what you need to know to capitalize on using this hypnotic archetypal trigger. As well as, you'll be learning the sequential steps necessary to implement a strategy using rarity change people's minds. Toward the end of this chapter, we will also be looking at some possible scenarios where rarity can be applied for other purposes.

Why You Might Want To Know About Rarity In Order To Utilize This Hypnotic Archetypal Trigger To Influence People To Take The Actions That You Want Them To Take

Back in time, perhaps during childhood, you may think to yourself about some pleasurable memories or some not so excellent memories you might have had, but one thing remains absolutely true, and that is you can never get those moments back. For this reason, these memories have intrinsic value for you. This is very personal. Other people have memories too, and it is these memories people have, which you can utilize the influence people to take actions the future actions you want them to have. Why...think 'rarity'? The rarer something is the more value it has. It furthermore, parallels the influence principle of scarcity. The more rare something is, the less of it available for the general public to possess. Rarity can be applied to opportunities and missed opportunities. It can be applied to limited product offerings. It can also be applied to any other type of opportunity, you can probably think up. This is why rarity work so well when it comes to selling ideas to people and getting them to buy those ideas, and then to take actions congruent with the direction you want them to take action.

What Do You Need To Understand First And Foremost About Rarity, Before You Implement In Whatever Application You Have Planned For It

On something that was given to you by someone who's passed away, that had some type of intrinsic value to, but you know firsthand the pain associated with losing something so valuable. Maybe it was a pocket watch passed down from your great, great, great grandfather. You had this pocket watch, and you stored in a secret place, only you knew about. Then one day you go to that hidden place, just to discover the pocket watch is no longer there. What do you do? Already the answer has probably come to you – you panic! You panic, because this is perhaps one of the most valuable things, you've ever possessed, and it has such a significant meaning to you, that when you no longer have possession of it, you experience a sense of trauma. Something rare is something that possesses so much value; that people are willing to pay astronomical rates just to possess it. Something rare is also often prohibited from other people owning. It's one-of-a-kind. Also, things that are rare can have sentimental value as well. This most often happens when things are passed down from one generation to the next; entrusted to be passed down to future generations as well. Like for example, the pocket watch scenario I told you about a moment ago. Understand things that are rare can also be priceless. By priceless I mean that they can command about any price so long as someone is willing to buy it and someone is willing to part with it. Something quite rare is often not always easily parted with, making it more valuable.

How Can You Use The Hypnotic Archetypal Trigger Known As Rarity To Hypnotize People Into Paying The Price You Want In Changing Their Minds

The way you change minds using rarity is by first presenting an offer to someone, and then setting a benchmark, on how long they have actually to respond and accept your offer. You force people to make up their mind, and in such situations impulse can kick in, and the person makes a decision without fully considering it one way or the other. You can accomplish this by simply offering something rare or at least presenting it in a way that makes it appear to be rare. Appearances can be deceptive—for example, people attracting a mate, usually put on their best face, and behavior, masking their true nature. We wonder why there are so many divorces, don't we? Finding someone with the attributes, values, and benefits we hope to find in a mate, is rare. For this reason, a potential life partner may give the illusion they are what you're looking for, hiding their true nature, acting instead as a chameleon to get you to accept them and buy them as a life partner. You can only hide your true self for so long, before your true colors start emerging. Sure it may be easy to sell you to someone and attract a temporary relationship, but keeping that relationship happy and enduring is the real challenge. Being honest, being your true self, might take you longer to attract the right mate, but when someone comes along and shows attraction and interest in you, chances are you'll have a much better relationship and a longer lasting one.

I remember one time talking with a gentleman who owned a rare book I had always wanted. At the time, money was a little hard to come by for me. The gentleman offered to sell me the book if I bought it within one hour's time. I tried negotiating the timeline, explaining to him I'd like to have at least a day or two to consider if I could even afford it or not. The gentleman told me it had to be then or never, and that I couldn't have any time to think about it. I just so happen to have enough money at that moment to cover the cost of the book, but that money was hard to come by, and was already allocated toward paying bills and other things. Knowing I had opportunities to come up with money through other outlets to pay my bills, and I didn't have the opportunity to buy the book probably ever again, I spent all the money I had and bought the book. I have never regretted that decision. I still own the book. Rarity causes people to want things that they can't have. When these things are presented to us as being rare, it is possible for someone to present us the offer, stipulating we make a decision right there and then to buy it or not.

I. The first thing you want to do to position a product as rare, is to market it as such and explain the product as being a very rare to come by, or very limited opportunity; one that will not come around again forever possibly.

II. The second step, after you've positioned the product as being rare and limited, is to decide on the price you want the customer to pay for it. One way you go about achieving this is questioning in your mind what can the customer or potential customer afford to pay for the item that you're selling. The idea here is to get them to come off the most amount of money possible.

III. The third step, and final step, is to present the offer, and ask for the sale right there and then, without giving the potential customer time to think about it. The customer must understand if they say no, they are forfeiting the possibility of ever being able to own the product ever again. You must stress the features of the product, the logical advantages of the product, in the emotional benefits the potential customer will gain when they make the purchase.

You must besides stress what the customer will be giving up in terms of the features, advantages, and benefits. The whole offer must be presented from an emotional view, where the potential customer becomes so hypnotized, they are literally unable to think and enter a hypnotic trance. In the state of hypnosis, they become reactionary, and they simply take decisions based on emotion alone.

How Else Might You Use Rarity To Change Minds And Get What You Want

I want to invite you to think about this question for a moment: What other applications can you think of where you could use rarity as a hypnotic archetypal trigger to influence people and even change their minds about things that they have said no to in the past? In an incident that happened several years ago; a close family member had invited me to come visit them. At the time, I told them no, because it simply was not what I wanted. Already settled in life, with a business to operate, and perfectly content with how I was currently living, it made no sense for me to go and stay with that family member for a few months' time. My family member told me they would be downsizing to smaller house later, and the opportunity for me to come and visit would essentially evaporate. They then lived in a beautiful part of the country, in a rather nice home. After thinking about the offer, and realizing it was truly an once-in-a-lifetime offer, I decided to go for it. I made the decision to go and did. It was a great time I had, and true to their word, they did in fact downsize, and it wouldn't have been possible for me to go and visit, without coming off of a lot of money to stay in a hotel room and so forth. So I am actually glad I went. This is one application I'm throwing out here where my mind was changed as a result of their argument the opportunity would likely never come around again. It was a rare opportunity, and one that if I hadn't taken up on, I would have forfeited forever. I changed my mind as a result of learning the opportunity wouldn't be offered me again.

Final Purport

In this chapter, we covered how rarity can be utilized to present offers, change people's minds, and position products as well as ourselves in a way, which encourages people to take action in the direction we want them to take those actions. When someone is presented with a 'rare' offer, whcih if they refuse they refuse they lose out on forever, they become hypnotized by their own thoughts, simply because there is so much pressure put on them. In this way, they are forced to make a decision without being able to think it through logically. When you present a rare offer to someone we've also said it's hard for them to not say 'yes' to that offer. The fear of loss kicks in, and for that reason people simply say 'yes'. The psychology of avoiding pain, which comes from not being able to have what you want, coupled with the ability to have something rare, is a strong synergistic hypnotic soup that can influence people to take action without them even thinking about it. I encourage you really to think about some of the past times in your life, when something was presented to you in an untimely fashion, which required you to say 'yes' or 'no' to an offer that would never come back around again. I want you to think about these times, because I'm sure, you'll find more often than not you said yes, even if it meant going against your better judgment at the time; simply because if you paused or hesitated, you'd be missing out on something.

Take Action Now

In order to get any value whatsoever from this book you must take action now on the instructions I'm going to be laying out for you. Do not be like most people—buy a book, half read it, set it aside, forget about it, never take action, never gain the advantages and benefits it has to offer you.

There is a reason you purchased this book. Do not forget that reason. If you attended one of my live training workshops, you would have participated in doing many exercises at the end of each module I taught you. This is because you get considerably more value practicing the techniques in a safe environment, before going out and practicing them in the real-world. Many people do not feel comfortable testing techniques they've just learnt blindly on real-life contexts. Do not be afraid to do these exercises: They are for your own good and self-development. Your personal power will increase when you proactively apply this knowledge to your specific contexts. Part of learning this information (the largest part) is applying it hands-on. Suspend your doubts and disbeliefs that you can do these exercises, because your insights will elevate to a higher level once you do them. You will only learn a fraction of what I teach in this book from reading the book. The great majority of your learning comes when you apply this information in whatever contexts you have been intentioned on learning it.

To prove this point: Think about your first kiss. You may have talked to friends about their first kiss to get some insight. Maybe you read a book on adolescent sexuality, where kissing was covered. You may have watched movies of actors kissing on the big-screen. Until you actually kissed a girl or guy for the first time, you didn't realize all that was involved in kissing, as you hadn't practiced it, and learned from that experience. I bet after you kissed for the first time, regardless how good or bad the kiss was; you felt pretty amazing afterward, and felt much more confident in kissing other people. I'm right, and you know it, so do these exercises!

In fact, make a promise to yourself; you will not move on to the next chapter until these action steps have been completed. You'll thank yourself. I promise.

I. Make yourself take out a piece of paper and a pen/pencil and write down exactly how you'll utilize the information found in this chapter to fit your particular persuasion context.

II. Find an opportunity to apply what you learned in this chapter and apply it. After you have taken this initial action, journal your discoveries and results.

III. Take a 3x5 index card and summarize the leading points from this chapter. Let this summary serve as a quick flash card to jog your memory once a day, as you continue reading this book, and doing future exercises. This is important, because this book has a lot of information, and a fast flash card to look at daily will help you not to forget what you have learned. Over time, this knowledge will become imprinted on your hypnotic mind, where you'll take action on this knowledge without thinking about it consciously.

IV. Teach what you have learned in this chapter to a trusted friend whom you think might benefit. Teaching information to others helps you gain greater clarity and insights you'd likely not have gained trying to keep it all in your own mind.

V. Discuss with the friend you've taught this information to and take notes on their thoughts and understanding of the material. This way, you'll gain another person's perspective and likely gain a deeper understanding of the material.

After you have successfully completed each of these exercises, only then, proceed in moving forward to the next chapter. Do not take shortcuts and tell yourself the lie you'll come back and do the exercises later. Statistically speaking the probability is improbable you ever will. Take a leap of faith and do the exercise, please! Trust me; it's worth it, if you want to gain true mastery in hypnotic persuasion.

===================xx=================

CHAPTER 9

POPULAR

There is such an innate attraction to everything that is popular. We look to people who are popular. We look at things that are popular. Whatever is trendy and hot, you can be sure some marketer is capitalizing on it, positioning their product in alignment with whatever is indeed popular at the moment. Popularity can be tricky. Some things never go out of style and are always somehow popular. Other things, on the other hand, come into popularity one moment, and before you even get to enjoy them, and experience them, they go out of style and lose their luster. I remember an incident in middle school where silk shirts became the craze. It was a trend, and everyone in my school, who was anybody, i.e. popular, owned these silk shirts. They were nice shirts, I must admit. Unfortunately, because of the popularity they were priced beyond what my mother was willing to pay for them. As you might imagine, I wasn't all that cool or popular myself. Popularity breeds popularity. What I mean by this is, if you want to be popular yourself, there is an unwritten rule that basically says you must position yourself in alignment with whatever else happens to be popular that moment. Because I was unable to align myself with the silk shirt trend, I myself was not privy to enter the world of the social elite, who were all popular kids in my middle school. An interesting thing happened. The next year, we were shopping at a local department store, and surprisingly enough the price of silk shirts had reduced astronomically. When I saw this, I insisted my mother purchase for me five silk shirts, so that I could wear a different one, every day of the week. Because we were shopping for school clothes, she agreed, since the price was so favorable. The first week of school I learned something very important. I realized none of the others kids in my middle school that were considered popular by definition, were wearing the silk shirts. Silk was out of style and a certain brand of cotton T-shirts was in style. This is the reason the price of silk had dropped, because the demand had lessened. I can't tell you the embarrassment and ridicule and unkind remarks I received as a result of having to wear those silk shirts all year long. Yet, I think you can imagine what I must've dealt with. So you have to be careful with popularity. You have to remain in check with the current styles and trends of the day, in order to enter the world of popularity. Even so, people are always drawn to what's popular and trendy. This is one reason clothes designers are able to charge such an exorbitant price for their outfits, because they have designed them for this purpose of creating this culture were popularity rules, and anyone else is flat on their luck when it comes to being popular themselves.

In this chapter, we're going to exploit popularity, and I'm going to show you why you need to understand how hypnotic 'popularity' can actually be. Then, I'm going to walk you through what you need to understand so you can utilize popularity to gain the upper edge and get people to pay a higher price for your items. I'm also going to show you how you can exploit what's popular to position yourself and your products in such a way people are forced to buy them. After all of this, I'm then going to open up the discussion to talk about that other contexts and applications you might be able to exploit this hypnotic archetypal trigger named 'popular'.

Why Do You Need Understand The Hypnotic Archetypal Trigger Called Popularity

If you go back to what I was talking about before, in a previous chapter, where I discussed about early human civilization and human beings deciding to join together into groups known as tribes, you'll remember a typical tribe consisted of an estimated 50 individuals. With a group of fifty people a tribe could withstand many of the dangers that stood in their way of surviving in replicating. Inside every group, there is a unique culture; that is to say, there are things the group values as a whole. Whenever someone has an idea that the group finds useful, this idea then becomes popular. When an ideas becomes popular its hard for those who disagree with its usefulness, to argue otherwise. Instead, these few individuals follow the herd mentality, and accept what's popular as approved. The same thing holds true in our modern society. When a fad or a trend catches on, it has a tendency to go viral, and an entire country and even the world may jump on the bandwagon and begin engaging in whatever activity is well-liked, whichever fad is popular, or even purchase whatever happens to be trendy at that moment in time. Popularity creates a contrast between what is valuable and what is not. By valuable, I simply mean what is likeable compared to what is not so nice. This can also be what is ugly compared to something that is fashionable. During the 1970s, shag carpeting was popular. Today it is not. During the 70s and early 80s bell-bottom pants were fashionable. Today no one would be caught dead wearing them—no one wishing to go along with the trends of society anyway.

The reason you need to understand the hypnotic archetypal trigger known as 'popular', is so when no one's buying your product, and everyone seems to be buying an inferior product, you'll know why. Your failure to position your product, self, and ideas in alignment with what's popular, and in good taste, can greatly hinder your sales, placement in your market, and even whether or not people accept your ideas or not.

What Do You Need Understand To Create A Value Proposition Utilizing The Hypnotic Archetypal Trigger Known As Popularity

Really, what you need to understand about popularity, is society determines the trends, just as much as marketers do. In order to make something popular, marketers must position the product in a way where consumers must buy that product or experience discomfort somehow (e.g., mental dissonance, or physical discomfort). Popularity is also a process, which requires a large section of society getting on board to agree something is popular or isn't. You need to understand popularity is closely associated with the influence principle known as 'social proof'. When enough other people believe something to be true, it's challenging for an outsider to disagree.

How Do You Create Intrinsic Value Utilizing The Hypnotic Archetypal Trigger Known As Popularity

For something to be popular, you must understand other people have to believe in the product, idea, or you. Just having a few close friends telling you they like your product, isn't enough. You have to position it to be approved among a large group of individuals. You must make your product irresistible, and position it so that not just a few people; but, rather, a widespread many people find it attractive, and desirable. If you are able to do this, you stand a chance your product or idea will catch on and become popular. Things, people, and ideas that elevate to a level of popularity, might also go on to become unforgotten, and be written about in the history books. If you take, for example, Albert Einstein, you know firsthand who this individual is, and even though he has been dead for years and years, he is still just as popular as ever. As I mentioned earlier, some things never go out of style or lessen in popularity. Other things are here one moment, and gone the next. There are a couple of steps you can take instantly to position yourself, ideas, and even products, so they reach a level of popularity.

The first step to positioning something as 'popular' is to understand other things, which are also popular, and then piggyback off of those things, associating your product with them. For example, I have a friend who makes pipes for a living. These pipes are handmade, and of the finest quality. When my friend asked me how he might be able to sell more of these hand-crafted pipes, I helped him by suggesting he associate his brand and product with other things, which were popular. My friend sent out free pipes to musicians and songwriters and other popular people. One musician loved the pipe so much he gave an endorsement. My friend has sense used the endorsement to sell thousands of his pipes. Overnight he had to hire more staff, just to be able to keep up with the demand.

Now you also want to create some buzz around your product, utilizing the power of the Internet, and special groups. For example, that friend I told you about, who makes handmade pipes, created an advertisement with that endorsement from that celebrity musician, and very quickly the advertisement was sent across the Internet through his friends, their friends, and their friends, and so on. Before long, everyone wanted their very own pipe that was endorsed by that popular musician.

How-Else You Can Harness The Hypnotic Power Of Popularity To Get What You Want

If you're in a sales call, you can talk favorably about the product you're pitching, exclaiming with excitement, how everybody loves the product, and cannot wait for the next product to come out from your company. You can talk about how quickly, and amazingly, the product has caught on with others, and how easy your job has gotten as a result. This starts imprinting the message that your product is popular amongst other buyers. The potential buyer you happen to be in front of, telling all this to, will likely get excited, and join the 'in-crowd' and purchase from you as well. You can even compound this by exclaiming how you will likely run out of product by the end of the week. Adding in the influence principle 'scarcity' will help you sell more, you can be sure. Just take a few moments to think about all the other applications you can apply 'popularity' to your particular context, and utilize it to affect people's minds, and get them to take actions you want them to take. I'm sure you'll come up with many.

There are many applications, such as, selling goods you create, which let you harness the power of popularity to create other outcomes you desire, as well. For example, if you're forming a cult, one thing you can do is create popularity for yourself within a group of individuals, and use that popularity to recruit other new members. I'm not suggesting you start a cult; however, I do use this to serve as an example to show you how out-of-the-box you can actually go with utilizing these hypnotic archetypal triggers. Human beings desire on a deeper level than they can understand, to be liked, valued, as well as avoid pain and discomfort. One reason school-age children wish to dress alike, wearing whatever happens to be popular at the moment is, so they don't get made fun of. Even if they don't like the trend, they still understand on an unconscious, hypnotic, level, that in order to remain well-liked, and not be messed with, it is important to group themselves with other people who are popular.

Final Purport

Popularity is an interesting paradox, given in our Western culture, most people prefer to maintain their own identity and individuality. This being said, our human ancestry realized early on we're dependent on other people for our survival and replication. For this reason, this paradox exists; namely: we know in order to fit into our tribe, successfully, we must conform to what the tribe values, likes and dislikes, and do our best to fit in with whatever is popular among the group. This affects us on a deep psychological level. In many Eastern cultures, collectivity is valued over individuality. They understand firsthand the importance of maintaining and assimilating within the tribal environment. For this reason, the individual is not as valued as much as the group itself is. The leaders of a group or the great majority of a group or tribe dictate what everybody else must value and appreciate, and perceive insofar as popularity is concerned. In Western culture, individuality may be praised, but even so, in the workplace, and our educational institutions, which we spend a great deal of our life's existence, not to mention our family groups; we learn firsthand being collective in our thinking and in how we present ourselves is valued on a far greater level than how we present ourselves as individuals and outcasts. There is an organizational behavior concept known as group-think, which is defined as: "Groupthink is a psychological phenomenon that occurs within a group of people, in which the desire for harmony or conformity in the group results in an irrational or dysfunctional decision-making outcome. Group members try to minimize conflict and reach a consensus decision without critical evaluation of alternative viewpoints, by actively suppressing dissenting viewpoints, and by isolating themselves from outside influences." This just goes to show that what's popular doesn't necessarily have to be rationally popular, only accepted by the great consensus of people in that group.

Take Action Now

In order to get any value whatsoever from this book you must take action now on the instructions I'm going to be laying out for you. Do not be like most people—buy a book, half read it, set it aside, forget about it, never take action, never gain the advantages and benefits it has to offer you.

There is a reason you purchased this book. Do not forget that reason. If you attended one of my live training workshops, you would have participated in doing many exercises at the end of each module I taught you. This is because you get considerably more value practicing the techniques in a safe environment, before going out and practicing them in the real-world. Many people do not feel comfortable testing techniques they've just learnt blindly on real-life contexts. Do not be afraid to do these exercises: They are for your own good and self-development. Your personal power will increase when you proactively apply this knowledge to your specific contexts. Part of learning this information (the largest part) is applying it hands-on. Suspend your doubts and disbeliefs that you can do these exercises, because your insights will elevate to a higher level once you do them. You will only learn a fraction of what I teach in this book from reading the book. The great majority of your learning comes when you apply this information in whatever contexts you have been intentioned on learning it.

To prove this point: Think about your first kiss. You may have talked to friends about their first kiss to get some insight. Maybe you read a book on adolescent sexuality, where kissing was covered. You may have watched movies of actors kissing on the big-screen. Until you actually kissed a girl or guy for the first time, you didn't realize all that was involved in kissing, as you hadn't practiced it, and learned from that experience. I bet after you kissed for the first time, regardless how good or bad the kiss was; you felt pretty amazing afterward, and felt much more confident in kissing other people. I'm right, and you know it, so do these exercises! In fact, make a promise to yourself; you will not move on to the next chapter until these action steps have been completed. You'll thank yourself. I promise.

I. Make yourself take out a piece of paper and a pen/pencil and write down exactly how you'll utilize the information found in this chapter to fit your particular persuasion context.

II. Find an opportunity to apply what you learned in this chapter and apply it. After you have taken this initial action, journal your discoveries and results.

III. Take a 3x5 index card and summarize the leading points from this chapter. Let this summary serve as a quick flash card to jog your memory once a day, as you continue reading this book, and doing future exercises. This is important, because this book has a lot of information, and a fast flash card to look at daily will help you not to forget what you have learned. Over time, this knowledge will become imprinted on your hypnotic mind, where you'll take action on this knowledge without thinking about it consciously.

IV. Teach what you have learned in this chapter to a trusted friend whom you think might benefit. Teaching information to others helps you gain greater clarity and insights you'd likely not have gained trying to keep it all in your own mind.

V. Discuss with the friend you've taught this information to and take notes on their thoughts and understanding of the material. This way, you'll gain another person's perspective and likely gain a deeper understanding of the material.

After you have successfully completed each of these exercises, only then, proceed in moving forward to the next chapter. Do not take shortcuts and tell yourself the lie you'll come back and do the exercises later. Statistically speaking the probability is improbable you ever will. Take a leap of faith and do the exercise, please! Trust me; it's worth it, if you want to gain true mastery in hypnotic persuasion.

===================xx=================

CHAPTER 10

CONTRARY

I think of the word contrary, and I associate that with the word contrast. I don't think a lot of people do, however, because if they did, I think they would understand more understand from a psychological perspective how important contrast really is. Sometimes we need to be able to compare certain situations to other situations, in order to be able to gain some perspective. When people make buying decisions often times sales professionals place three options in front of them with three different price points. One price point may be toward the right hand tail of the bell curve. One option is usually right in the middle of the bell curve. And another option is usually toward the left-hand curve (tail of the bell curve. Just like a bell curve and statistics, most people tend to fall within the middle range of the bell curve. Each tail represents the outlying area where small percentage of people will fall into. By giving a contrast, people are able quickly to discern which is the best solution for them. It also keeps them from having to think about every solution out there, which they haven't yet considered. Most humans fall within the middle of the bell curve. We comply to social expectation. We want to fit in. We tend to value the same values. We tend to be attracted to the equivalent things. We all happen to be like each other. In many respects, societally, we have become conditioned to believe if we are like someone, then we can more trust that individual, rely on that individual, predict that individual's behavior, and feel more at ease with that individual. Some may be wondering, where am I going with all of this? In this chapter we are going to be exploring the hypnotic archetypal trigger that will refer to as 'contrary'.

We have all known people who went against the grain. By this, I mean it almost seemed as though they were predisposed to disagree, and stand out, not so much in a positive way, but in a way, which conflicts with the thinking of most individuals. You might say these individuals are the outliers on a bell curve. They are the exception to the rule. There is, however, something valuable to be gained by understanding this hypnotic archetypal trigger known as 'contrary'. Whenever we're presented with an idea that something is contrary to our expectations, beliefs, or the way in which we think things should be, we may not at first grab hold tightly to such a contrary idea or individual, but we are triggered psychologically to consider it none the less, and this can even be after the fact. For example, I if a sales professional visits you, gives you a presentation, let's say, and you dismiss him or her, and they go about their business; after they leave, you'll still be thinking to some extent about their proposition. There is a lingering effect that stays with you. People who are in conflict with our way of being, get us thinking about our own beliefs—sometimes even having us questioning those beliefs, due to the contrast presented us.

My significant other has a friend whom was born a few generations back from us. This gentleman is perhaps one of the most contrary individuals I have ever met. The first time I met him, my defenses kicked in and my red resistance flag popped up. This happened, because this individual is a contrarian, going against the current; that is, which I'm accustomed to following, I had to take a backseat, reveal less of myself to this individual, and wait for some time to pass to warm up to him. Today, this individual is someone I trust, and someone I have come to like. In the beginning, however, I really couldn't fathom how this would ever be a possibility. Let me tell you what happened.

This individual never became affected by my silent coldness toward him, the first couple times we met. He didn't take the time to agree with me on my points and ideas either. Instead, he truthfully told me the way he viewed things, and he did it in a manner that was anything but easy going. Now that I have become cognizant of the way this individual typically responds, and communicates, I have come to respect his ideas, even though they are quite different from my own.

Sometimes when we are presented with contrarian views and ideology, it helps us to become self-aware of our own core beliefs. Furthermore, it causes us to appreciate observing another perspective in order to gain perspective ourselves. If everyone always agreed with you, it would be hard for them, and hard for you, to see the world from any other vantage point. When someone makes it a point to play devil's advocate with us, at first it can be alarming, but the truth remains that the shock value alone compels us at least to consider ideas from those individuals in a different light. In this chapter, I'm going to teach you why you need to understand the hypnotic archetypal trigger known as 'contrary'. I'm also going to teach you what you need to know in order to utilize contrarian behavior to ignite a fire inside someone's mind, which causes them to rethink things. I'm as well going to show you how to use this hypnotic archetypal trigger in order to convince and win people over to your side of a persuasion, by contrasting to them the complete opposite. After we explore all of this, then will look at some different contexts in which this hypnotic archetypal trigger may be used.

Why Do You Need To Understand This Hypnotic Archetypal Trigger Known As Contrary

When someone is contrary the main thing to understand is it can affect other people's beliefs and ideologies. The contrarian may have strong formed opinions, which the great majority of us will not get behind. Perhaps we all know someone who is contrary to the way we think and behave. Think of someone with a personality outside left base, to where it's almost unbelievable the things they say, and reactions they give. By this I mean unfathomable that someone would even make such a suggestion, or act in a certain manner. In other words it just doesn't make sense to us. The natural inclination is either to hear the person out, or instantly reject whatever it is they're telling you. We're left wondering how in the world this individual came up with this perspective. Even so, there are advantages of seeing things differently, in the way that we are accustomed to seeing them that give a contrast. Contrast has a major benefit to the hypnotic persuader. This benefit is, contrast does two things for us: (a) the first thing contrast does is it reduces resistance toward an alternate perspective, which further solidifies one's own belief and attachment to their own idea; and (b) the second thing contrast does is it hypnotizes us by the shock value of the contrast. When ideas come out of left field we're taken off guard. This is a hypnotic phenomenon, which occurs when a stage hypnotists overloads a person's critical faculty. If you have studied hypnosis for any length of time, you're probably familiar with the 7+ or minus 2 rule. Simply put, human beings can only process consciously 7+ or -2 bits of information at any given moment. Present more information to an individual than this and they will not be able to consciously keep up with what you're saying. The shock of this overload drops them under the spell of hypnosis instantly. For them, at this point, it is easier for them to go with the flow, and let you lead the way, than for them to try and resist you. They just cannot handle the lead, because they cannot keep up with you. It's the same thing, which happens when a high level intellectual engages someone without a clue, about his or her specialty. The person unfamiliar with the material doesn't stand a chance against this person. They're over powered. Instead they just do their best to listen and keep up.

As human beings we are socially conditioned to be respectful of other people's beliefs and ideas. I'm being general here, talking from the point of view of what the educational systems teach and tries to indoctrinate and instill in our children. In the educational systems we are both taught and indoctrinated. Learning happens through both mediums. Being indoctrinated we're being told what to believe, and what not to believe. Some people may perceive this as a form of manipulation. The reality is, however, we are manipulated, and indoctrinated from the time we're born all throughout our lives. We are also 'educated' through teaching. Teaching occurs when we're allowed to think for ourselves. Thinking is different than merely having a thought about something. Thinking requires we go deep within ourselves and contemplate and question what information we're being presented with. When we question and contemplate we make distinctions that lead us to formulate an understanding about something. We start to believe our contemplations and these beliefs are the answers we arrive at through the process of thinking and contemplating. Asking the right questions can direct another person or group of individuals to adopt thinking that will lead them down the path to the answers we want them to believe and attach themselves to. This is a very powerful method of persuasion. It's very mental, and can be very emotional, and for this reason it becomes very hypnotic. But we recall and remember information better when we're allowed to do our own thinking, and arrive at our own answers, because what we learn we actually believe, and what we believe, we perceive is true. Whenever something is presented to us contrary to what we believe is true, the tendency is for us to reject it. If something is so contrary to what we believe to be true we start to question the individual who presented the idea to us as well as that idea itself. When we question that idea presented to us we start to engage in the act of thinking, and as we are thinking we start to arrive at answers. Now it doesn't really matter what these answers are necessarily, as these answers will either be used as a tool for debating the individual making such a wild accusation or claim, or these answers will become our new beliefs, and what we associate as true. So you see how this system works. When we are told something, enough times, over and over again, it can lead us to believe it is true (even if it isn't). Repetition is also hypnosis inducing. Hypnotism can result from many techniques, and later in this book we will be exploring what some of those techniques are —specifically, tools used for conversational hypnosis.

Before we chart off course, just be aware and understand that contrast helps us make choices. When people are given the illusion of choice, resistance is reduced. Desired outcomes can also be easier to achieve from your hypnotic subject as well. Let me give you an example: when I said Yellow Pages advertising one of the tricks of the trade is to come up with three unique value propositions. The proposition you want the customer to buy is the middle proposition. And you can think of these propositions as low medium and high. When you think of high, you can associate that with a higher price tag. When you think of low, you can think of that with having a lower price tag. And when you think of medium, you can think of the perfect balance between value and cost. It is the equilibrium pricing strategy. Most people want to get a deal, but they don't want to buy something cheap. In the same regard, they don't want to buy something outside their comfort zone contrasted to what they're used to spending. By presenting a contrast to the customer I gave them the illusion of choice. When you give someone choice, you give them options, and you put them in the driver seat where they feel as if they have control. The reality is you already know what you want to sell the customer. It's that middle package that is a perfect balance of value and savings. It's not too low to where the customer perceives the product is being cheap and thus having little or no value. However, its also not overpriced to the extent they are uncomfortable making the decision to buy something that pricey. What's inside most people's comfort zone is the middle of the bell curve. Between is where you make most of your sales. Now, let's step back for just a moment. Let's imagine for a moment, that I didn't present any choice or contrast to what I believed was in the customer's best interest. Let's assume I presented only the middle offer most people decided to buy. By not giving any contrast it is as if I'm making the decision for the customer, claiming to know what's in their best interest. In order for this type of sales scenario to work what I'm going to have to do is constantly reiterate and repeat myself while I explain to them that this is in their best interest. Most people don't want to be talked down to, so the only way, in this type of scenario, I will be able to sell this customer is if I hypnotize them through the principle of repetition. If you hear something enough times, eventually you believe it. This is one reason I don't watch the news. Because everything you hear on there is repeated bad news. That's for another book. By presenting options, which are in clear contrast to that medium offer, I put the ball in the customer's court. At this point, the only options I'm giving them are the low medium and high options. Of course if human beings weren't so predictable and socially conditioned, we would quickly fathom that there has to be an infinite amount of choices outside of just the three choices we're being presented. The problem with presenting too many choices, goes back to this idea that the human mind can only process 7+ or -2 bits of information. You will still create a hypnotic effect in which you can implant suggestions into the mind of your potential customer, but you also lessen the chances a sale will be made, because a customer might become so overwhelmed, and thus their rejection trigger kicks in to protect them from being taken advantage of. Often times when this happens, the potential customer will suggest to you they need time to think about all these options, before they can make up their mind. The idea with presenting only three suggestions is to allow the potential customer to decide without having to over think things. In this regard, they feel more comfortable, because they believe the decision, they're making is a logical decision – one which is rational. For most people, their comfort zone is when they feel as though they have control over their thinking. A good conversational hypnotist can narrow their potential subject's focus by directing it on that middle offer through communicating to them repetitively and hypnotically the relevant features or attributes of their product, as well as the logical advantages and the emotional benefits attached to those advantages. Stimulate someone emotionally and they start to fall under the spell of hypnosis. So you understand now why contrast is so useful to the hypnotic persuader. The main attribute of contrast is the illusion of choice. The advantage to giving someone a false choice or false sense of choice is that it triggers the impulse to decide. When someone is forced to decide amongst three things, i.e. low medium and high offers, they enter what is known as a double bind. This simply means regardless of whatever choice the customer makes in deciding, in terms of which offer to buy; the salesperson still achieves the result of making a sale. The option not to buy is never a consideration presented to the customer. Choices make it easy for the customer to decide to take action. It also takes away discomfort associated with buying. This is done to ensure the customer doesn't experience cognitive dissonance, or what is commonly referred to as buyer's remorse.

What You Need To Understand In Order To Apply The Hypnotic Archetypal Trigger Known As Contrast

Now you understand a great deal as to why it is important to utilize contrast when positioning your product or offer in the marketplace. We also need to understand though the emotional side to contrast. Contrast can besides build trust. And trust builds confidence in you from the vantage point of your customer or anyone you're trying to persuade for that matter. Contrast can be a wonderful way to frame agreement. For example, let's pretend there are two individuals. Let's refer to them as John and Jane. Let's pretend John is the leader of a cult, and he is trying to recruit Jane to join his cult. As you might imagine if John were simply to approach Jane and start having a conversation with her and start talking about is cult, and then ask Jane to join, chances are she probably would say no. Of course, this is all theoretical. Now were John to ask Jane questions to get information from her and get her thinking, and at the same time start leading her with his questions to certain desired outcomes or answers, then John could begin to frame a persuasive argument to make it easier for Jane to want to join his cult. Let's assume hypothetically John discovers through his question asking Jane has just experienced a bad breakup with her boyfriend. Let's also assume Jane has revealed she feels less connected to her parents now that she's gone away to college. And lastly, let's entertain that Jane is not doing so well in college. As a result of these three conditions Jane reveals her discord and depression. Depression is the emotional state of mind the Jane happens to be enduring at this present moment in her life. Her erratic mind is causing her to feel less sure about her direction in life. Empathetic John says he wants to utilize this weakened state Jane finds herself in, by presenting her with the solution to join his cult. In order to position the idea of joining his cult as a good idea, or even the best idea Jane could ever conceive of, John decides to take the contrarian approach to recruiting Jane. John is going to contrast and paint a pretty picture of his cult against the backdrop of all this negativity and depression going on in Jane's life. So John quickly formulates in his mind that he is going to tell Jane or suggest to her rather that she should join the cult, which he makes out to be the best solution to Jane's problemed lifestyle. The first thing John decides to do is to contrast three different options in order to create the illusion of choice. Incidentally not taking one of these three options is not a choice John is going to present to Jane. So the three choices are: (a) come take advantage of a free dinner and meet some of myfriends, (b) you should stay in your room and keep thinking about how depressed you are, and (c) the last choice might be something ridiculous like you might want to join the circus. I realize that the obvious choice, most people are going to choose is going to be that of coming and having a free meal and to meet some John's friends. The reason this choice seems like a no-brainer, is because it gets Jane out of her slump in order for her to meet some more uplifting and positive people, so that she can get a better grasp of all the things going on in her life at that particular moment. Jane is looking for a friend, and because John was willing to listen and empathize with her the three choices he presented and constructed in this way to make it easy for her to continue associating with John. At this point, Jane trusts John, and so when John throws out three ideas, it causes Jane not to think for herself about what it is she might want to actually do, but it creates this dynamic situation in which she feels compelled to give something back to John; to reciprocate the friendship he has shown her. By coming up with two out-of-the-box ideas, and the middle idea being something quite within most people's comfort zone, Jane is not going to at this point want to disappoint John, so she will agree with that choice that is most within her comfort zone. And, this choice will feel like a good idea to her. Her resistance flags won't therefore outright reject John's invitation for her to come and meet his cult buddy friends and enjoy the free carbohydrate laden non-nutritious meal they're going to be feeding her. If Jane were to still make up an excuse as to why she couldn't go and meet John's friends and have a free meal, John has enough ammunition to present an argument to contrast why she should. For example, John might say, "I mean, Jane, I don't want to tell you what to do, but it seems to me you can either continue being depressed and be by yourself, or you can get out of your apartment, come out with a new friend and meet some really cool people in the process and have a free meal. I mean, which seriously makes more sense Jane? I insist that you let me help you get out of this funk you happen to be in at this time in your life. I'm afraid if you stay here by yourself, things are not going to be getting any better. I mean they haven't gotten any better yet, have they? So you're coming with me. I'm going to introduce you to some cool cats, and the food's free. You will have a blast I promise." Contrast the idea of having a blast, with continuing to remain depressed. No other choices are really being presented to Jane. So John is capitalizing on the things he already knows about Jane. Now Jane feels as though she owes John an opportunity to help her. This is because she has already revealed her problem to him, or should I say 'problems' in this situation, and to get help, Jane to be willing to let someone help her.

How Do You Use The Hypnotic Archetypal Trigger Contrary In Order To Persuade People Hypnotically

The first step to using the hypnotic archetypal trigger known as contrary is just outright disagree with someone to bring in some contrast, so they question their own beliefs, while insisting and building on the fact their belief is true. In order to feel as though their belief is true, they must consider why your belief is false. In the process of doing this it reinforces their belief as being true, and at the same time causes them at least to open up their minds to considering other possibilities. Most often when this happens, your hypnotic subject will automatically start to consider all the reasons why your belief is false, and their belief is true. They won't tell you this; however, it will happen in their mind automatically, as a result of this contrary trigger. The shock value of this contrary perspective, is also enough to shock them into hypnosis. You can use your contrary idea to focus their attention in a direction away from where you want it actually to go.

The second step to utilizing the hypnotic archetypal trigger known as contrary, is to create a false sense of choice. This is by presenting a strategic series of things to consider, so your hypnotic subject doesn't think about all the things you don't want them thinking about. In the case of John and Jane; John didn't want Jane to think about the idea his friends might be members of a cult. He wanted her to think only of the appeal, i.e. the free meal. This was used to bring her one step closer to joining John's cult. Instead, he presented the illusion of choice, so that Jane felt compelled to give into one of those choices; namely, the most logical one which was 'come meet some of my friends and have a free meal'. This choice seemed less risky, because it presupposes there are going to be other people besides just John---a person she's just met. And food is usually an anchor for a mental safety blanket, because it's on the bottom of Maslow's Heirarchy of Needs Pyramid. People need food, more than they need just about anything else. So food is anchored psychologically to mean something that's safe and sensible. This is one reason why people who find themselves depressed, and worried about all the things going on in their lives, tend to eat more. Food becomes a crutch. In the scenario with John and Jane; John has already positioned himself as the crutch Jane is going to lean on so this is symbolic on many levels.

The last step to utilizing contrast to persuade your subject hypnotically is to follow through. Once you have a commitment out of someone, don't give the individual time to think about any other possible out. There are no more choices, a commitment has already been made, and

Jane's promise to go and meet John's friends and have a free meal, is now binding. It would be socially disgraceful at this juncture for Jane to bow out unless she had a good excuse. So at this critical moment, you have to be absolutely sure you don't give the individual an opportunity to come up with another alternative to the suggestions you presented them with.

What Other Contexts Can Contrary Be Applied In Order To Hypnotically Persuade Other People To Do What You Tell Them To

When people are contrary, they're often perceived as being radical. However, you have to be careful not to be too radical, because then the great majority of people will feel uncomfortable following you. However, by being just radical enough, people perceive you as being ideas oriented. People love ideas, and ideas can be very hypnotic in nature. Many people will follow other people's ideas, just so they don't have to do any thinking on their own, or present choices to individuals, which could fail. There is a psychology to all this. If you present a solution to someone, and that solution doesn't pan out for them, you are, then held personally liable for their loss. For this reason, many people don't want to assume responsibility for leading other people. If their ideas fail, they will be perceived by others as being a failure. Most people don't want this. For this reason, a contrarian viewpoint can still be sold as being the right solution. And people will blindly follow your idea, only so they don't have to present the idea that is so radically different than the idea that you have presented to them. Because there is such a disparity in difference in the two ideas, many people will assume their idea is a bad idea, and your idea is the best idea. Even if they feel somewhat uncomfortable with your idea, they will still act like sheep and obey your orders, just so they don't have to take responsibility. So you see, there are many assiduities for applying the hypnotic archetypal trigger known as contrary. There have been psychological experiments done in which a group of people all sit around a table, and were asked a series of questions, where one of the questions was clearly wrong. One of the individuals sitting at a table was unaware all the other individuals sitting at the table were already predisposed before the meeting and told to say 'no' to the right answer being 'yes'. Whenever the interviewer got to that individual that the individual sided with a group and responded by giving the incorrect answer, even though the individual clearly knew the answer was wrong. Because everyone else seemed emphatically to say the answer was right even though it was wrong; or wrong even though it was right, that individual felt it better simply to agree, because they didn't want to be perceived as a contrarian in the group.

Final Purport

In this chapter, we've covered a lot of ground. We discovered many ways utilizing contrariness can hypnotically persuade other individuals to do what you want them to. You discovered why contrast and contrary can be a useful tool for both hypnotizing people and persuading them. You learned why people are socially conditioned to respond in predictable patterns when other ideas are contrasted in front of them. We plus explored what you need to know about 'contrary' in order to be able to utilize it to influence and persuade people to do what you want them to. Then we covered how exactly to do this, and rounded off this chapter with this hypothesis that contrast and contrary can besides be used in a multitude of other applications, as you see fit. We also discussed why individuals can position themselves as contrary to the mainstream, and still gain a following of supporters.

Take Action Now

In order to get any value whatsoever from this book you must take action now on the instructions I'm going to be laying out for you. Do not be like most people—buy a book, half read it, set it aside, forget about it, never take action, never gain the advantages and benefits it has to offer you.

There is a reason you purchased this book. Do not forget that reason. If you attended one of my live training workshops, you would have participated in doing many exercises at the end of each module I taught you. This is because you get considerably more value practicing the techniques in a safe environment, before going out and practicing them in the real-world. Many people do not feel comfortable testing techniques they've just learnt blindly on real-life contexts. Do not be afraid to do these exercises: They are for your own good and self-development. Your personal power will increase when you proactively apply this knowledge to your specific contexts. Part of learning this information (the largest part) is applying it hands-on. Suspend your doubts and disbeliefs that you can do these exercises, because your insights will elevate to a higher level once you do them. You will only learn a fraction of what I teach in this book from reading the book. The great majority of your learning comes when you apply this information in whatever contexts you have been intentioned on learning it.

To prove this point: Think about your first kiss. You may have talked to friends about their first kiss to get some insight. Maybe you read a book on adolescent sexuality, where kissing was covered. You may have watched movies of actors kissing on the big-screen. Until you actually kissed a girl or guy for the first time, you didn't realize all that was involved in kissing, as you hadn't practiced it, and learned from that experience. I bet after you kissed for the first time, regardless how

good or bad the kiss was; you felt pretty amazing afterward, and felt much more confident in kissing other people. I'm right, and you know it, so do these exercises! In fact, make a promise to yourself; you will not move on to the next chapter until these action steps have been completed. You'll thank yourself. I promise.

I. Make yourself take out a piece of paper and a pen/pencil and write down exactly how you'll utilize the information found in this chapter to fit your particular persuasion context.

II. Find an opportunity to apply what you learned in this chapter and apply it. After you have taken this initial action, journal your discoveries and results.

III. Take a 3x5 index card and summarize the leading points from this chapter. Let this summary serve as a quick flash card to jog your memory once a day, as you continue reading this book, and doing future exercises. This is important, because this book has a lot of information, and a fast flash card to look at daily will help you not to forget what you have learned. Over time, this knowledge will become imprinted on your hypnotic mind, where you'll take action on this knowledge without thinking about it consciously.

IV. Teach what you have learned in this chapter to a trusted friend whom you think might benefit. Teaching information to others helps you gain greater clarity and insights you'd likely not have gained trying to keep it all in your own mind.

V. Discuss with the friend you've taught this information to and take notes on their thoughts and understanding of the material. This way, you'll gain another person's perspective and likely gain a deeper understanding of the material.

After you have successfully completed each of these exercises, only then, proceed in moving forward to the next chapter. Do not take shortcuts and tell yourself the lie you'll come back and do the exercises later. Statistically speaking the probability is improbable you ever will. Take a leap of faith and do the exercise, please! Trust me; it's worth it, if you want to gain true mastery in hypnotic persuasion.

====================xx==================

CHAPTER 11

DIFFERENCE

The last hypnotic archetypal trigger that I wanted to discuss with you is difference. Sometimes things that are different are captivating. There's intrinsic value in something that is positioned as unique and different. Something which is different than other products in its category has the potential to entice buyers simply due to its being positioned as different. You have to be careful utilizing this hypnotic archetypal trigger, because something so different may actually be perceived as having less value. It doesn't mean it won't attract attention, which can be highly hypnotic, in and of its self, but it may not be the right type of attention you are seeking. In this chapter, we will look at why you need to understand the power of 'difference'. We will look at what you need to understand in order to utilize this hypnotic archetypal trigger to influence and persuade people hypnotically. Then, I'll teach you a step-by-step formula for ensuring you use this hypnotic archetypal trigger in a way that is sure to be hypnotic. Finally, we'll look at some other applications and case studies where difference has made all the difference in the world, as far as hypnotic persuasion is concerned.

'Difference' works is because of the human inclination to own things, and associate themselves with things that are unique. Ideas parallel the very essence of 'difference'. This is hypnotic, because everybody loves a good idea, and quickly become captivated.

What You Need To Know In Order To Persuade People Hypnotically Utilizing The Hypnotic Archetypal Trigger Known As Difference

What you need to understand regarding difference, and positioning your ideas and products as being different, is that when all else fails simply presenting an idea as being different than anything else a potential client has ran across, can be exactly the right thing you need in order to sell your idea or solution. You also need to understand people resonate with differences. Many times people shopping in a department store seek out items that are unlike other items. They then buy these items. I was associating the concept of difference as being the sister to ideation. Ideation is presenting information in a way that is different, so people find it interesting. The easiest way to position the product or service or persuasion is to present it in a way that is unique and different from anything your hypnotic subject has ever encountered before. The last thing you need to understand about difference, in terms of how they can be used to hypnotize your subject, is everybody has a different spin and way of presenting information that is different from anybody else. Just knowing this opens your mind to the possibility you can trust yourself to deliver information in a way that is different and refreshing than anything else out there. People pay good money for fresh ideas.

How To Hypnotize Someone Utilizing The Hypnotic Archetypal Trigger Known As Difference

In order to hypnotize anyone you have to be able to focus their attention narrowly, to block out all external distractions. For the sales professional, this technique will be beneficial, because one problem sales professionals often have is walking into a sales call, and the person whom they are presenting their sales spiel to begin being bored and interrupted by outer distractions. Utilizing this technique is one way you can minimize your hypnotic subject from becoming distracted, and focused on other things, besides what it is you have to present to them.

I. Step one: the first step to hypnotizing someone utilizing the hypnotic archetypal trigger known as difference, is simply to understand that, however, you present information is already going to be different than the one way and approach that anyone else who happen to be in your same situation would be presenting. What this does, by understanding you already have inside you everything you need in order to present information differently than anyone else is the 'inner knowing' you will be hypnotizing people without having to even try. The key thing with this first step is just let the flow of the conversation happen, and let ideas come to you naturally.

II. Step two: the second step to presenting something differently, so that it focuses your hypnotic subjects attention is to utilize the hypnotic language pattern I have an idea.... You simply do is preface the next words out of your mouth vocalizing the words, "I have an idea."

III. Step three: the third step in this process is to pause. By pausing it forces your potential customer to engage and focus back in on you. You will continue pausing until which time your potential customer says, "okay, so what's your idea?"

IV. Step four: the first step in this process of hypnotizing someone is simply to present any idea naturally that comes out of your mouth. After you have presented your idea do not try to sell it by continuing speaking. Instead silence yourself and pause again.

V. Step five: the final step is to wait until your potential customer has responded. In more cases than not you will find that your hypnotic subject will embrace whatever idea has happened to come out of your mouth. The idea itself does not matter so much necessarily, as much as the idea being an idea. People love ideas, and the very nature of an idea denotes difference, and originality. People are often quick to grab hold of ideas, because they presuppose that the idea presented is already a good idea. After they have accepted your idea, simply close the sale, continue to present more information to your hypnotic subject. The additional information should be in alignment with furthering your desired outcome. Once you achieve what it is you have set out to achieve, then you are finished.

How Else Can You Apply Difference To Captivate People's Attention

When people are captivated, they are drawn into a level of awareness about something to the extent they block out everything else. We often hear people say something like, "She captivated my attention." When people talk like this, they're essentially saying it was difficult for them to concentrate on anything else other than the person or thing that captivated their attention. It is important that you understand the power behind captivation. Essentially hypnosis and captivation are the same. There is, however, a different intensity concerning captivation, which causes people to substitute hypnosis in place of captivation. You want to be able to intensify the value of your persuasions, by linking the attributes of a belief, product, idea, or whatever the case happens to be to a logical advantage that will be gained when someone takes hold of ownership of whatever it is you're advocating. You must also link and emotional benefits to such a logical advantage. Often time's sales people only get this sequence half right. They teach their potential customer about the features of their unique product offering, and then explain the logical advantages that are gained as a result of taking possession of those attributes. However, what many salespeople fail to do is connect an emotional benefit to the relevant logical advantages. Let's look at an example: let's pretend that were selling a Yellow Pages advertisement to a potential customer. Let's pretend that one of the features of the advertisement is the ad is in full color. This is differentiated or different than other company's advertisements, who only position their product in black and white, or one or two colors. The advantage that is linked to a full color ad is that the ad stands out more from other ads in the Yellow Pages directory. Another logical advantage is that more people are likely to see a full color ad when contrasted against other black-and-white ads. Most salespeople would stop at this. They would leave it up to the customer to draw their own conclusions about what the ad will do for them while it runs its course. The next step is to associate an emotional benefit to the logical advantage of being in full color and more people seeing the ad. And an emotional benefit to more people seeing the ad can be attached to making more sales. How you might attach this emotional benefit would be to say something like: "This ad is in full color, so it stands out against all the other ads in this Yellow Pages directory. It will get you more customers as a result, and thus more sales. You will feel good to know because you're making more sales, it gives you the opportunity to do more of the things in life you want to do; such as feeling amazing when you're spending more quality time with your loved ones. Notice we're capitalizing on the emotional value that's inherently linked to the logical advantage, which is linked to the unique attribute, which is that the ad is in full color. These causal links, only need to be plausible, for someone to become captivated and drawn into your presentation. It doesn't matter what your persuasion is, you can use difference, as a contrast to everything else your hypnotic subject has been exposed to, so you increase interest and desire, which will lead ultimately to them taking action. Differentiation in any context possesses a hypnotic quality by which to influence and persuade your potential customer.

Final Purport

In this chapter, we looked at how difference can be utilized effectively to hypnotize and persuade your hypnotic subjects in a way, which is captivating and mesmerizing. We explored all the different reasons why it is important to differentiate and draw a contrast to your persuasions versus everything else. There is intrinsic value in something being unique and different from everything else. This value makes even an ordinary persuasion extraordinary. We also looked to what you needed to understand to be able to differentiate your product, idea, or persuasive belief, so you position it differently, so as to draw attraction to it. Then we covered the steps and sequential logic that literally showed you how to create such a proposition. In the last section we further explored other contexts and applications, showing how this can be applied to sales, marketing, cult building, or any other type of application in which you want to persuade someone to believe something is true.

Take Action Now

In order to get any value whatsoever from this book you must take action now on the instructions I'm going to be laying out for you. Do not be like most people—buy a book, half read it, set it aside, forget about it, never take action, never gain the advantages and benefits it has to offer you.

There is a reason you purchased this book. Do not forget that reason. If you attended one of my live training workshops, you would have participated in doing many exercises at the end of each module I taught you. This is because you get considerably more value practicing the techniques in a safe environment, before going out and practicing them in the real-world. Many people do not feel comfortable testing techniques they've just learnt blindly on real-life contexts. Do not be afraid to do these exercises: They are for your own good and self-development. Your personal power will increase when you proactively apply this knowledge to your specific contexts. Part of learning this information (the largest part) is applying it hands-on. Suspend your doubts and disbeliefs that you can do these exercises, because your insights will elevate to a higher level once you do them. You will only learn a fraction of what I teach in this book from reading the book. The great majority of your learning comes when you apply this information in whatever contexts you have been intentioned on learning it.

To prove this point: Think about your first kiss. You may have talked to friends about their first kiss to get some insight. Maybe you read a book on adolescent sexuality, where kissing was covered. You may have watched movies of actors kissing on the big-screen. Until you actually kissed a girl or guy for the first time, you didn't realize all that was involved in kissing, as you hadn't practiced it, and learned from that experience. I bet after you kissed for the first time, regardless how good or bad the kiss was; you felt pretty amazing afterward, and felt much more confident in kissing other people. I'm right, and you know it, so do these exercises! In fact, make a promise to yourself; you will not move on to the next chapter until these action steps have been completed. You'll thank yourself. I promise.

I. Make yourself take out a piece of paper and a pen/pencil and write down exactly how you'll utilize the information found in this chapter to fit your particular persuasion context.

II. Find an opportunity to apply what you learned in this chapter and apply it. After you have taken this initial action, journal your discoveries and results.

III. Take a 3x5 index card and summarize the leading points from this chapter. Let this summary serve as a quick flash card to jog your memory once a day, as you continue

reading this book, and doing future exercises. This is important, because this book has a lot of information, and a fast flash card to look at daily will help you not to forget what you have learned. Over time, this knowledge will become imprinted on your hypnotic mind, where you'll take action on this knowledge without thinking about it consciously.

IV. Teach what you have learned in this chapter to a trusted friend whom you think might benefit. Teaching information to others helps you gain greater clarity and insights you'd likely not have gained trying to keep it all in your own mind.

V. Discuss with the friend you've taught this information to and take notes on their thoughts and understanding of the material. This way, you'll gain another person's perspective and likely gain a deeper understanding of the material.

After you have successfully completed each of these exercises, only then, proceed in moving forward to the next chapter. Do not take shortcuts and tell yourself the lie you'll come back and do the exercises later. Statistically speaking the probability is improbable you ever will. Take a leap of faith and do the exercise, please! Trust me;

it's worth it, if you want to gain true mastery in hypnotic persuasion.

====================xx=================

CHAPTER 12

HYPNOSIS

Now that we have covered ten of the most significant hypnotic archetypal triggers, it is time to investigate what exactly we mean by hypnosis. To hypnotize someone is the art of hypnosis or hypnotism. But, what exactly is hypnosis? Hypnosis is a process of inducing attention, which ultimately leads to trance. When someone is trance, they are experiencing the same state someone experiences when they cannot concentrate except on one thing. Sometimes people, when they fall in love, they become obsessive about their relationship with that individual, to the point where they lose interest and focus on all the other aspects of their lives, which require attention. They can't think, about anything else. They're hypnotized. The same thing is true when you take a long trip in your car. You're driving along, and at some point, you blank out, and when you arrive at your destination, you don't even remember the ride or journey. We call this highway hypnosis. You become lost in your thoughts, to the extent you can't focus on your driving.

Driving then becomes a hypnotic experience because you're driving unconsciously, but still competently. When new drivers take to the wheel, they must first undergo conscious incompetence. This means because they have little or no experience driving, they must give all of their attention to their driving, and take it quite seriously to avoid an accident. They can even start to have a slight fear of driving, or what can happen as a result of driving poorly. Their desire is to drive competently, but because of their lack of experience this is not yet possible. Because they over think everything, driving becomes a real task for them. As a new driver gains some experience become better and better at driving eventually to drive unconsciously and competently. It is a process. When they're unable to think about all the steps required to operate a motor vehicle, ironically they drive better. They are no longer over thinking their driving, i.e. what's required, as it has become an unconscious action at that point. Eventually, all drivers begin taking their driving for granted, and don't have to think about driving. Chances are you have got into your car at some point today, and driven somewhere, and you didn't even think about it. You probably haven't even thought about it until I've brought it to your attention. You do this all the time, unconsciously, and/or hypnotized and not even aware that you're hypnotized.

What other activities do you engage in that you have taken for granted, and I hypnotized every day doing. We call this going through the motions of life. From the time we wake up in the morning, for instance, we put on our clothes, take a shower, brush our teeth, eat our food, drive to work, start our work, come home, engage in watching television, eat our dinner, go to bed, dream, and wake up and do it all over again the next day. Life has become routine for most people. This routine has become an unconscious way of living our lives. From this end, we are hypnotized to this routine, which is repetitive. Now, remember back to when I brought it to your attention in an earlier chapter that a huge part of hypnosis and inducing hypnosis conversationally is through the use of repetition. When something is repeated enough times, it becomes subroutine, that it becomes accepted and therefore, believed automatically and without question. This is the nature of hypnotism.

But, you say, "I am conscious of everything going on in my life." Throughout your waking hours, you do experience certain aspects of your life consciously. You take ownership and comfort in the state where you're able critically to think, logic, and rationalize things that come into your awareness. Whenever something new enters your awareness, immediately it affects you and your critical faculty kicks in, and though it may not reject it outright, an idea or suggestion presented to you stands a far greater chance of being rejected, being a part of your everyday routine. We trust things that are familiar, and consistent. Even though something might come along that could benefit us, we are most often satisfied without regulated life. For this reason alone, it becomes challenging for many sales professionals and persuaders effectively to gain someone's confidence and trust and influence them to believe their persuasions as being true and worth pursuing. The hypnotic archetypal triggers which we have covered in the previous ten chapters can help you overcome these issues, because they instill value that is beyond mere practical value indulging in intrinsic value. They also carry the weight of affecting people on an emotional level, which is a hypnotic level.

In the next chapter, I will outline and explain what conversational hypnosis is and how it differs from your standard hypnotism. For now, I want to educate you on what you need to understand about hypnotism so you can better understand conversational hypnotism, as I go through that information in the next chapter. I also want to give you the reasons why it is important first to understand about hypnosis and what it is, before learning about conversational hypnosis. After I've given you these reasons and what you need to know, I'm going to teach you the actual formula for hypnotizing anyone in its most basic form. Then I'm going to explain to you some of the applications in which hypnosis or hypnotism can help people improve the quality of their lives.

Why Do You Need Understand Hypnotism, Before You Understand Conversational Hypnotism

So I've already hinted at what hit that Susan is. Hypnosis is the unconscious behavior that is caused from going into trance. When someone is entrance, they are focused elsewhere, while their actions are put on autopilot. This is why your thinking about one aspect of your life, while another aspect of you is driving your car taking you to your destination. You're not consciously thinking about the next turn to make or exit to get off of. Your hypnotic mind is taking care of all those details and activities for you. If you can get someone to think about something to work it captivates their attention so much so that they can't think about anything else, their actions will come about automatically without them thinking about doing them. If you can slip in a suggestion to someone's hypnotic mind, while you have captivated their attention, their hypnotic mind will act on it in the same automatic fashion that they would act on any other suggestion planted by the individual into their hypnotic mind. When you hypnotize someone else you are essentially relating suggestions to the individual's hypnotic mind. The suggestions go under the radar of consciousness, because you have distracted that individual's consciousness and focused it on something totally unrelated to the instructions you have given their hypnotic mind. When someone comes out of hypnosis, they act on things from the unconscious level, without even understanding why they're doing what they're doing. To their conscious mind, it just seems like a good idea, and the right thing to do. When someone pays money and goes to hypnotherapists to stop smoking, what that hypnotist is doing is focusing their attention elsewhere, in order to create the same daydream like or trancelike condition, so they can slip hypnotic instructions into the individual's hypnotic mind; telling them they are not a smoker—they dislike smoking. After the person has come back to conscious awareness, what many people call 'reality', they are usually unaware at a conscious level the hypnotist has done anything, except help them into a quiet relaxed state.

I mentioned quiet and relaxed, as this has been proven to be an effective means of helping induced trance. When you are a child, and your mother read books to you and lulls you off to sleep in her arms, this lulling back-and-forth motion comforts you. You are so absorbed in the story, your mother is telling you, you quickly fall asleep. Before you fall asleep, however, you entered a hypnotic trance. You didn't think about anything except living in the moment, there in your mother's arms, engaged fully in the story. You disengaged from everyday normal reality, and enter the fictitious world, where the characters of the story come live. As a child, paying attention and being absorbed into the story, you found yourself empathizing and caring about the characters, even though in your conscious world they are unreal. These characters emotionally affect you and cause you to feel certain emotions; all happening at the unconscious level as you enter hypnosis. The values and morals of these early childhood fairytales have been imprinted onto your hypnotic mind. They are so deeply rooted in your mind; they have become your values, beliefs, and the benchmarks upon which you use to make all your decisions throughout life. Whenever a character in a fairytale disobeyed their parents, and found themselves quickly endangered and experiencing distress and chaos, imprinted into your psyche was the importance and value of respecting and obeying your parents and other figureheads. As you go through your life, you are innately conditioned to honor and respect your parents. You take their advice when they give it. As you get older, around your friends and peers, and are given other perspectives, ideas and philosophies, these become imprinted on your hypnotic mind as well. You may experience going through a rebellious stage during this time. Throughout your teenage years, you might, like many teenagers do, disrespect and dishonor your parents many times. You find yourself in conflict with your beliefs, because of new impressions, which have been imprinted by associating yourself with other people besides just your parents and teachers. Their ideas, influences, and persuasions, you begin to adopt as your own. You might even hear someone you care about, such as a parent, tell you, "You don't seem like yourself lately."

Our brains are like computer systems. We are being fed by our environment certain instructions, which metaphorically could be considered computer code. This information comes through at a deep unconscious level. As I've mentioned in a previous chapter, we can only process consciously 7+ or -2 bits of information at any given moment. However, there is an infinite or seemingly infinite amount of information bombarding us all the time. This information is going on around you, even though you're not consciously aware of it.

Let's do a little thought experiment to prove this. I want you to focus on all the noises going on around you right now. And I want you to notice all the things you were not conscious of before doing this thought experiment. It is pretty amazing if you continue focusing on the things and happenings going on around you, that you quickly discover a great bit of information about your environment, you never had any clue about before. You are aware of everything; yet, not aware. What this means is your hypnotically aware of everything going on around you all the time. But, you're just consciously aware of the little bit, a tiny amount only. In other words, you're hypnotically aware and in tune with aspects of yourself and your environment, though, for most people, it is difficult to see the 'big picture' because we're focused on only a fraction of that picture. When people logically sit down and plan out goals for themselves, and later come to the realization those goals have been completed, they often wonder how in the world did they do it. The reason for this is because most of their actions were taken unconsciously. This is what is meant when people say, "Let go, and let God." They are essentially telling themselves what they want, and then releasing their conscious mind from getting in the way, so their hypnotic mind will operate to take care of fulfilling that big picture.

Ultradian Rhythms

Switching gears just for a moment, to slip this in, because I feel it's very important to do so. Our lives are regulated cyclically. Everything happens on the cycle. From the time human beings are born as tiny babies, they undergo changes that are dominantly consistent overall with the way other human beings live their lives. Cycles are systems. Systems are automatic revolutions that happened throughout life. From the time we are born, until we die, life is one big cycle. We enter life until one day we exit. Everybody endures this reality. Our day-to-day routines are cyclical for the most part. There are anomalies of course, but I'm talking holistically here. When you look at the big picture from the time you wake up in the morning, until the time that you go to bed, it is a replication, on average, of the other days which have heralded this day. The seasons are cyclical. There is a cooling-off period known as winter, a cycles that happens annually for summer when it is blaring hot outside. Trees lose leaves every autumn---another cycle. Spring takes in new life, and new leaves bud, and everything become fresh and green again. This happens in a cycle. Even, the female anatomy undergoes monthly changes which can be measured in days. Each day begins with the sun coming up, until which time the sun goes down and the moon becomes visible. The same cycle repeats itself daily. It is all a processes, a system, something that is cyclical and hardly changing. It's predictable. We are consciously aware of many moments throughout our waking state too. Even sleep itself is a cycle. We are awake so many hours, until it's time to go to bed. Then we sleep for so many hours, on a cycle, and awaken again. It is a habit. A routine. A cycle that is rarely broken. It's measurable, and it's predictable. You can assume the sun will eventually set, and the night sky will dominate the outside world you see. It's predictable. Routines become dependable as well. People's behaviors are also foreseeable. When someone has a tendency to do the same thing every day, you can foretell, with high probability, when they will do that very activity again. This is important to understand, but there's one more thing you need to really understand as well. Let me explain.

Have you ever been at work, going through your daily routine, after all you have it down, don't you(?), because you do it every day, and it's the same activities, perhaps with only subtle changes to your routine? If you're a personal banker you're counting money day in and day out, waiting on customers, counting your till, until it's time for you to go home and engage in other routine activities. Have you ever found yourself though slipping off into a daydream? A daydream is when your body is somewhere, but your mind is thinking about either being, doing, or experiencing some other activity altogether different than the routine you're consciously doing whenever you're not daydreaming about doing something else. I bet you have. Because everybody does. These daydreams happen to us approximately every 90 to 120 minutes of our waking day. They last for roughly twenty minutes. And then we go back to refocus our attention onto routine activities, in which we're consciously engaged in at any other time. The cycles are known as ultradian rhythms. They are rhythms similar to your sleep rhythms, which tell you when you're tired and when it's time to get up in the morning. During these periods of time your body is telling you it's time to take a break. In other words, it's time to recharge your batteries, and take a break from all the heavy conscious activities you've been doing over the last hour and a half. If you fight this daydream like state, it creates the same issues you face when trying to fight your sleep, when it's late at night, and you're trying to finish watching that movie. The state or cycle, by the way, is no respecter of persons. We're physiologically conditioned this way. It's a same type of comparison situation when your cell phone goes in the hibernate mode. When you need it and you're pressing buttons, it's utilizing more energy, especially when you're talking to someone else on the phone. The battery life of your phone gets used up much more quickly than it does when your phone is not being operated – when it's in hibernation mode. For you smart phone users out there, the same thing happens when you have applications running in the background, and your phone is losing energy quicker. These applications, running in the background, use up more battery life, than when you shut these applications off. Human beings experience the same type of phenomena. When you're engaged in heavy thinking and critical analysis you are using up a lot more energy than when your mind is clear, and you're allowed to rest. If you happen to work outside in construction or do some type of physical activity for your work, you are also using up for more energy than when you're sitting idle doing nothing, and thinking nothing. So rest is important. Rest is synonymous with comfort, which is the same experience which happened when you are a child and your mother lulls you off to sleep at night. You are comforted by her, you enter into a state of relaxation or hypnosis, and soon find yourself waking up the next morning.

I'm sure you've experienced times in your life when you exceeded the time that you should offend yourself falling asleep. Maybe your job required you to stay up because there was a task that needed to be completed as soon as possible. If you're working alongside other people, you may find that your conversations become quite interesting when you haven't been allowed to get enough sleep. You start talking what some people might call "crazy talk," or start speaking simply in an irrational way.

We use the excuse, "I'm sorry. It's just I'm tired, and I haven't had enough sleep to be able to function properly." In other words you haven't had the opportunity to enter a state of hypnosis, where you've been allowed to relax and operate at the hypnotic level or unconscious level. When you're hypnotized you're often able to accomplish a lot more work, that when you're consciously trying to do the work. Whenever you try to do something, it denotes failure, and it lessens the likelihood you will be able to achieve what it is you've set out to achieve. When you're operating in the flow or at the hypnotic level, you're not trying any longer to do something; you're simply operating on autopilot, completing tasks without even being aware you're completing them.

What You Need To Understand In Order To Be Able To Hypnotize Someone

You have to understand that hypnosis is synonymous with trance. When you start to daze, blank out, or find yourself slipping out of consciousness, you are entering a state of hypnosis. When you enter this state, and other conscious people are around you, feeding you instructions, these instructions are being impressed into your hypnotic mind, to be followed out later. Often times people don't give direct instruction; rather, they infer what they want you do. When someone appears to be tired or not in the mood to focus on what it is they're supposed to do, they are unconsciously protected by their critical faculty, from these types of outside influences slipping in covertly. We tell people, "Not now," or "I'm busy. I will have to get back with you at a later time." We do this because we know we're communicating with that person while under the spell of hypnosis. In this state, their influence over us would be far greater than it would be if we were able to critically think about their arguments. When we are able to critically think, our resistance protects us from poor decision making. Ironically, most people believe in order to get their way and influence someone, the person they're trying to persuade needs to be in a conscious state; able to critically think about the rationality and logic behind what's being proposed. I'm going to suggest to you in this book this isn't necessarily the case, and that in more instances the not, waiting for someone to be in a completely conscious state of awareness, will actually hinder your chances and opportunities to influence and persuade them to accept what you say as being true. When someone is in a conscious or logical state, as a hypnotist you want to first mirror that exact conscious state they happen to be in. Then you want to start slowly transitioning the conversation in a way, which creates the hypnotic state. Once this is accomplished, you can then feed instructions to their unconscious mind or hypnotic mind, and then bring them back up out of trance and back into the conscious world most people prefer to live in.

How-To Hypnotize Someone

Hypnotizing someone is a four-step process. It doesn't require a lot of time. It doesn't require a lot of fancy words. The essential premise is the same process, which gets applied to different applications of hypnosis.

I. Step one: the first step to hypnotizing someone is getting them to focus on one item or idea completely. This is important, because it prevents them from being able to focus their attention anywhere else.

II. Step two: the next step to hypnotizing someone is to bypass their critical faculty or resistance mechanism. In order to do this is simply requires that you build in trust into your communications with them. When they trust you they allow themselves to be hypnotized by you.

III. Step three: the next step to hypnotizing someone requires that you stimulate them emotionally. Emotions are powerful thing. It's hard to describe or even actualize emotions. We understand emotions by the labels we give them. We understand the essence of happiness, even though we cannot define it outside the scope of an abstract definition. The same thing goes for sadness. We get mental images in our mind about what these words mean, but a reality is the images that we formulate in our minds, our different person-to-person. When you stimulate someone's emotional mind you are stimulating their hypnotic mind.

IV. Step four: the last step in the hypnotic process is to implant instructions or suggestions to the individual, while they are trance induced. Keep in mind their focus and attention is not on you or what you're saying anymore. It is completely focused on the object or idea that you had them focus on intensely. For this reason there not aware of the traffic outside your building, any more there than they are aware of the instructions that you are feeding their hypnotic mind. The importance of stimulating their hypnotic mind or emotional mind utilizing emotions to do so, is to alert their hypnotic mind that you are going to be feeding it certain instructions, which are to be acted out at a later time that day were at some other.. The last up, where your feeding them instructions, his last phase of the hypnosis session, before the extra action where you will be bringing them back out of hypnosis allowing them to focus on anything and everything, they wish to, where they can rejoin the rest of the world and consciousness.

This is all that is required to hypnotize someone. The process never seriously changes for any context you might want to apply hypnosis. Even getting someone to stop smoking, the only thing that changes are the actual instructions you will be feeding their hypnotic mind. If you're trying to get someone to lose weight, those instructions certainly will be different from the instructions you give the client who is trying to stop smoking. The process doesn't change only the instructions you feed the hypnotic mind. For this reason, I have made this final step 'general' so as to imply whatever instructions you wish to give.

What Other Applications Can You Use Hypnosis To Help People

Hypnosis is a valuable tool for helping people to do numerous things to improve their lives. You can help people stop smoking, lose weight, stop blushing uncontrollably, fight off disease, attract the right life partner, improve their driving skills, and the list goes on and on. I personally have used hypnosis to help me learn math problems that were quite complex, without even having to try to learn them. As I said before trying denotes failure anyway. I was never a really good math student, until which time I hypnotized myself to be excellent at math. I suppose any type of limiting belief or experience that is continually replicated in a person's life, to the extent they have believed it to be true about themselves, can be altered and changed utilizing hypnosis. Hypnosis can be used for helping people achieve self-confidence, learning foreign languages, becoming better sales professionals, and so much more. It really is up to you first to discover what you might need help with, and then either hypnotize yourself, or go to a hypnotist to help you self-improve.

Final Purport

In this chapter, we discovered what exactly hypnosis is. I give you many insights into the times in your life you have been hypnotize, and didn't know it. It may even be safe to say most of your life you have been hypnotize. We become so focused on one thing, that everything else in our life becomes unnoticed. When we're young and in love we can only think about the person we love. It's challenging for us to think about the other people in our lives that are equally important. This can breed contempt and frustration from family members and it can even disrepair relationships that have been firmly rooted since childhood. It can cause conflict, and for most people they do not have any understanding about what is causing someone to behave in a certain way. They don't understand the effects of trance, to draw conclusions about what is actually happening, so they can fix or improve an individual's behavior. What's even more important to take stock of is the fact we ourselves are not consciously aware of our own problems and the effects happening when we are so focused on one thing, so much so that were hypnotized and unable to consciously focus on anything else going on in our lives. Sometimes we can lose sight of what's truly important.

When you think about falling in love for the first time though a smile might appear on your face. That feeling or rather feelings associated with love can be a natural high, and something unforgettable. And experiences can leave an indelible mark on a person's personal history, to the extent it becomes impossible to forget. Of course, good experiences, like falling in love, can have secondary or tertiary consequences that are not always positive; like for instance, when your mom and dad have a challenging time getting you to get off your butt and get a job. When your parents are giving you money to take a girlfriend out on dates, or your boyfriend, whatever the case happens to be, this can be one of those situations this can lead to one of those secondary consequences that may have some negative repercussions on your relationship quite quickly. It's not because your parents are jealous of your relationship with your partner, it is simply because they don't wish to support your relationship financially. Of course, you can't focus on that, because you're hypnotized by love.

Notice also how love is an abstract emotion that is hard to define—like happiness or sadness. The act of love, sadness, or happiness, is a trigger that penetrates the hypnotic mind, where suggestions and ideas become impressed by other people you happen to be in love with at a time. So if you're a guy and your girlfriend is giving you instructions about what she wants you to do for her, these become hypnotic suggestions more so than they become conscious instructions given to you by anyone else. When you're in a conscious state of functioning, of course you rationalize differently. Under hypnosis, however, these ideas go under the radar and penetrate your hypnotic mind, and then you act on these ideas and instructions, believing they are good ideas, even though your parents may not agree.

We also covered why you need understand what hypnosis is, before you can actually learn how to use hypnosis conversationally in order to be able to persuade people to believe you and act on your instructions. We will be covering this in the next chapter, as we talk about hypnotic conversations, and how you can do those without the person you're talking to knowing you're hypnotizing them. We also talked about what you needed to first understand about hypnosis before you could understand the steps to take to hypnotize someone. This was the information necessary to know so when I did deliver to you the essential sequential steps they would make sense to you. After I gave you this information I then covered with you the actual process that comprises the act of hypnotism. These are the steps you can take to hypnotize anyone regardless of the application of hypnosis. Finally, we rounded off this chapter by looking at some different types of benefits that can be achieved utilizing hypnosis as a tool for self-improvement and helping other people. I had a friend, once who suffered from OCD. It was an extreme case of OCD, which had greatly affected this person's life, and caused him to almost commit suicide. One night he invited me over to his apartment, and in ten minutes time I hypnotize him and he has not experienced the side effects of OCD since then. He's since become a productive member of society, unaffected by the disorder, and no longer exhibiting the side effects of having OCD. So take the story, just to give you some depth in terms of how you can utilize hypnosis to help other people live more productive and fulfilling lives.

Take Action Now

In order to get any value whatsoever from this book you must take action now on the instructions I'm going to be laying out for you. Do not be like most people—buy a book, half read it, set it aside, forget about it, never take action, never gain the advantages and benefits it has to offer you.

There is a reason you purchased this book. Do not forget that reason. If you attended one of my live training workshops, you would have participated in doing many exercises at the end of each module I taught you. This is because you get considerably more value practicing the techniques in a safe environment, before going out and practicing them in the real-world. Many people do not feel comfortable testing techniques they've just learnt blindly on real-life contexts. Do not be afraid to do these exercises: They are for your own good and self-development. Your personal power will increase when you proactively apply this knowledge to your specific contexts. Part of learning this information (the largest part) is applying it hands-on. Suspend your doubts and disbeliefs that you can do these exercises, because your insights will elevate to a higher level once you do them. You will only learn a fraction of what I teach in this book from reading the book. The great majority of your learning comes when you apply this information in whatever contexts you have been intentioned on learning it.

To prove this point: Think about your first kiss. You may have talked to friends about their first kiss to get some insight. Maybe you read a book on adolescent sexuality, where kissing was covered. You may have watched movies of actors kissing on the big-screen. Until you actually kissed a girl or guy for the first time, you didn't realize all that was involved in kissing, as you hadn't practiced it, and learned from that experience. I bet after you kissed for the first time, regardless how

good or bad the kiss was; you felt pretty amazing afterward, and felt much more confident in kissing other people. I'm right, and you know it, so do these exercises! In fact, make a promise to yourself; you will not move on to the next chapter until these action steps have been completed. You'll thank yourself. I promise.

I. Make yourself take out a piece of paper and a pen/pencil and write down exactly how you'll utilize the information found in this chapter to fit your particular persuasion context.

II. Find an opportunity to apply what you learned in this chapter and apply it. After you have taken this initial action, journal your discoveries and results.

III. Take a 3x5 index card and summarize the leading points from this chapter. Let this summary serve as a quick flash card to jog your memory once a day, as you continue reading this book, and doing future exercises. This is important, because this book has a lot of information, and a fast flash card to look at daily will help you not to forget what you have learned. Over time, this knowledge will become imprinted on your hypnotic mind, where you'll take action on this knowledge without thinking about it consciously.

IV. Teach what you have learned in this chapter to a trusted friend whom you think might benefit. Teaching information to others helps you gain greater clarity and insights you'd likely not have gained trying to keep it all in your own mind.

V. Discuss with the friend you've taught this information to and take notes on their thoughts and understanding of the material. This way, you'll gain another person's perspective and likely gain a deeper understanding of the material.

After you have successfully completed each of these exercises, only then, proceed in moving forward to the next chapter. Do not take shortcuts and tell yourself the lie you'll come back and do the exercises later. Statistically speaking the probability is improbable you ever will. Take a leap of faith and do the exercise, please! Trust me; it's worth it, if you want to gain true mastery in hypnotic persuasion.

=====================xx==================

CHAPTER 13

MILTON ERICKSON'S INDIRECT, COVERT, CONVERSATIONAL HYPNOSIS, AND NLP MODEL OF PERSUASION

The anomalous recommendations utilized as a part of conversational hypnosis are intended to misdirect or confound, and power you to contemplate what the roundabout recommendation may mean, what the diverse conceivable outcomes are, and how it applies to you by and by.

The Milton Model proposes that indirect suggestion inserted in conversational hypnosis is more viable than immediate recommendation. The Milton Model is a series of methods utilized as a part of conversational hypnosis, a method for placing somebody into daze unnoticed as a feature of an ordinary discussion. This manifestation of "mystery" aberrant recommendation system is known as the **Milton Model**. Conversational hypnosis frequently joins together Milton Model hypnotic wording with Analogical Marking and Tonal Marking.

Advantages Of Conversational Hypnosis

While doing conversational hypnosis the Milton Model is utilized to put hypnotic words into an indirect suggestion.

An direct hypnotic proposal is a particular instruction, for example, 'You will now go into a deep trance' or 'You are now a person of normal weight. An example of a circuitous proposal is : 'Eventually you'll end up wondering about going into a deep trance. Moreover, you may do that all of a sudden or gradually' - would it say it is the "wondering" or the 'going into trance' that you 'may do'? And while you are considering which it is, your brain is actually going into trance.

Because hypnotic words are not exactly characterized, amid conversational hypnosis the customer must stop and consider the meaning of those hypnotic words. This causes the customer to search their hypnotic mind to fill in the missing bits, or to choose how to apply the words to their own particular personal experience (known as a **transderivational search**). Because the hypnotic mind has to invest time contemplating many distinctive conceivable meanings, it is substantially more probable that the customer will discover something in their past that fits, and will be more practicable than a direct suggestion would be.

In conversational hypnosis the Milton Model recommendations require some more work to prepare, yet have the advantage of avoiding resistance. Some people have such low regard toward oneself that they will not accept immediate direct proposals, for example, *'You deserve to be treated well, you are respected and loved by many.'* Yet they will accept an aberrant proposal in conversational hypnosis, for example, *'I wonder how aware you are that many people have deep admiration as well as respect for you... then there are other individuals, ...who like you as the person you are'*.

Conversational Hypnosis Suggestions

The following cases of indirect hypnotic words and phrasing utilized within conversational hypnosis show how the Milton Model of hypnotic suggestion is completed. Each one portrays how conversational hypnosis functions, and gives illustrations of that type of hypnotic wording as utilized as a part of conversational hypnosis interactions.

Cause & Effect Implied

The therapist creates an impression that infers that one thing causes an alternate, or states that one thing is genuine; thus making the following thing definitely genuine. The announcement may be untrue, or there may be no immediate connection between the one thing and the other.

'What's more realizing that you can stop provides for you the right to change.'

'Snapping that closed, implies you are picking an alternate life"

'You don't have to gain weight any more in light of the fact that such a large number of individuals love you and rely on you for support'.

You can distinguish an implied cause/effect result by articulating – 'Does A truly prompt B?'.

Complex Equivalence

This is the place a Milton Model proposal is given that one thing is the same as or identical to some other thing. It isn't that one thing reasons an alternate, however the ramifications is on the grounds that if one thing is genuine the other thing must be genuine.

'When I see you on that bridge, it shows that you have settled on a choice today'.

'Snapping that tape implies you are picking an alternate life"

'Since you have control... you have decision in everything that you perform'.

You can distinguish a complex equality by substituting *'is the same as'* concerning the joining verb, although the statement *'causes'* does not fit.

Conversational Postulate

A conversational proposes an inquiry that, on the face of it, obliges a Yes or No reply; however, which is truly requesting a particular conduct. *'Might you be able to pass me the cream?'* is a solicitation for activity, not an enquiry about capacity. *'Do you truly need to remain there?'* is a solicitation for somebody to move. So also, inquiries could be postured in hypnosis that is truly directions.

'I think about whether you can review a period when you were truly unperturbed?'

'Will you envision some quiet, serene spot?"

'I think about whether you could envision a huge old house in some place?"

'Might you be able to start to unwind while counting backwards from ten?'

Conversational inquiries could be tried by attempting a 'yes/no' response to check whether it fits.

Embedded Commands

Immediate orders could be inserted inside normal discussion. This is the quintessence of a conversational pretension, or concealed hypnosis induction. For instance the hypnotist could start a discussion with

'I can see that you are open to lying there, **unwinding** in that seat, **quietly sure**, looking **so agreeable** as though you are prepared to **simply release things** and **unwind** while I discuss various stuff. You know, **you don't need to think, you don't need to hear** me out or do anything truly with the exception of **unwind** and **permit you brain to float away** like a little tyke **cuddling agreeably down** in a warm calm spot, **easing off**, additional quiet and **more in liesure**...' etc.

Embedded commands are normally shown by some manifestation of analogical or tonal marking—for instance by talking louder or looking specifically at the customer while utilizing a specific manner of speaking, or pausing just before and after the embedded command.

Extended Quotes

On the off chance, that you attribute an instruction to another person this can eliminate resistance from the clients. By utilizing, one or more levels of citation you can say very nearly anything to the clients, and will likely baffle their hypnotic mind simultaneously, making the proposal more prone to be acknowledged and complied with.

Milton Erickson once recounted the tale about how he advised a man *'you can learn to relax instantly'* and the man discovered he could unwind quickly and maintained, *'Everyone can relax faster than they think.'*'.

I met a man from Bombay who said the mystery of trust is *'Fake it until you make it'*.

What's more, as you flow around that gathering you catch somebody saying *'I am so pleased with her. She is the best little girl I could ever have longed for. She has become everything to me.'*, and the other individual answers *'Yes, possibly, we didn't say it frequently enough, perhaps we thought she would simply know it'*.

Lost Performative

An instruction is presented to the subconscious expressing that some supposition is true, however does not say exactly how it is known to be true, or who is stating it. The psychotherapist means that the intuitive nature of a person will acknowledge the revelation as being irrefutable and not request validation. Samples are:

"Your hypnotic mind will discover the right reply."

"You are never going to have an issue with your beliefs again."

"No habit can stand up to the power of the psyche."

You can just test for a lost performative by asking *'Says Who?'*.

Mind Reading

The Milton Model plans the recommendation as though recognizing what the hypnotic subject is thinking or feeling (cognition, affective response predicting) when in all actuality the psychotherapist, or conversational hypnotist has no possibility to know with certainty what the hypnotic subject is thinking or feeling. Illustrations of how this might be applied include:

'You are thinking about how quick you are going into hypnosis right now...'

'You are more curious about how that change is happening, aren't you...'

'Your mind is more open to the thought of transformation...'

You can tell apart a mind reading pattern by asking, 'In what way could you possibly know that?'.

Modal Operator

These are expressions that use words that infer things could happen or must happen. Normal Milton Model modal operators incorporate words like, *'ought to, can, can't, should, shouldn't, must, mustn't, may, could, couldn't, would, wouldn't, will, and won't'*. Modal operators may be the most frequently utilized hypnotic language pattern. Here are some examples:

*'You **can** do many things to more relax.'*

'You must be astonished at how rapidly you fall deep into trance.'

'You may perceive your left foot heavier than the right foot....'

A modal operator is typically recognized if it makes sense to add ...*'or possibly not'* or 'or maybe not' at the completion of the statement.

Negative Suggestions

Negative proposals are similar as conversational postulates in that they request one thing (usually a 'yes' or 'no' questions) yet infers and expects an alternate behavior to be the resulting answer/solution. The Milton Model works in light of the fact that the oblivious personality does not manage negatives well, and has a tendency to disregard the words *'don't and not*' and rather concentrates on the object of the sentence. The sentence *'Don't think about a black horse running in heavy rain*' must bring out a memory or figment of ones imagination (caused by remembered associations pieced together) before it could be not considered mentally, so negative inquiries might be utilized to give positive directions.

'What's more I don't need you to feel that you are going into dazed state now'.

'You ought not to be excessively inquisitive about how you will feel yourself going into a hypnotic trance.'

'You don't need to think too much about a solution coming; it can come to you when you least expect it.'

Nominalizations

The Milton Model is about utilizing words as a part of an 'artfully vague' way of communicating ideas to the hypnotic mind, under the radar of consciousness. A nominalization is a statement formed from a process. For instance, the verb 'to confine' might be nominalized into the thing 'confinement'. The statement confinement is then treated as though it is a "thing" and the way that it implies an action is overlooked. By utilizing the nominalization, the thing is dealt with as though it is over and done with, or some concrete finality, when indeed the activity may in any event remain an ongoing happening. Nouns ending in '-ship', '-ment', '-ion' or '-ings' are regularly nominalizations, for instance 'relationship', 'revocation', 'learnings', 'shipment' or 'decision'. By treating the word as a tangible thing, you are hiding the fact it is a fluid ongoing experience, for the purpose of letting your hypnotic subject assume an obstacle can be stepped over, and things can return to normal. Again, here are some examples:

*'Your **learnings** are mounting up, more and more, as you listen to my voice.'*

*'You affirm your permanent **choice** and **decision**, by moving exhibiting unconscious movement.'*

*'...you must acknowledge your **accomplishment** and own some ego.'*

You can test for a nominalization by asking of the thing nominalized, *'is it be able to be placed in a wheelbarrow?'* Nominalizations are abstractions and have no physical structure so cannot be placed in a wheelbarrow.

Non Sequitur conclusion

A Milton Model non sequitur avowal is an message introduced as 'cause prompts effect/result', A > B, however where there is actually no rational associated linking between A and B. The structure of the message tricks the hypnotic subject by beginning with a statement that something is true and afterward defining a result that does not consistently take after. Getting the client to concentrate on their breathing has nothing to do with unwinding, yet by expressing something that is true, the mind is tricked into thinking a causal linkage exists between the two parts of the argument. If I say, 'You're here, which causes you to feel better already,' the psychotherapy subject takes this statement to be true, without reflecting on its validity.

'....giving careful consideration to your slowing breathing can help you unwind significantly more.'

'You will be coming back to the present, and bringing with you everything you have absorbed today.'

'...as I count backward to you, you will go deeper into hypnosis'.

These could be recognized by testing *'Goodness, truly? Furthermore how does that work?'*

Presuppositions

A Milton Model presupposition discusses the outcomes of something and deliberately abstains from specifying the underlying idea. The proposal begins from a supposition that thing is true and afterward examines the results of that thing being true. By concentrating on the results whether the thing is true or not is disregarded and never tried.

Adverbial	...And now as you unwind all the more profoundly you feel something special.
Alternatives	I don't know whether you will go into mesmerizing before unwinding is completely finished or start right away.
Awareness	The easily overlooked details you perceive help you to remember how you have relaxed.
Causality	Because your eyes are shut, your consciousness will open to the thought of profound unwinding.
Equivalence	Coming here today implies you have settled on a choice to relax.
Ordinal	It may not be until the third breath that you recognize relaxing.
Possibility	...And you may find that every breath unwinds you more.
Time	You may not feel you are at the right level of unwinding yet.
Existence	It may be fascinating to consider the level of your unwinding.

A supposition may exist if the argument bodes well when you include "*I suppose*" tagged onto the end of it.

Inanimations

These Milton Model verbalizations appoint feelings or actions to things that can't have any. Actually, these are called *Selectional Restriction Violations*. A couch cannot think, a plant cannot verbalize and communicate, yet sentences might be developed that sound that way and on the grounds that our awareness is astonishingly tuned to the metaphoric representation. This kind of reference will be acknowledged by the unconscious mind.

'That seat knows the privileged insights of numerous customers'.

'The part of you that makes you smoke is embarrassed and needs to change.'

'Listen to the wind in the trees and assimilate its knowledge'.

Selection restrictions are at all times a type of metaphor.

Tag Questions

These are Milton Model inquiries swaying the customer to affirm reality through words, right? When you read the preceding statement it makes you want to say 'Yes', does it not? It is generally great to get the customer into a positive attitude, I am certain you would concur, would you not? If the tag question is delivered with a falling voice tone, it reinforces the statement and discourages opposition.

'Unwinding is extremely pleasant, isn't it?'

'Some individuals truly appreciate unwinding, isn't that so?'

You may ponder what you will appreciate most, mightn't you now?'.

Tag questions are undeniably agreement-getting, wouldn't you agree?

Truism Sets

A Truism is an apparent truth. In the Milton Model truisms are utilized as a part of sets to deliver spurious cause and effect statements. The customer listens to the first truism explanation, and concurs with it. The customer listens to the following truism, and concurs with that as well. The following recommendation is then made while the concurrence with the truism is still as a main priority, so it disproportionately will be acknowledged as true also and perceived as plausible enough to be regarded as a true statement, regardless of the fact it has nothing to do with the first rationalizations. A mockup of a truism set may be –

'Individuals are at their happiest when they feel not only cherished, but needed.'

'*There are times when everybody belittles their own abilities*'

'*Everybody needs to be loved, and everybody needs to be adored, and you are figuring out how to listen to your feelings*'.

You can recognize a truism set by asking 'Yes, **A** is true, and **B** is undisputable, however how does that make **C** legitimate?'

Universal Quantifier

Milton Model expressions like, 'all, every, never, any, everyone, no one, nobody, always, and everybody' demonstrate a generalization that may or may not be quantifiably true. Universal quantifiers always make sense, and can be persuasive when used, but almost never are verifiably true statements. Again, here are some examples:

'***All*** *that has come before has made you what you are today.*'

'***Each*** *expression you hear might be an indicator to your hypnotic mind, you're ready for change to happen now.*'

'***Nobody*** *can fall flat once they truly choose to change*'.

You can recognize a universal quantifier by questioning the quantifier, e.g. 'each expression; that is, each and every one ever heard by me?'

Unspecific Comparison

A common Milton Model articulation will utilize words to intimate something, and depends on the mind being excessively caught up with listening to the following words to truly address reality or rationale of what was simply taken note of. In a definitive Milton Model assertion, an association is made, but does not specify what is being likened with.

'You will end up shifting quicker'.

'Furthermore you may discover you are significantly looser'.

'Consistently all around, you are improving and becoming better.'

An unspecified comparison might be recognized by asking '-----er than what?'

Unspecific Object

These are words that sound great however are really very unclear. Milton Model words, for example, 'learning's, conclusions, assets, discoveries, attention' and so on, could be utilized to ground practically anything, which makes the recommendation unable to be argued. By utilizing inclusive words, the hypnotic subject uncovers and finds closure from their own particular resources. In the event you have concur with the past sentence you may need to re-read it, and consider whether it means anything whatsoever.

'..And after that return to the present with all the learnings you require.'

'Your comprehension will help roll out the improvements clearer'.

'You can open your intellect to full attention of everything that matters'.

Listen deliberately to any government official dodging a sticky issue for a lesson in how to say nothing utilizing unspecified verbs, nominalizations and unspecified objects.

Unspecific Verb

Like the Milton Model unspecified objects, Milton Model verbs sound great however are tricky to pin down. The unconscious mind acknowledges the expression in setting and supplies its own particular importance. Words, for example, 'marvel, change, comprehend, think, feel' and so forth, are non-particular and can be applied to anything.

'..In addition, you may be pondering about how best to go into hypnosis.'

'...also soon, the time will come when you get a handle on this.'

'..Your hypnotic mind will realize all that it needs'.

Analogical Marking

Analogical Marking is a method of applying the Milton Model. Analogical Marking conveys hypnotic commands buried covertly inside typical normal discourse as a component of a conversational impelling. Milton Erickson found that he could blend hypnotic orders into a standard discussion and have somebody follow up on them given the command words were subtly diverse somehow. This understanding is the premise of the Milton Model and of NLP securing. In ordinary discussion a hypnotic affectation is possible clandestinely by utilizing a deeper voice tone for the order words, or stopping quickly previously, then after the fact the words, or touching the customer while the charge words were being said. The customer subliminally enlists that these analogically stamped words were by one means or another distinctive keeping in mind the cognizant piece of the psyche is listening to the progressing discussion the intuitive piece of their brain is as of now pondering the analogically checked words and expressions. The accompanying area demonstrates to do a conversational impelling focused around Milton Model systems.

A Conversational Induction

This style of hypnosis is named 'conversational hypnosis', or 'covert hypnosis', and is regularly used to prevent triggering resistance in the hypnotic subject, who won't acknowledge formal hypnosis, or in applications which require the hypnotic subject not knowing they're being hypnotized (e.g., sales hypnosis scenarios/cult indoctrination). It is rarely utilized as part of treatment because standard techniques are speedier and simpler in most psychotherapeutic contexts. Notwithstanding it is pushed forcefully on the Internet by individuals asserting to have the ability to uncover the mystery of 'undercover hypnosis' and 'how to get other individuals to do whatever you want them to' or to 'subtly hypnotize ladies into bed'. Truth be told, there is nothing perplexing or mysterious about the procedure of analogical and tonal marking. Anybody can learn it. Everything can be mastered with a bit of practice.

In order to assert a covert command, demand, or instruction, so that it goes unnoticed in a normal conversation, the statement must be short, not over used, and not emerge as something unusual or odd in the context of the conversation it is installed in. It needs to be unobtrusive and not overused, because you don't want your hypnotic subject to suspect any funny-business going on. The summons might be blended in with any subject whatsoever, in spite of the fact that the conversational hypnotist would generally pick a point that the customer happens to be acquainted with, however decide to discuss it in a marginally equivocal or inexplicable manner, in order to hypnotize the hypnotic subject through captivating their attention.

Fundamental Procedure For Analogical And Tonal Marking

The first thing you want to do is choose what embedded commands (i.e., short instructions) you want to put into your hypnotic subject's hypnotic mind utilizing analogical and tonal marking techniques. This would relate to your purpose, outcome, or desired end result.

Then, write out the instructions sequentially, in the way and order you wish to suggest them.

After that, select a hypnotic theme that will captivate the subject's attention. I usually choose a topic that they have indicated is important to them, or one they happen to bring up in course of conversation.

Tell a hypnotic narrative rooted contextually around the theme of the conversation. The story ought to be fascinating, ambiguous, and indirect in nature; namely, keeping in mind the end goal, but telling it in such a way the hypnotic subject begins to wonder where it will end. In the couple chapters from now I'll be teaching you more about narration and hypnotic storytelling. For now just understand that you want to tell your story in a way that gets the hypnotic subject thinking and pondering where it may be going. Hypnotic narration of a hypnotic story, will make the hypnotic subject to quickly become hypnotized. Once the hypnotic subject falls under your hypnotic spell, you can then pause for a couple seconds before and after the embedded command you deliver. Keep in mind, the shorter the embedded command, the better, and better chance it will stick and become imprinted on your subject's hypnotic mind. For this reason, don't get caught up too much in proper grammar usage, or over think the process of tonal marking your embedded command. It should be subtle and go unnoticed by the conscious mind; yet, get the attention of their hypnotic mind. You'll know when this happens too, by the nonverbal cues you'll receive from them. When someone is hypnotized their body language is usually calm and relaxed, and they slow down and enter a day-dream like trance. When the emotional hypnotic mind is communicating back to you that the embedded command has been accepted, it will be through sudden movements, or an indication of 'yes' from the head shake of the hypnotic subject. Body language doesn't lie or hide behind words.

As you're communicating hypnotically remember to speak rhythmically, two-thirds slower than you normally speak (gradually decrease your speed over the course of the conversation). Remember to deepen your voice, and start talking in a monotone. Use conjunctions and bridge words (e.g., 'that is to say', 'meaning', 'rather', 'after which', 'yet', 'and', 'or', 'because', 'more so', 'becomes', and 'makes'). The main thing is you divert the conscious, analytical, logical, rational mind into the story; that is, so you hypnotize your hypnotic subject, and proceed to communicate with their hypnotic mind.

Step By Step Instructions To Marking Embedded Commands

Embedded commands can be marked in numerous ways, and likely ways hypnotists have yet to consider. There is no right or wrong approach to doing a conversational induction, so long as the analogical and tonal marking is smooth and consistent throughout the duration of the conversation.

Voice Tone

Voice tone is the most helpful method for marking out particular words and hypnotic fragments. People perceive that the manner of speaking intimates something far beyond the actual words utilized. Saying an short fragmented command with a descending tonality, makes it a command, and at the very least marks it as something important to take note of at the hypnotic level. At any rate marking your embedded commands in this way make them something you ought to be giving careful consideration to. Then again, saying an expression with the voice climbing at the end transforms it into an inquiry. So pay attention to how to state a command, and replicate this in your hypnotic interactions with the hypnotic subject.

When talking to a hypnotic subject, with the intention of performing a conversational hypnosis induction, the conversational hypnotist can speak the command words more audibly, or with a exacting stress on the words, or in a another inflection, or by turning their head either towards or away from the client—even, my preferred method; namely, looking into the left eye of the hypnotic subject (the left eye is connected to the emotional or hypnotic brain). All of these forms of analogical and tonal marking are easy to do and many persons even now do it innately and involuntarily. Politicians are taught to 'lean forward and grin' while delivering their hypnotic messages to the interviewer or their publics.

Word Of Caution

Analogical marking has to be done with proper measures. If the whole thing is performed in a very messy pattern, then the listener will realize that they are being affected. They will right at that moment refuse to accept anything the speaker says from that moment on. When this happens, any sort of faith or trust in the hypnotic communicator is faded away forever. You'll not be able to recover, as rapport is compromised.

Similarly, as with all unknown recommendations, the mind inside will not perform anything that is against that person's moral balance. It is commonly said, "A hypnotist cannot make you do anything against your will;" however, what's not often spoken is, "A hypnotist can bend your will to make it what they want." In business, cunningly done analogical and tonal marking can be used to plant ideas such as 'good value' or 'decide today' or 'buy now' or similar types of short and sweet embedded commands, because these are part of the normal buying and advertising process. Though, irrespective of the process a suggestion is made, you cannot force anyone to do things they would not ordinarily do. You can bend their will to make them want to do what you want them to do, though. Any recommendation, command, demand, or order, even if introduced subtly and increasingly, will be discarded if it contradicts the subject's moral beliefs and inner values.

Creating NLP Anchors

NLP Anchoring refers to the nature of an association between an affection and a sensory experience such as a touch or a noise. NLP Anchoring works because individuals form normal relations between feelings and external objects every day. And every day our anchors remind us of those feelings. For instance a smell might well trigger a memory of a past event in your personal history. A place you re-visit may trigger a strong connection to a past emotion you felt for someone dear to you. Most often we are unaware of the physical associations linked to emotions and memories. A child is anchored to safety when holding a stuffed animal, for example. It creates a sense of security. The security may be lacking whenever the child misplaces the stuffed animal. The child feels love for the stuffed animal, because it represents paternal love given by a parent. An NLP anchor is something an NLP practitioner purposely establishes to link a feeling to something else for the purpose of helping the client get to a better state, or experience more self-confidence, as possible examples. Anchoring can be achieved in or out of hypnosis. The last example, I'll share is money being an anchor for good times or irreligiousness; that is to say, it would depend on the association someone has made with money. Often times someone who obtains a large quantity of money, may go out and have a good time, knowing they have the money to enjoy life, and the physical 'money' (e.g., debit card, cash, etc.) will naturally link to this emotional state of feeling abundant and happy. This is one unconscious reason people might become 'attached' to money; rather than being attached to what their money buys them (although this doesn't have to always be the case).

Anchoring in NLP

The NLP Anchoring system is focused around unintentional anchorage, a common intuitive learning knowledge. For instance, assume you go on vacation, have an extraordinary time and the same tune is playing all around where you go. In years to come, listening to that melody brings back the knowledge of that occasion. You didn't do anything to make the connection, and you can't stop it happening - that is a characteristic stay. In any case, stays ordinarily get overwritten. On the off chance that you hear that same melody in numerous better places later, then the programmed grapple between the tune and that occasion experience is broken. The NLP tying down system utilizes this characteristic capacity to make and break affiliations.

Unintentional Anchoring generally happens when you are in a specific passionate state. At that point, something happens amid that state and your brain structures a moment relationship between the two. Case in point phobias, for example, a youngster could create apprehension of a certain food, from adult figures in their life, before ever trying or even seeing the food. The youngster goes into a state of alarm, and afterward sees the food and the mind structures the affiliation: this food = nasty.

Anchors are set all the time. The more occasions an anchor becomes reinforced, the stronger that anchor gets to be. Delight can get connected with numerous types of unessential things. Smokers have an espresso and a cigarette in the morning. Before long, they can't appreciate an espresso without the cigarette, and thinking about an espresso naturally triggers the requirement for a cigarette. These are unconscious anchors that hold power of us at the hypnotic level. Individuals who got their first serious sexual feeling in a certain circumstance may end up anchored to certain stimulus' which trigger sexual desire. Adolescent boys may become aroused by looking at mostly naked women in a magazine, and then become subscribers of that magazine, long after the fact. They become attracted not so much because of the nudity, but because of the anchor having been set earlier in their life.

NLP Anchoring: Directions To Make NLP Anchors

The following instructions will help you master the skill of NLP anchoring. Additionally, I have included some different types of techniques you can use to anchor your hypnotic subject. Some of these various techniques will work better in some contexts; others, in different contexts. The key is to recognize 'when' and 'how' to use the different techniques presented, so you maximize the probability of achieving the desired result.

Survey The Target State

Ask your subject to survey a period when they felt 'in control', or "proficient" or 'in control' or some other constructive state of mind. Have the hypnotic subject revivify the state fully, by asking them to re-experience it from memory, feeling the emotions they felt back then, and insist that they really go to great lengths to put themselves back in that situation. Have them notice their body movements, what was going on around them, what people were present then, and so on.

Increase The Target State

By then ask that they build upon those emotions. You can do this by saying to them, "Double the intensity of that emotion... Now, double it again. You are strengthening this emotion even more now than that." As an NLP practitioner you should be able to see physiological changes happening in the hypnotic subject, as they indeed tune into that emotional state of being. These physiological signs will happen unconsciously and will reflect that physiology they originally experienced when the event first took place.

Anchor The Target State

When they give off an impression of experiencing the state you require, attach the anchor. This may be something you do, or something they do. An ordinary anchor is to press on the shoulder or knee of your hypnotic subject, for five seconds. Keep in mind, I'm walking you through how to set anchors using NLP practitioner techniques; not to be used in covert indirect contexts when applying conversational hypnosis inductions. Anyway, this five seconds, gives the subject's body time to work together the emotional stimuli with the top most emotional experience. This association is what is meant by anchoring the target state. Other techniques can be thought up for differing contexts. For covert contexts you can bring in an out-of-the-ordinary anchor and associate it to your hypnotic subject when they are emotionally experiencing a state you wish to easily have them access again in the future. For example, if you happen to be selling them something, and they buy, and they will be a recurring customer, make sure you anchor with a hand-shake, a shoulder touch, and a smile, when they happen to be highly emotionally satisfied with the purchase. Next time you visit them to sell them something else, the first thing you can do is shake their hand, touch their should (like before) and smile. This will trigger the same buying state emotions they experienced the first time they bought, and it will help assist you selling them again.

Test The Anchor

The next step is to test the anchor to determine its efficacy. The first time or two you test the anchor it may not work to recreate the same affective state they were in when the anchor was set. For this reason it is often necessary to set the anchor several times, reinforcing the anchor to the emotional state. How you test an anchor is simply to redo the physical stimulus to see if the emotional experience occurs again automatically. It should be an automatic physiological response that occurs. This is what is meant by testing the anchor.

Setting Verbal Anchors

It is also possible to set verbal anchors. These types of anchors work best with covert indirect persuasion contexts. Suggestions could be anchored verbally in diverse ways. There is no right or wrong approach to do it, as long as the anchor is consistent and not plainly obvious. This is known as analogical or tonal marking. I covered this with you already. The principal thought behind this technique, however, is to get your words to trigger the anchor connected to some state or feeling so that an automatic reaction is achieved by your hypnotic subject.

The last point I want to cover with you on verbal anchors is to become aware of certain words your hypnotic subject tends to lean on. People are anchored to words; explicitly, words that have deep emotional connections to past experiences or mental imaginings. When we're young, the words we learn first, remain with us throughout our life, and have a stronger emotional bond, than synonyms we learn later on. We are connected to our language through emotional connections attached to these words. There is a different emotional connection with the word 'baby' than with the word 'infant'. We learnt 'baby' first, and it carries a deeper connection in our hypnotic mind, than does the word 'infant'. To prove that these anchors exist just think about the word 'love' and discover what first comes to your mind. Now think about how your physiology changed when you considered what came to mind. You probably didn't pay too close attention, did you? Guess what...you did think of something in your mind when you thought of the word 'love' didn't you. The mentioning of the word 'love' was attached to something other than the four letters l, o, v, and e, was it not? Incidentally, the word love, is the anchor.

Voice Tone

Voice tone is the most important methodology to catch specific words. People see that the way of talking surmises something a long ways past the genuine words used. Saying an interpretation with a falling, creating way of talking converts it into a request, or in any occasion something you should be giving cautious attention to. On the other hand, saying a representation with the voice moving at the end changes it into a request.

Exactly when chatting with a customer, the hypnotic authority will speak the request words more uproariously, or with a particular nervousness, or in an interchange stress, or by turning their head either towards or a long way from the client. These securing procedures are not hard to do and various people starting now do it normally and unwittingly. The group of onlookers will unwittingly see that a couple of words and declarations are not the same as others and will focus on them remembering the final objective to class them.

The switch technique for mirroring with the voice is to misspeak, stammer or be indecisive over particular words or outflows. If the orator says: "There is no smoke whereas not um... as well I will be able to tell you..." The cluster of onlookers will endeavor to fill in the missing word, and will say the representation "fire" in their psyche, will consider it, be aware of it, all without any direction from the speaker.

Essential Keyword Word Marking

Sometimes, depending on the context of course, it may be that you objective is simply to anchor some crucial keywords. One context this might be useful would be Sales. A sales professional may wish to anchor certain keywords by simply patting the shoulder of their potential customer while saying the keywords—for example, the keyword 'buy' may be repeated several times over the course of the conversation, and each time the sales professional may tap the arm, raise a finger, click a clicker-pen, or something else, simply to set the anchor. When it is time to get the customer to buy, the sales professional may simply trigger the anchor by touching the arm, or clicking the pen, and the anchor should be set, and the customer should likewise buy. You can also utilize this same type of anchoring technique in other applications as well. You need only to decide it this technique is applicable to your particular purposes or not.

Gesture Marking

Sometimes a simple gesture can communicate hypnotically on several levels. For example, when public speakers are giving a speech, they may unconsciously use body language that represents visually what they are trying to convey with their words. For example, a politician running for an office, may use a pointing forward gesture to represent his agenda, while using a downward pointing gesture to represent his opponents agenda. The abstract hypnotic metaphor of moving forward is anchored to the gesture. Whenever the politician is unable to directly speak with many in his audience verbally, who have supported his or her campaign by coming out to rally support; the politician may make eye contact, and use that gesture of moving forward to reignite the same excited emotions which came about when he was delivering the speech. This can be a useful anchor to set as it can be a reinforcement that builds and sustains the right emotional state to ensure that the desired outcome comes about.

Priming Behavior Anchors

A substitute related system for influencing people unwittingly is to use 'get ready' as a means of priming their future behavior. When someone says to their teenage child, who plays sports, "Get ready to show them what you've got tomorrow!" they are priming them mentally for success. This verbal priming technique causes the child to future pace, which means see the outcome they've been wanting, before the day of the big game. This mental maneuver has been used by many coaches, to help their clients and team play better, and win their desired outcomes more. Thoughts are results not yet realized outwardly. By encouraging people to excel and go after the results they seek, through presuppositions, and assumptive language patterns, people tend to achieve more.

Respondent Conditioning/Anchoring V. Shaping Behavior

Sometimes people get confused or mistaken by their understanding of 'shaping behavior' for anchoring/respondent conditioning. There is a difference though and so let me explain: Anchoring is connecting an emotional experience to a specific stimulus, called an anchor. Shaping on the other hand is using rewards to shape your subject's behavior toward a desired behavioral outcome. Punishment may also be used to curb behavior whenever the subject moves away from or resists moving in the right direction, desired by the shaper.

Respondent conditioning or Anchoring is best illustrated by the famous Pavlovian experiment using dogs, conditioning them to salivate (as they did when they were presented with food) by anchoring this behavior to the sound of a tuning fork. Eventually, it only required hearing the tuning fork, and the dogs would begin salivating, expecting food. They were conditioned to react hypnotically to the tuning fork.

Shaping is often a technique employed by parents to get their children to behave. When the child is doing 'right' a parent may reward this behavior by providing something to the child that is desired. When the child misbehaves a punishment may be used to curb the behavior back into alignment with what is required by the parent.

Cult leaders oftentimes use shaping to provoke the behavior and thinking that is desired by the leader. When a new person is getting involved with the cult the behavior is generally positive and accepting. As the new recruit becomes initiated into the culture of the cult, the use of negative reinforcements may be employed, as a punishment, to redirect behavior back into alignment with the cult's objectives. When a new member joins, they are often met with praise, friendship, etc. The new member quickly learns that this 'happy friendship attitude' toward them is what they desire, so they are shaped slowly, almost unnoticeably by the cult, to comply with the expected behaviors if that new recruit wishes to met with this 'happy friendship attitude'. If they resist being shaped into the cult's agenda for them, then they are met with a 'not-so-nice attitude' which may create discomfort, and psychological distraction, which will lead to the raising of questions. When the recruit doesn't get answers, they simply learn to obey, instead of disobey, in order that they will be liked, and honored by other members of the cult.

On the other hand, certain anchors are generally set by the cult, which are constantly being reinforced—for instance, a cult may require their members engage in a regular daily activity with all the other members, which is anchored to a certain emotional response. One such anchor may be chanting, anchored to a 'spiritual feeling'. This is one way a cult may evoke a 'spiritual truth' connection to their cult and the will of a god or idol. Members start to believe that the cult has all the spiritual answers for them, because they're anchored to the 'spiritual feeling' by the activity.

Hypnotic Words Create Post Hypnotic Anchors

Under hypnosis, a hypnotic anchor can be connected to an emotional state brought on by a past event the hypnotic subject earlier experienced—for example, the subject may be asked, under the spell of hypnosis, to revivify a past experience in which they felt empowered. This empowered state is already associated to the previous experience. However, you can set up an alternate anchor, while the subject is hypnotized to trigger the feeling of 'empowerment' whenever a future event or stimulus is encountered. You can set-up these hypnotic anchors using hypnotic language—case in point, a sales professional can subtly inquire using interrogative techniques, a past experience a potential customer experienced. The potential customer can be provoked using hypnotic interrogative language patterns to revivify the emotions experienced. A sales person may wish to, for example, have the potential customer experience a state of excitement, brought on by revivifying an earlier experience, which is anchored to the state of 'excitement'. When this happens, the sales professional may suggest, hinting using hypnotic language patterns that the subject will likely have a similar experience whenever he/she experiences using the product the sales professional happens to be selling. When the potential customer experiences using the product, the experience will trigger the same strong emotions previously had during the other experience. This will create hypnotic intrinsic value in both the product, yet also the sales professional. The next time this sales professional revisits the customer, to sell another item, it will have created so much goodwill that the hypnotic subject will want to buy over and over and over again—making the sales person's job easier, and him richer for it. The customer will gain the value of experiencing on a deep emotional level something far more valuable than the actual product purchased.

Trancelike words for Post Hypnotic Suggestions

At whatever point you see the shade blue, you will rapidly become more and more relaxed, and think clearer—accomplishing far more than you think.

At whatever point the possibility of eating food, before mealtimes, comes into your thoughts, you will feel uneasiness toward the food, and not be able to eat it, making mealtime more exciting and desirable to wait for. Each time you look in the mirror you will see a minor change that evokes more self-confidence.

The trigger itself is not all that important. The main thing is that it is something your hypnotic subject will without fail encounter. Also important is the repetition of the encounter with the trigger. A mirror, looked into every morning and evening (after waking and before bedtime) helps to reinforce and strengthen the anchor, making it more powerful and effective. What matters is that the hypnotist, setting the anchor, uses the right hypnotic words to continue through to the end of the therapy session, or hypnotic encounter, so the events and affective responses trigger on cue.

Final Purport

In this chapter you learned about aspects of the Milton Model, and how to use conversational hypnosis in a myriad of applications. It is fair to relay to you, now, exactly what some of these applications are, by profession, which I have alluded exist across multiple career paths. Knowing some of the applications, will perhaps help you beginto see the value in learning how to communicate hypnotically through indirect covert means.

Some of the jobs where hypnotic persuasion language is useful are: advertising, acting, activism, argument, auctioneering, brand management, buying, change management, working with children, communications, conflict resolution professions, consulting, counseling, diplomacy, financial advising, human resources, interrogation, job-hunting, journalism, lecturing, lawyers, leadership, marketing, mediation, management, networking, parenting, protesting, romancing, screenwriting, teaching, therapy, and writing. In fact, a different book could be written on any of these occupations, to teach the group how to utilize advantageously, and beneficially hypnotic persuasion techniques. It is even possible to completely change the culture of an organization by harnessing the power of this model of communication, and the techniques described in this chapter, but also throughout the rest of this book.

Please take your time studying this chapter, because the more you know how this stuff works on a practical level, the more intuitive you can work with it when applying it to other applications you wish to adapt it to. In the next chapter, I'll be presenting you with some specific hypnotic language patterns that can be learnt and memorized, and instantly utilized to help you influence and hypnotically persuade anyone you wish to. Memorizing and regularly using the language patterns I'll be sharing will also help to make you a much more persuasive speaker, writer, and all-round communicator.

Take Action Now

In order to get any value whatsoever from this book you must take action now on the instructions I'm going to be laying out for you. Do not be like most people—buy a book, half read it, set it aside, forget about it, never take action, never gain the advantages and benefits it has to offer you.

There is a reason you purchased this book. Do not forget that reason. If you attended one of my live training workshops, you would have participated in doing many exercises at the end of each module I taught you. This is because you get considerably more value practicing the techniques in a safe environment, before going out and practicing them in the real-world. Many people do not feel comfortable testing techniques they've just learnt blindly on real-life contexts. Do not be afraid to do these exercises: They are for your own good and self-development. Your personal power will increase when you proactively apply this knowledge to your specific contexts. Part of learning this information (the largest part) is applying it hands-on. Suspend your doubts and disbeliefs that you can do these exercises, because your insights will elevate to a higher level once you do them. You will only learn a fraction of what I teach in this book from reading the book. The great majority of your learning comes when you apply this information in whatever contexts you have been intentioned on learning it.

To prove this point: Think about your first kiss. You may have talked to friends about their first kiss to get some insight. Maybe you read a book on adolescent sexuality, where kissing was covered. You may have watched movies of actors kissing on the big-screen. Until you actually kissed a girl or guy for the first time, you didn't realize all that was involved in kissing, as you hadn't practiced it, and learned from that experience. I bet after you kissed for the first time, regardless how good or bad the kiss was; you felt pretty amazing afterward, and felt much more confident in kissing other people. I'm right, and you know it, so do these exercises! In fact, make a promise to yourself; you will not move on to the next chapter until these action steps have been completed. You'll thank yourself. I promise.

I. Make yourself take out a piece of paper and a pen/pencil and write down exactly how you'll utilize the information found in this chapter to fit your particular persuasion context.

II. Find an opportunity to apply what you learned in this chapter and apply it. After you have taken this initial action, journal your discoveries and results.

III. Take a 3x5 index card and summarize the leading points from this chapter. Let this summary serve as a quick flash card to jog your memory once a day, as you continue reading this book, and doing future exercises. This is important, because this book has a lot of information, and a fast flash card to look at daily will help you not to forget what you have learned. Over time, this knowledge will become imprinted on your hypnotic mind, where you'll take action on this knowledge without thinking about it consciously.

IV. Teach what you have learned in this chapter to a trusted friend whom you think might benefit. Teaching information to others helps you gain greater clarity and insights you'd likely not have gained trying to keep it all in your own mind.

V. Discuss with the friend you've taught this information to and take notes on their thoughts and understanding of the material. This way, you'll gain another person's perspective and likely gain a deeper understanding of the material.

After you have successfully completed each of these exercises, only then, proceed in moving forward to the next chapter. Do not take shortcuts and tell yourself the lie you'll come back and do the exercises later. Statistically speaking the probability is improbable you ever will. Take a leap of faith and do the exercise, please! Trust me; it's worth it, if you want to gain true mastery in hypnotic persuasion.

======================xx==================

CHAPTER 14

HYPNOTIC PERSUASION PATTERNS

As we live our day to day lives, having the ability effectively communicate our ideas and feelings to others can mean the difference between leading lives full of frustration; or satisfying, fulfilling, and successful ones. Key to effective communication is the ability to get our point across to and influence others. This means understanding how to apply the power of language patterns that can be described as hypnotic.

In the last chapter we covered many facets of the Milton Model and NLP. In this chapter we'll be taking that complex model, and making it more useable for you to indirectly persuade anybody hypnotically. What I have done is create a number of hypnotic persuasion patterns, complete with examples, so you can simply fill in the blank adapting the hypnotic persuasion patterns to your specific contexts. This cookie-cutter approach makes learning how to speak hypnotically a much faster process. I think it is fun learning these patterns, and hope you will gain great value from them, and make learning conversational hypnosis much simpler.

These patterns of speech have been proven over and over to be effective, and they work because of the way our brains are structured. Our brains developed gradually over time, have specific subdivisions of structure, and these structures each process information and language in different ways.

The first and the most primitive structure is the reptilian brain. This part of the mind processes fight or flight reactions in situations which may be perceived as threatening. The second part to develop was the limbic or emotional brain. This section processes information in an emotional matter, tending to perceive situations based on their benefits. The last section is the cortex, or the logical brain. This area processes language and logical thought, and perceives situations based on the advantages that may be gained.

Properly using these language patterns will result in the communication being unconsciously processed by the emotional mind. This enables the pattern user's communications directly to access the minds of others at a deep level, bypassing unnecessary resistance and allowing unprecedented influence.

These patterns should be used in a basically verbatim form. Using them in this way will ensure that the unconscious minds of the ones being spoken to will automatically be engaged and influenced in the desired manner, and will guarantee that other people believe true your persuasions.

For your learning benefit, I am including 54 of these covert, indirect, linguistic, persuasion patterns. I will also be putting together a deck of flashcards, comprising these same exact language patterns, which will be for sell at: www.indirectknowledge.com. I highly recommend you purchase a deck, if you're a serious student of hypnotic persuasion. As I've mentioned earlier in this book, in a previous chapter, repetition is a powerful means by which to induce hypnosis. By practicing, repetitively, these patterns using the flashcards, you'll quickly and effortlessly master these 54 persuasion patterns before you've had time to realize it. I will provide a short purport explaining each pattern, as well as examples of usage with each provided pattern. Let us begin.

1. **You might be aware of___.**

This statement causes the listener to consider what it 'might' be that they are aware of.

"You might be aware of that hot new IPO."

2. **I'm wondering if___.**

Deflects attention from the fact that you are making a suggestion, and causes listener to wonder as well.

"I'm wondering it you might be better off with a lower mortgage."

3. **You probably already know___.**

Causes listener to consider whatever statement comes next on a deep level.

"You probably already know how much money people are making with this product."

4. **Don't __ too quickly.**

An effective reverse tool, which causes the hearer to want to do whatever they were advised not to.

"Don't lose weight too quickly."

5. **Can you imagine__?**

This will cause the listener to imagine what is being described, especially if the subject is emotional.

"Can you imagine how much safer this will make your child?"

6. **One can (name)__.**

This conceals the fact that you are making a suggestion for action.

" One can, Phyllis, save much more money by refinancing one's mortgage."

7. **You might notice the feelings of__ as you __.**

Causes the listener to think about the feeling of what is being suggested.

" You might notice the feeling of relief as you finally make that stock trade."

8. **One could__ , because.**

Adding 'because' to the statement gives it emotional weight.

"One could use Dr. Benson, because he's never had a malpractice suit."

9. You can ___, because.

Has the same effect as the above statement, but even more forcefully.

"You can buy this product, because it has a money back guarantee."

10. You can__, can you not?

Invites subconscious agreement from the listener.

"You can see the benefit of this 401k plan, can you not?"

11. You might notice how good it feels when you__.

This assumes that what I am about to suggest feels good.

"You might notice how good it feels when you turn on this state of the art alarm system."

12. One doesn't have to ___.

Casually suggests something to the listener.

" One doesn't have to overdo it on the sugar."

13. **You may not know if ___.**

This can set the stage for a suggestion for action.

"You may not know if the bottom drops out of that stock without this software."

14. **It's easy to __, isn't it?**

This causes the listener to consider the suggestion.

"Its easy to see that, isn't it?"

15. **You are able to __.**

Assumes the listener can do something.

"You are able to afford this service."

16. **(Fact, fact, fact) and ___.**

This gets the listener to agree with the last statement.

"It's almost Winter, and your roof is quite old, snow can add quite some weight to it, and you can get a new one through our finance plan."

17. ___ once said___.

This is a great way to make a suggestion.

"Henry Ford once said, "A dollar saved is a dollar gained."

18. **If you__, then__.**

A simple cause and effect assumes that if one part is true, so is the other.

"If you use this galvanizing product, then you will never have to worry about rust."

19. **When you__, then__.**

Whatever is mentioned is the first part is factual, so the suggestion is accepted.

"When you take this class, then your earning potential will rise."

20. Will you__now, or will you__later?

Gives only two choices, implying both are valid.

"Will you open this account now, or feel sorry later?"

21. You don't have to__.

A veiled command.

"You don't have to continue to suffer with that washer."

22. You may__.

Subconsciously giving approval.

"You may hold that meeting anytime."

23. You might__.

A powerful suggestive.

"You might want to do that now."

24. You could__.

Can remove pressure, because you're not saying they will, must, or have to do something.

"You could purchase that tomorrow."

25. One might, you know__.

Listener will consider what is 'known'.

"One might, you know, postpone that get-together."

26. Maybe you haven't__ yet.

Assumes that they eventually will.

"Maybe you haven't put in that order yet."

27. People can, you know___.

It puts the responsibility on others, but is processed as a command.

"People can, you know, apply for that course."

28. I'm wondering if you'll ___ or not.

Get around needless resistance.

"I'm wondering if you'll take advantage of this sale or not."

29. You may or may not___.

Listener will consider what it is they may or may not know.

"You may or may not have heard about that great merger."

30. You might notice the sensation__.

Directs listeners attention to emotion.

"You might notice the sensation of comfort when you put these shoes on."

31. **What happens when you__.**

Causes listener to consider the suggestion.

"What happens when you decide to retire?"

32. **Can you really enjoy__.**

Does not ask if something can be done; only if it can be enjoyed.

"Can you really enjoy going on this vacation?"

33. **Some people__.**

The listener is made to imagine what others are doing.

"Some people choose the Brown Fund."

34. **You might not have noticed__.**

Directs attention where wanted.

"You might not have noticed the huge depreciation."

35. **Try to resist__.**

Implies listener won't be able to.

"Try to resist having too much of that cake."

36. **Eventually__.**

Implies certainty.

"Eventually, that water heater will rupture."

37. **Sometime__.**

Encourages listener to imagine something in the future.

"Sometime, this situation will rectify itself."

38. **Sooner or later__.**

Implies something will definitely happen.

"Sooner or later, you'll have to sell that stock."

39. I could tell you that, but__.

Helps overcome resistance.

"I could tell you that this vehicle is a great value, but I'm sure you know that."

40. How would you feel if you__?

Causes listener to consider proposed scenario.

"How would you feel if you went on that romantic cruise?"

41. You might become aware of __when you__.

This assumes the existence of something.

"You might become aware of the amazing profits when you read this report."

42. I wouldn't tell you to__because__.

Listener is compelled to process what you wouldn't tell them to do.

"I wouldn't tell you to use that new medication, because I'm sure you'll look into it."

43. **However much you are already exploring__.**

Assumes listener is exploring something.

"However much you are already exploring weight loss supplements, you may not know of this one."

44. **As you may have considered__.**

Listener will focus on what they may have considered.

"As you may have considered, this investment position gives the highest return."

45. **Whatever way this will work for you__.**

Assumes that something will work for the listener.

"Whatever way this will work for you, we'll make sure to do it."

46. Either way__.

This predicts a certain outcome.

"Either way you do this, you'll come out ahead."

47. You are going to think___.

A useful suggestive.

"You are going to think this is the best you've ever seen."

48. How would you feel if___?

Causes listener to focus on emotions.

"How would you feel if you could ensure your child's safety?"

49. What happens when you___.

Causes listener to imagine what would happen.

"What happens when you get sick without insurance?"

50. **By the time you've started to___ you will__.**

Assumes certain outcomes.

"By the time you've started to lose weight, you will wonder why you didn't start this plan sooner."

51. **When you really begin to, ___ then__.**

First, this assumes that they have begun something, and then adds an effect to the cause.

"When you really begin to use this trading strategy, then you will see huge returns."

52. **You should recognize___.**

Assumes there is something to be recognized.

"You should recognize the size of this market."

53. Once you get going___.

Assumes something is going to be started.

"Once you get going with this class, you'll never look back."

54. After you__, you may want to___.

Assumes that one thing will be done, and then suggests another.

"After you finish making dinner, you may want to serve the wine."

Want More Hypnotic Language Patterns?

If you enjoyed these hypnotic language patterns, you'll really love the selection we offer at:
www.indirectknowledge.com

We offer physical flashcard decks of many varieties. Flashcards make learning these patterns much faster and simpler.

Take Action Now

In order to get any value whatsoever from this book you must take action now on the instructions I'm going to be laying out for you. Do not be like most people—buy a book, half read it, set it aside, forget about it, never take action, never gain the advantages and benefits it has to offer you.

There is a reason you purchased this book. Do not forget that reason. If you attended one of my live training workshops, you would have participated in doing many exercises at the end of each module I taught you. This is because you get considerably more value practicing the techniques in a safe environment, before going out and practicing them in the real-world. Many people do not feel comfortable testing techniques they've just learnt blindly on real-life contexts. Do not be afraid to do these exercises: They are for your own good and self-development. Your personal power will increase when you proactively apply this knowledge to your specific contexts. Part of learning this information (the largest part) is applying it hands-on. Suspend your doubts and disbeliefs that you can do these exercises, because your insights will elevate to a higher level once you do them. You will only learn a fraction of what I teach in this book from reading the book. The great majority of your learning comes when you apply this information in whatever contexts you have been intentioned on learning it.

To prove this point: Think about your first kiss. You may have talked to friends about their first kiss to get some insight. Maybe you read a book on adolescent sexuality, where kissing was covered. You may have watched movies of actors kissing on the big-screen. Until you actually kissed a girl or guy for the first time, you didn't realize all that was involved in kissing, as you hadn't practiced it, and learned from that experience. I bet after you kissed for the first time, regardless how good or bad the kiss was; you felt pretty amazing afterward, and felt much more confident in kissing other people. I'm right, and you know it, so do these exercises! In fact, make a promise to yourself; you will not move on to the next chapter until these action steps have been completed. You'll thank yourself. I promise.

I. Make yourself take out a piece of paper and a pen/pencil and write down exactly how you'll utilize the information found in this chapter to fit your particular persuasion context.

II. Find an opportunity to apply what you learned in this chapter and apply it. After you have taken this initial action, journal your discoveries and results.

III. Take a 3x5 index card and create your own flashcards (one for each pattern). Let this help to jog your memory once a day, as you continue reading this book, and doing future exercises. This is important, because this book has a lot of information, and a fast flash card to look at daily will help you not to forget what you have learned. Over time, this knowledge will become imprinted on your hypnotic mind, where you'll take action on this knowledge without thinking about it consciously.

IV. Teach what you have learned in this chapter to a trusted friend whom you think might benefit. Teaching information to others helps you gain greater clarity and insights you'd likely not have gained trying to keep it all in your own mind.

V. Discuss with the friend you've taught this information to and take notes on their thoughts and understanding of the material. This way, you'll gain another person's perspective and likely gain a deeper understanding of the material.

After you have successfully completed each of these exercises, only then, proceed in moving forward to the next chapter. Do not take shortcuts and tell yourself the lie you'll come back and do the exercises later. Statistically speaking the probability is improbable you ever will. Take a leap of faith and do the exercise, please! Trust me;

it's worth it, if you want to gain true mastery in hypnotic persuasion.

=====================xx=================

CHAPTER 15

NARRATIVE TRANSPORTATION THEORY: A PERSUASION MODEL FOR HYPNOTIC STORYTELLING

Every cult needs a good story. One of the most moving aspects of a cult is its back story. The story can be true, possess half-truths, or be entirely fictional. What matters most is the way the story is told. It needs to be able to make an impact on new and potentially new members, so they will get caught up in the story, be intrigued, mystified, captivated, hypnotized, and both empathize with the protagonist character(s) and be subjected to alterations in beliefs, intentions, and thought patterns through the narrative transportation aspect of this psychological persuasion model, which causes affective and cognitive responses, beliefs, and attitude and intention adaptations. Also, the transport should cause changes to identify through some type of attachment to the narrative. When a cult has an interesting historical foundation, it becomes easier for new entrants to want to become indoctrinated into that cult abandoning their individual identities, and past history, in lieu of identifying themselves as part of something bigger than themselves. Most people are not famous. Many people have lived seemingly normal existences their entire life. Just as people will abandon this normalcy and boredom to immerse them in a book's storyline, new entrants to a cult will likewise adhere to and attach themselves to a cult for the same reason. When people join a cult, the story that defines a cult becomes their story, and their great escape. When people have become dissatisfied with their ordinary lives, and wish to move on to something more exciting and attractive, one of the first things they do unconsciously is try to do their best to understand the mystery behind the cult's history. As new entrants typically have little information and knowledge of the storyline, it becomes real important for them to learn as much as they can about this story, so that they can have meaningful conversation with other cult members. The story is left unanswered intentionally, and your members become like the 'Scoobydoo Mystery Gang' in a sense. This sense of incompleteness creates the need for more answers. In order to get more answers the cult member(s) must turn to other cult members and cult leaders to get those questions answered. Until which time these new members are satisfied, they tend psychologically to continue remaining associated with the cult itself. What they don't know, is the story/mystery is never complete, so satisfaction never comes. This is intentional by design. Cult leaders don't want their members going elsewhere. They want them right there, i.e. in the cult.

People want to know what they don't know. If you remember back to many of the hypnotic archetypal triggers that create intrinsic value in offers, individuals, and even cults, you see this pattern that emerges of wanting what someone can't have as being closely linked to wanting to know what you don't know. It creates more value intrinsically for the cult itself. It keeps new members interested and loyal enough to continue affiliating themselves with the cult. It is also what draws outside individuals into the cult. This is a drawing in attraction for many people to want to uncover secrets, and understand the mysterious nature of the cult.

In persuasion psychology there is a persuasion model which has become labeled narrative transportation theory. I remember when I was a kid in high school, how there were news stories surfacing at that time around kids who would engage in these dangerous experiments, because they had seen these acts done in movies and in cartoons. These children have become attracted, much in the same way that I had become attracted when I was a child to the mysterious world of the martial arts. These kids would do things like lying down in the middle of the highway until which time an automobile ran them over, killing them. There was debate surfacing at that time in the news media where specialists would come on the air and talk about how watching television had such powerful influence over these children. There was even debate on what should be shown on television and what should not. It was being encouraged at the time that parents should watch their kids and monitor what they view, and not allow them to watch what might be label 'dangerous programming'. The mysterious nature of such programming creates internal excitement inside the mind of the individual watching the programming. This is the same phenomenon that happens to suck people into joining cults when stories are told by cult leaders.

Narrative transportation theory is a persuasion model, which explains the phenomenon of what happens when people become transported into a story. One of the first things that happens is they depart their normal existence and enter into an alternate reality mentally. It is important to note also that when leaving the story and coming back to reality the individual arrives changed. There was a famous hypnotist known as Milton Hyland Erickson. Erickson was a doctor of psychiatry and he lived from 1901 until 1980. In my opinion, he is perhaps one of the most prolific storytellers the world has ever observed. He utilized storytelling as an indirect means of hypnotizing his psychiatry patients in order that he could help them therapeutically. Though Ericksonian psychotherapy consists of much more than mere storytelling, it was storytelling that often times Erickson employed to help his clients. Storytelling is a powerful method through which to hypnotize another individual in order to change their mind, and get them to see an idea differently. Storytelling is the gateway to the hypnotic mind. This direct entryway into someone's mind allows the conversational hypnotist to bypass resistance, stimulate a person's hypnotic mind, drop them under their spell, and then manipulate their mind any way they see fit. You may be able to recall and experience are two or more from your past where you started watching some type of movie or engaged in reading some book, and got so wrapped up in the book or movie that you wished it would never end. Likewise, you've probably read a book or seen the movie, which you could not wait for the movie to end and in some instances you may have actually gotten up and ended the movie, or put the book to the side never to return. Not 'every' story is necessarily hypnotic. Some stories aggravate us, bore us, and cause us to formulate opinions about that story, which one might explain harshly. The most hypnotic stories are the stories that literally transport us from our reality into a new reality, keep us captivated, and make us forget ourselves. We start to take on the characteristics of the characters mentally. Their thoughts, beliefs, and environment even, become hours. In order to achieve this type of affect on an individual both effectively and cognitively, it is important that the storyteller's words in such a way so as to structure this false reality in a way that it becomes perceivable he real. The more descriptive a writer or verbal storyteller is the more hypnotic the story becomes. Storyteller can also employ such mnemonics as voice inflection, rhythm, body language, then pauses, and other devices to increase the affect that the story has individual watching and listening. Actors in a movie can likewise convince the watcher that they are in fact the characters being represented in the story.

Narrative transportation theory suggests that when people lose their selves in a narrative, their own thought patterns and motives alter to reflect that story. The mental state of narrative transportation can easily clarify the persuasive effect of stories on people, who may go through narrative transportation when certain contextual and personal preconditions tend to be met, as Green and Brock postulate for the transportation-imagery model. We won't, by the way, be discussing the imagery-model in this book, but the research is fascinating, should you choose to persue it independently. As Van Laer, De Ruyter, Visconti, and Wetzels elaborate even more, narrative transportation occurs whenever the hypnotic subject experiences a feeling of stepping into a world evoked by the narrative as a consequence of 'empathy' with the story characters and imagination of the plot. Given the implications of stories for the persuasion of men and women, **nothing is less innocent than a hypnotic story.**

The majority of research on narrative transportation follows the initial definition of the construct. Scholars in the persuasion psychology discipline unceasingly reaffirm the relevance of three unique attributes.

Narrative transportation requires that people process stories-the acts of receiving and decoding. Story receivers become transported through two primary ingredients: empathy and mental imagery. Empathy implies that story receivers try to understand the experience of a story's character, which is, to know and feel the world in a similar manner. Hence, empathy offers an reason behind the condition of detachment from the world of origin that's narrative transportation. In mental imagery, story receivers produce vivid images of the storyline, in a way that they feel as though they are experiencing the events themselves. When transported, story receivers forget reality in a physiological sense.

Relative to these features, Van Laer et al. define narrative transportation as the extent to which an individual empathizes with the story's characters and the story plot actuates his or her imaginative resourcefulness, leading him or her to experience suspended reality throughout story reception.

Since narrative transportation's conceptualization, studies have demonstrated that the transported "explorer" can come back transformed and even converted by the passage. Subsequent research has authenticated that a story can absorb the story receiver in a transformational encounter, whose side effects are robust and long-lasting. The transformation that narrative transportation accomplishes is persuasion of the story recipient. More specifically, Van Laer et al.'s literature review unveils that narrative transportation can result in affective and cognitive responses, beliefs, and attitude and intention modifications. However, the running pattern of narrative transportation is markedly not the same as that in well-established models of persuasion.

Analytical persuasion and narrative persuasion vary with respect to the role of involvement. In analytical persuasion, involvement depends on the extent that the message provides personally relevant consequences for a receiver's money, time, or other resources. If these consequences are adequately severe, receivers evaluate the arguments meticulously and produce thoughts relevant to the arguments. Yet, as Slater notes, despite the fact that serious consequences for stories are relatively rare, "viewers or readers of an entertainment narrative typically appear to be far more engrossed in the message." This type of involvement, or narrative transportation, is arguably the crucial determining factor of narrative persuasion.

Though the dual-process models provide a valid description of analytical persuasion, they don't encircle narrative persuasion. Analytical persuasion identifies attitudes and intentions produced from processing messages which are explicitly persuasive, such as most lessons in science books, news reviews, and speeches would tend to be. However, narrative persuasion refers to attitudes and intentions developed from processing narrative messages that aren't brazenly persuasive—for instance: novels, movies, or even video gaming. Addressing the strength and duration of the persuasive outcomes of processing stories, narrative transportation is really a state of mind that produces long-lasting persuasive effects devoid of careful evaluation of arguments. Transported hypnotic subjects are immersed in a story in a way that neither is inherently critical nor will involve great examination.

Sleeper Effect

Narrative transportation appears to be more unintentionally affective than intentionally cognitive in nature. This way of processing leads to most likely intensifying and long-lasting persuasive effects. Appel and Richter use the term "sleeper effect" to label this paradoxical property of narrative transport over time, featuring its increasingly pronounced alteration of attitudes and intentions along with a higher surety that these attitudes and intentions are right.

Plausible Answers For The Sleeper Effect Are Twofold

With respect to poststructural enquiry, language's articulation in narrative format is capable not merely of mirroring reality but also of building it. Consequently, stories could cause serious and durable persuasion of the transported story receiver as a result of her / his intensifying internalization. When stories transport story receivers, not only do they provide a narrative world but, by reframing the storyplot receiver's language, they also durably change the world to which the story receiver returns after the transportation experience.

Research reveals that individuals analyze and hold on to stories differently from other information formats. By way of example, Deighton et al. show that analytical advertisements stimulate cognitive responses whereas narrative ads are more inclined to activate affective responses.

After this line of reasoning, Van Laer et al. establish narrative persuasion as the effect of narrative transportation, which usually establishes itself in the story receivers' affective and cognitive responses, beliefs, attitudes, and intentions from being carried away by a story and moved right into a narrative domain that modifies their perception of their own world of origin.

The conceptual distinction between analytical persuasion and narrative persuasion and also the theoretical construction of sound elucidation of narrative persuasion evenly support the expanded transportation-imagery model (ETIM). Again, we won't cover the imagery model in this book.

In this chapter, I'm going to teach you why you need to understand the pure fundamental nature of narrative transportation theory as a hypnotic persuasion model. I'm then going to give you what you need in order to put into action this persuasion model successfully; namely, so that you may more easily hypnotically persuade your subjects indirectly and covertly. Then I'm going to teach you how to actually integrate narrative transportation theory 'simply' into every hypnotic story you'll ever tell to increase the intensity of these stories. You'll be able, when you're finished with these learnings, to apply the principles of narrative transportation theory to transport anyone into any reality you see fit. We're then going to look at some other applications where narrative transportation theory might be applied successfully, with the incitement that you continue your learnings by thinking about other applications on your own. These other applications might be more in alignment with your particular purposes for wanting to hypnotically persuade people.

Why You Need To Understand The Pure Fundamental Nature Of Narrative Transportation Theory As A Hypnotic Persuasion Model

Narrative transportation theory lies at the foundation of three attributes. The first of these attributes come into play, when the hypnotic subject processes a story through the receiving and decoding of messages that are laden throughout the story. The second attribute of narrative transportation theory is the transportation into a narrative caused by empathy, which detaches the hypnotic subject from their own world and transports them into the fictional world of the story. The last attribute is the mental imagery aspect that naturally happens when a story is told. The act of mentally imaging something creates such vivid images to become so strong that the hypnotic subject feels as if they are actually experiencing those images personally as reality. Hypnotic stories tend to be more affective and less cognitive.

Receiving and decoding information causes the hypnotic subject to begin a journey into unknown territory. This processing that happens is the receiving of new information that is decoded against knowledge and thought-patterns, which are already present in the mind of the hypnotic subject. When you can get your hypnotic subject to start thinking thoughts in a particular direction, this is the first step in taking control of their thought patterns. Being able to take control of the mind of your hypnotic subject empowers you to feel more in control of that hypnotic subject, letting you more easily persuade the hypnotic subject, without resistance happening.

Empathy is where transportation into a story actually begins. When your hypnotic subject begins to empathize with the characters of your story, she or he will start to understand and experience the world from the vantage point of the character(s). This empathy detaches us from our own world and transports us into the world of the story. When you are able to transport your hypnotic subject into a new world you start to become the puppet master pulling their strings. Nothing is less innocent than a story; namely, because of its indirectness. Most of what we believe have come from stories people have told us. We remember stories much easier than we remember logical facts. For this reason, hypnotic stories are wonderful devices, because they change our perceptions and beliefs, in a way that is non-confrontational, nor direct.

Mental imagery is the same thing children do when they're playing make-believe and pretend. They are transporting themselves into the realm of possibility, where anything is achievable. When anything is imaginable, doubt and resistance don't become limiting factors that impede others from believing your persuasions, and therefore they don't stand in the way of hypnotic persuasion. To take what you envision in your mind, until those images are so strongly imprinted on your hypnotic mind, your hypnotic subject starts to perceive a new reality as a true possibility, apart from the original reality they existed in before the story was told.

With a narrative you can change anybody's attitudes by simply getting them to immerse themselves in a whole other reality. According to the research, people who exit a story to re-enter their previous reality, come back altered. These changes last a long time when compared to analytical and systematic models of persuasion. What this means is people are more persuaded by a story than they are when explained logically why something makes sense. This is the great secret why people often times do illogical actions, even after being explained why taking a different course makes more sense rationally. No wonder colleges advocate critical thinking skills; most people don't critically think things through logically when making a decision to take a certain course of action.

What You Need To Know In Order To Put Into Action This Narrative Transportation Persuasion Model

Now that you understand the benefits and why you need to understand narrative transportation theory as a persuasion model, it's now time to discover what you need to know to make this model actionable. Astonishingly, you don't have to be the most prolific storyteller in the world, to get what you want from people. Just knowing a few simple principles is enough.

The first thing you need to realize is you've been telling stories, in fact hypnotic stories, your entire life. The next thing you need to know is even through 'language' is a very rational and logical function, we combine the logic of language with the creativity of strong internal pictures, to create highly imaginative stories people can vividly image and make sense of. This is part the paradoxical nature of stories; that is, they possess an element of logic and creativity. In truth, the better you are with using your language, the better storyteller you can become, because knowing how to use language and your words to vividly paint a picture in someone's mind is a useful skill for anyone wishing to be more persuasive.

The last thing you really need to know is when you tell a story it is very important that your characters be well developed and believable and able to be interpreted and empathized with by your hypnotic subject (or: audience). Empathy is the catalyst for real change to happen. Whenever your hypnotic subject starts to empathize with your protagonist or antagonist they start to internally chance their thought patterns, beliefs, ideas, and overall experience the life inside the story differently. When your hypnotic subject leaves this inner world to return back to their everyday conscious reality they return changed. These changes are usually long lasting, possibly permanent, and knowing this can be useful for internally shaping behavior through the use of reward and punishment metaphorically applied to the characters in your story. The empathy one feels for the character's behavior is what one tends to project outward after the story is over.

I remember once when I went to the movies: I forget exactly what movie I went to see, but I remember it was a movie that had a lot of deep metaphoric meaning hidden inside the general message. It was difficult to make perfect sense of the movie's deeper meaning; yet, I knew them somehow on a hypnotic level. When I walked out of the movie I was deeply affected, and I had become more pensive and absorbed in thought and internal dialogue. I was definitely hypnotized, and I think I had become more agreeable as well. The movie had something to do with these behavioral changes.I want to encourage you to let your stories have a same or similar affect on your hypnotic subjects.

How-To Actually Integrate Narrative Transportation Theory 'Simply' Into Every Hypnotic Story You'll Ever Tell To Increase The Intensity Of Impact These Stories Have On Your Hypnotic Subjects

In this section I want to take you through the sequential steps necessary to implement narrative transportation theory successfully as you begin to start telling more hypnotic stories. Because, in the next chapter we'll be discussing in greater depth the deeper intricacies of hypnotic storytelling as an artform and strategy for hypnotizing and persuading our hypnotic subjects, I won't get into too much detail now about hypnotic stories and how to tell them. Instead I want to give you the steps to get you thinking in the right direction, more holistically, and to precondition your hypnotic mind to hypnotically be in the right place mentally for when you are telling hypnotic stories. Consider this section more about the hypnotic 'mindset' needed to make your stories far more captivating and hypnotizing.

> I. The first step to integrating narrative transportation as a persuasion model, when telling extremely hypnotic stories, is to first be hypnotized yourself. 'Going there first' is a common theme stressed in hypnosis training

schools around the world. When you are hypnotized, others become hypnotized. It requires less conscious effort on your part, as conscious effort is not as powerful an an inducer as simply being in the presenece of someone who is already hypnotized.

II. The second step to integration is starting your story with a hook. A hood is something that grabs your hypnotic subject's attention, and sucks it into the story immediately. A good hook can be a powerful interrogative sentence. When you ask a question people pay attention because they know they may be required to answer. Nobody wants to answer a question unintelligently or wrongly. For this reason they pay attention so they might process every word being spoken. Another way of creating a hook is to begin your hypnotic narrative with something relatable. When someone relates with the story from the get-go, it is easy to pace them into the story slowly, and then lead them to whatever outcome you wish. Remember: Nothing is less innocent than a story; or rather, a hypnotic story!

III. The third step is to bypass their resistance. In this type of scenario resistance would not be the resistance to your persuasions, directly. Rather, resistance would come from wasting someone's time, and when people start to hear a story coming, they start to resist getting involved, because they don't know how long the story will last, and perhaps they have things they need to be doing besides listening to your story. One way of bypassing resistance is simply to preface your story with an inferred indicator that your story is a quick one. You might say something like: "Real quick, let me share this with you...". The indicator 'real quick' indicates you will be respectful of their time, and not be longwinded. If you are longwinded, and your story starts to develop slowly, you will have already bypassed their resistance enough, and hopefully captivated their interest with your story, that you'll be allowed to finish. Of course, by taking them on this adventure, or through some altering experience, you'll be hypnotizing them into changing their mind, value, ideas, perceptions, motivations, thought patterns, and beliefs; thus, persuading them hypnotically.

IV. The fourth step is to use your hypnotic subject's empathy for your characters to create an deep emotional connection with the story. This can be done by using literary devices like 'climax' and mental 'storyboarding' techniques, to ensure your hypnotic subject become emotionally involved with the story. You'll also want to use vivid descriptive language (adjectives/adverbs) to create vivid images in the hypnotic mind of your subject. Remember, empathy and vivid imagery are essential to narrative transportation and creating the mental environment inside your subject's mind to essentially hypnotize them into falling into your story. This is the same hypnotic deepening effect caused through traditional hypnotherapy inductions.

V. The fifth step is to utilize some of the hypnotic language patterns mentioned in an earlier chapter, for the purpose of embedding post hypnotic suggestions into your hypnotic subject's hypnotic mind (unconscious mind). These suggestions can be subtly and covertly repeated, as you tell your hypnotic story, and through this whole process of telling your story, you're hypnotic subject will be more apt to comply with such instructions, after exiting the the story and returning back to their normal reality.

After returning back to normal reality the hypnotic subject will be changed. These changes will be longer lasting than more systematic persuasion models. The last thing I want to mention is that, depending on what hypnotic affect you're seeking, will depend on which hypnotic archetypal triggers you'll be framing inside your story.

For illustration purposes, you may think of this book as possessing an element of forbiddances, because of the title, and due to the rich content that can be used to persuade people to do anything you want them to. The repetition of 'cult' strategies helps to reinforce the intrinsic value of this book, which has been done intentionally.

How Else Narrative Transportation Theory Might Be Applied Successfully To Other Hypnotic Persuasion Contexts

People have told stories since forever (well you get the idea). There is evidence of stories told from ancient cave paintings of early human ancestors. This was the first type of alphabet used to represent experiences human beings went through. These experiences were such that humans back then felt it intriguing to record such events in the form of pictures and symbols. Then we see early alphabets emerge in China, India, and Egypt, which were pictorial in nature. They weren't the same types of symbols for letters that we know and use today. The essence of the story, and the mental attachments human beings have to them, cannot be underscored enough. Stories are embedded in our human DNA. They touch on the aspects of human communication that are more indirect and less critical. We can believe a fictitious event in our minds as having happened, or happening, when we let our defenses down and engage in the enjoyment of a good narrative or movie plot. People enjoy stories, because they take them out of their humdrum everyday realities and give them someplace to go that's fun and exciting, without the danger of actually having to experience the happening.

There are many contexts with which to apply a story, besides just for the purpose of influencing and persuasion, which are still considered highly hypnotic contexts. For instance, if you want to change someone's state of mind or their mood a humorous story can do this. The value of telling stories can also be for the purpose of remembering something that needs to be remembered. Memory experts use a technique of associating the events of a story to whatever it is they want to memorize in order to remember longs chains of information. It may seem like a feat of magic to watch someone recall what is seemingly too complex a data set to remember, but there really isn't any magic to it. The secret is in using stories to help them recall the data. As I've mentioned, stories are easier to remember and more unforgettable in nature than most things logical and rational. When logic is intertwined and mixed with storytelling, it becomes more useful oftentimes, because it can be harmonized for the reasons I've mentioned here. The more stories are repeated, the more hypnotic they become. We've all heard of someone who tends to tell us the same stories over and over again until they become word-for-word repeatable back to the storyteller. These types of stories are heavy useful in hypnotism contexts. A good hypnotherapist is usually one who has repeated the same hypnotic scripts and inductions over and over again and again to where it becomes second nature for them to hypnotize someone using them.

Final Purport

In this chapter we learned about narrative transportation theory as a hypnotic persuasion model. I walked you through the reasons why it is important to understand this model of persuasion; namely, listing the attributes, then explaining to you both the advantage and benefits of these attributes, for using this model in crafting your persuasions so people believe them as true. I then gave you what you needed to know upfront before you actually implement this model in a practical application of hypnotic persuasion. After supplying you with this, I then gave you the necessary steps to successfully implement hypnotic stories around this hypnotic persuasion model. After all of this, I provided you with some insights into other hypnotic contexts you can investigate using this model.

I just want to conclude this chapter, by encouraging you to think outside the box for a few moments, before moving on to the next chapter. This is important because you need to be able to think about how you can benefit fully from knowing about narrative transportation as a hypnotic persuasion model. In my opinion, through much experimentation, I believe this is one of (if not) my favorite persuasion models. I want you to start thinking strategically, because simply learning this information doesn't help you, unless you are able to fully integrate it into actual applications to benefit yourself.

Take Action Now

In order to get any value whatsoever from this book you must take action now on the instructions I'm going to be laying out for you. Do not be like most people—buy a book, half read it, set it aside, forget about it, never take action, never gain the advantages and benefits it has to offer you.

There is a reason you purchased this book. Do not forget that reason. If you attended one of my live training workshops, you would have participated in doing many exercises at the end of each module I taught you. This is because you get considerably more value practicing the techniques in a safe environment, before going out and practicing them in the real-world. Many people do not feel comfortable testing techniques they've just learnt blindly on real-life contexts. Do not be afraid to do these exercises: They are for your own good and self-development. Your personal power will increase when you proactively apply this knowledge to your specific contexts. Part of learning this information (the largest part) is applying it hands-on. Suspend your doubts and disbeliefs that you can do these exercises, because your insights will elevate to a higher level once you do them. You will only learn a fraction of what I teach in this book from reading the book. The great majority of your learning comes when you apply this information in whatever contexts you have been intentioned on learning it.

To prove this point: Think about your first kiss. You may have talked to friends about their first kiss to get some insight. Maybe you read a book on adolescent sexuality, where kissing was covered. You may have watched movies of actors kissing on the big-screen. Until you actually kissed a girl or guy for the first time, you didn't realize all that was involved in kissing, as you hadn't practiced it, and learned from that experience. I bet after you kissed for the first time, regardless how good or bad the kiss was; you felt pretty amazing afterward, and felt much more confident in kissing other people. I'm right, and you know it, so do these exercises! In fact, make a promise to yourself; you will not move on to the next chapter until these action steps have been completed. You'll thank yourself. I promise.

I. Make yourself take out a piece of paper and a pen/pencil and write down exactly how you'll utilize the information found in this chapter to fit your particular persuasion context.

II. Find an opportunity to apply what you learned in this chapter and apply it. After you have taken this initial action, journal your discoveries and results.

III. Take a 3x5 index card and summarize the leading points from this chapter. Let this summary serve as a quick flash card to jog your memory once a day, as you continue reading this book, and doing future exercises. This is important, because this book has a lot of information, and a fast flash card to look at daily will help you not to forget what you have learned. Over time, this knowledge will become imprinted on your hypnotic mind, where you'll take action on this knowledge without thinking about it consciously.

IV. Teach what you have learned in this chapter to a trusted friend whom you think might benefit. Teaching information to others helps you gain greater clarity and insights you'd likely not have gained trying to keep it all in your own mind.

V. Discuss with the friend you've taught this information to and take notes on their thoughts and understanding of the material. This way, you'll gain another person's perspective and likely gain a deeper understanding of the material.

After you have successfully completed each of these exercises, only then, proceed in moving forward to the next chapter. Do not take shortcuts and tell yourself the lie you'll come back and do the exercises later. Statistically speaking the probability is improbable you ever will. Take a leap of faith and do the exercise, please! Trust me; it's worth it, if you want to gain true mastery in hypnotic persuasion.

====================xx=================

CHAPTER 16

HYPNOTIC STORYTELLING

Now that you've garnered some insights from the previous chapter on Narrative Transportation Theory, this chapter will focus on taking you one final step further, as it relates to explicitly hypnotic storytelling. Namely, you'll be studying the intricacies and art form of what has become termed 'Hypnotic Storytelling'. You'll learn why you need to be able to tell hypnotic stories, what you will need to know before you can start learning how to tell hypnotic stories, how-to tell hypnotic stories using several storytelling models which have been adapted for telling hypnotic stories, and after which you'll be given an opportunity to expand your thinking, as I discuss with you some other application where hypnotic storytelling may be useful and feasible. I am really excited for you, because you are really doing a fantastic job learning everything in this book. I remember when I first began my study of this information, and then began testing it out. The results I've gained have been nothing less astonishing. Let me explain...

Why You Must Learn Hypnotic Storytelling To Help You Hypnotically Persuade Anyone

When we think of hypnosis, we don't usually think about storytelling. Likewise, when we think about storytelling, we don't think about hypnosis. The truth is, we should! You see hypnotism is the act of doing only a few things well. How we do these things depends on what tools we wish to draw on. Stories are the best tool, given the context of covert persuasion tactics we're covering in this book. I think the reason for this has to with the passive nature of a story. Stories are less than innocent. We perceive stories as harmless, most of us. The essence of a hypnotic story are the indirect hypnosis implements and psychologies we employ. Also, the types of stories we tell.

When you can communicate something indirectly you gain the advantage of people actually paying attention. There's something about this type of communication where people somehow perceive that there's more to it than meets the eye. For this reason people are drawn hypnotically into what it is you're conveying. It's almost metaphorical in a way, because people tend to naturally draw their own conclusions, gain their own insights, and spark their own creative processes. You benefit when people do this, because you can feel a connection between you and your hypnotic subject. It's miraculous to experience this type of connection, because it makes people more drawn to you magnetically. This magnetic connection separates you from your competition, and brings out your uniqueness, which is astonishing to learn of.

The ability to tell different types of hypnotic stories give you an incredible edge over everyone else communicating, in the general sense. Marketers are always seeking and exploring new ways to position their offers in a way that bypasses the noise and clutter in the marketplace. Noise is a term which means distraction from what the marketer is trying to convey to the marketplace. Sometimes noise is the result of too many messages being conveyed. Sometimes it is caused from too many marketing communication messages that the culmination of too much is noise; that is to say, too much presenting can cause no message to be conveyed. Another term is clutter. Clutter is both an advertising and marketing term, which is defined as too many messages competing in a marketplace—for instance, your message may be lost in the clutter of all your competition's marketing communication messages. When this happens attention is not gained, and sales are lost as a result. It doesn't matter even how perfect your message is, because at the end of the day nobody is paying attention. In hypnosis, attention is the first step, to achieving the state known as hypnosis. If you cannot gain attention, you can't hypnotize your hypnotic subject. It is imperative you be able to attract attention, even with your words—hypnotic stories are the answer often times. Everybody loves a story! And, everybody loves ideas. The advantage you gain when you tell a hypnotic story in the right way, is an instant magnetic attraction towards you and your message. You benefit, as people start to love you, and in some cases—worship you!

What You Should Know About Hypnotic Storytelling

There are three types of hypnotic stories we'll be covering in this chapter. The first is a simple three part hypnotic story you won't forget. The second is the hypnotic hero's journey narration. This is a complex narrative with many parts. These types of stories can be told quickly sometimes, but often you'll want to save these types of hypnotic stories for when time permits you to tell them. They are deeply penetrating and hypnotizing. The last is the nested loops hypnotic stories. These take some practice mastering; yet, leave your hypnotic subject wanting more, while unaware they are unconsciously becoming more and more hypnotized.

When you're telling a hypnotic story, there are some questions you need to keep in mind. The first question is,

How relatable is your story to your audience? This may sound basic, but you'd be surprised how many people tell a story without considering their audience. Quite often people think about themselves, and tell a story that is one they can relate with, and this is the reason many people are put off from listening to someone else's story. You have to think about your hypnotic subject and their map of reality. One way to do this is to tell more general stories, where you leave too much detail left out, providing a means for the hypnotic subject to fill in the blanks. I talked about deletion, distortion, and generalization in an earlier chapter. The reason people naturally leave out details, distort information, and infer information in a way that is generalized, is because our conscious mind can only keep up with so much. When you generalize information, in your stories, it lets the hypnotic subject draw their own conclusions, relatable by their own unique maps of reality. Of course, you also want to guard against being too generalized, too. This is because people can adapt and make associations to what you're saying, when they have something from which to start forming mental pictures in their minds from. If you don't give them some detail, that they can work with mentally, it doesn't make for a very compelling story. You want to keep a balance.

Another question, Does your audience empathize with the main protagonist? In other words, Do they feel a connection to the main character in your story? When we empathize we put ourselves in the shoes of the character, and determine how we might handle the situation, or how we might feel. Seldom in life is there one particular way or set standard for handling life's situations. Some people will cry at a funeral; others, will remain silent and seemingly emotionless. We're all different, and for this reason, it is easy to empathize with other people, because we all recognize our differences from other. Your audience doesn't need to sympathize with the protagonist, as much as empathize with him or her. Empathy is aligning yourself and your feelings with the other person; sympathy is feeling sorry for the other person, without being able to put yourself in their shoes, or feeling what they feel, per se. It is very important that your audience, listening to your story, relate with what the characters are feeling, and experiencing.

Another question, Is your message getting through. By this, I mean, more specifically, Is your hypnotic subject imperceptibly getting the hidden meaning of your story, i.e., the moral of the story. This is important, because the deeper meaning of the story is linked to the hypnotic mind of your subject. The hypnotic subject may not be necessarily making sense of everything consciously; yet, they are getting information more profoundly, at the unconscious-hypnotic level. Incidentally, this is the level of awareness where emotions underpin hypnotic affect. When emotions get triggered people tend to lose their logic, and become more emotionally reactive—more under the spell of hypnosis too. So, this brings us to the last question, Does your story elicit emotional states, and if so, to what extent? The more emotionally invested your hypnotic subject is with your story, the more influence you will naturally have over them. A big 'part' of being a great hypnotic storyteller is being able to express your story's character's emotions, through your own non-verbal communication. The best hypnotic storytellers express or echo emotions in a way that the hypnotic subject empathizes with, and starts to feel something for. Minds get changed, when emotions get evoked. As a hypnotic storyteller it is your job to evoke those emotions. Emotions are contagious, and easily transferable to other people.

These things I've so far mentioned are the precursor to becoming an excellent hypnotic storyteller. They are the foundation from which everything is built upon. Now I want to tell you what you need to know specifically as it relates to the three types of hypnotic stories you'll learn in this chapter.

The first story is a very basic hypnotic story. It has three parts: (a) beginning, (b) middle, and (c) an end. The beginning is a background moment leading up to some problem happening. The middle is the transformational aspect of the story; namely, where the protagonist undergoes some adventure and solves the problem. The ending is the effect of the problem being solved in the greater scheme of the environment.

The second story is a bit more complex version of the first story. This is a sequential story structure, called the Hero's Journey, discovered and expanded on by the late Dr. Joseph Campbell. Campbell was a prolific storyteller, who studied philosophy, as well as mythology. He discovered insightfully that most narratives follow a certain underlying shape, where the protagonist begins in a normal environment, gets called on a quest, undergoes certain picturesque mini-adventures, along the way to solving his or her great mission, and eventually, but not always, finds his or her way back home, a changed individual. Our adaptation of this Hero's Journey, is called the Hypnotic Hero's Journey, as we'll be layering into this storytelling framework, many hypnotic elements to make a greater hypnotic impact. Make no mistake: All stories tend to have a natural hypnotic quality to them. We are simply extending the natural hypnotic qualities, using more structured tools, to parallel alongside the natural elements. What this does is, create potently hypnotic stories that drop your hypnotic subjects deep into the waters of unconscious hypnotisms, where your unsuspecting hypnotic subject enters an altogether deeper level of trance.

The third story, and last story we'll cover, will be what has been coined as nested loops. These are stories, within stories, which allow conversational hypnotists to implant suggestions, create a type of hypnotic fractionation effect, and opens the doorway to letting the hypnotic storyteller have more flexibility with storytelling;

namely: to be able to add-in such techniques as confusion patterns, anchoring, switch of referential index, and so on.

What I want you to understand upfront is each of these stories serves a purpose, and can be made hypnotic, simply by utilizing and adding in hypnotic elements already taught throughout this book. Once you know how to tell these stories, it will be left up to you to modify and add-in various hypnotic elements you have taken favor to, or find will be useful, for your particular purposes. Were, I to cover all of the ranges of possibilities in this book, I'd likely have a book written that would serve a primary function of serving as a door-stop—it would be so thick, most readers wouldn't read it.

How-To Tell Hypnotic Stories To Affectively Move People To Take Action, Change Their Minds, And Give You What You Want

As I previously mentioned. There are three stories we will be covering in this chapter. In this section we'll be covering each of these three types of stories in great detail. You'll learn how to tell each type, and how to make-up your own stories as you see fit, to correspond to your particular context for wanting/needing to tell hypnotic stories. Some contexts will require you tell your story quickly, and for this reason, a basic transformational story will suffice. Other contexts will give you an opportunity to tell or recount a longer Hypnotic Hero's Journey account. Still other contexts will be open to letting you tell multiple stories inside of other stories, leaving open loops, what you can choose to close or not. We'll discuss more about the pros and cons of this last type of story later.

Basic Transformational Story

A transformation is when a character undergoes a type of experience that leaves them altered as a result. Life is about change, so the essence of a 'story' is a metaphor to represent the experiences that lead to these changes. This is ironic, in a sense, given that a metaphor is a type of story. Your whole life you have undergone many experiences. Each of these experiences is a different story. How you tell a story today, will likely be vastly different than the way you tell a story at a later future date, as you will have had many more experiences, and changed, and therefore tell stories in a different light from what you tell them today, in the present. I want you to have a thought on this, because what this fundamentally means is you will never run out of stories to tell. By the time you have recounted every experience you've ever had, you'll have had many more experiences yet to tell stories about. You must also realize that your stories will always be unique from everybody else stories. No two people tell a story exactly the same, even if they recite it word-for-word; clearly, because storytelling involves more than the mere recitation of words—it requires non-verbal communication, body language, and verbal expression. What you can therefore deduce from knowing just this is, there are no bad stories, or bad storytellers, only 'different' stories. If you remember back to the hypnotic archetypal trigger—difference—I suspect you'll start to draw some inferences, insights, and possibly even insights into why every story possesses a hypnotic quality. Hint: Every story is different.

The first step to telling a basic transformational story is to start your story on a normal footing. What normalcy does is create suspense. Suspense creates intrigue. When someone it telling a story the audience listening to that story is wondering constantly what's going to happen next. Because of this engagement with the story, attention is narrowly focused on the story, and what's to come next. People naturally identify with normalcy, and associate it with day-to-day life. Normalcy is nothing really exciting, or glamorous, but, and this is key to keep in mind, the very act of telling a story is a presupposition that infers something is about to happen, or that a change is evidently coming, or some experience is about to take place that is going to rock the character's world, so to speak. Really understand this tiny, barely noticeable point, because it is something profound. The insight to gain is, you're hypnotizing someone, just by starting a story, as the subject is already primed to follow along, be intrigued, and want to know more. You're captivating the hypnotic subject's attention straightaway. You're also the puppeteer pulling the hypnotic subject's strings. Nothing is less innocent than a hypnotic story.

The second step is creating a conflict or climax where something happens—something problematic. The conflict creates both an inner and outer conflict with the character. What this means is the problem may be an outwardly identifiable problem anyone can relate to, yet it also carries with it an internal emotional disturbance, that gets exacerbated by secondary and tertiary effects that come about as a result. This relates back to logical advantages, and emotional benefits, only not we're observing the opposite—logical problems, and emotional problems.

Here's a short story to illustrate: I knew someone once, who hated someone else I knew, and so one day, they went up to this person, callously and calculatedly ready to launch an attack, and so they took out a sledge hammer, and intentionally broke the other person's leg, shattering it into multiple bone fragments. Person 'B' had to be rushed to the hospital. After a grueling surgery, and plenty of recovery time, the person finally walked again. After some time had passed, person 'A' came to wish they'd never taken such actions. Person 'B' got the last laugh, for sure.

The story I just told you isn't complex, and represents a basic transformational story. The logical problem came at the climax, where person 'A' sledgehammers person 'B'. How dreadful, right! Person 'B' definitely encounters a problem that even hurts just thinking about it, doesn't it? Can you imagine someone coming up to you and sledgehammering your shin bone? Wow! That would definitely hurt badly. What is the logical problem person 'B' has? The problem is they cannot walk and take care of ordinary tasks they usually could before the incident. Not being able to walk is a logical problem. What is the emotional problem? Emotions aren't so logical in nature, so this question might be a bit more challenging to answer. We have to 'empathize' in order to really answer this question. To do this, we think of the emotions that well-up inside of us when we find that we cannot walk. Will we be able to ever walk again? This causes emotional stress and concern. Will we be able to function doing things we're accustomed to doing? This causes emotions to surface like depression, boredom, isolation, and fear we might lose other things important to us. It is deeply psychological to say the least. Some of the emotional changes that might affect us would be anger and resentment. We may feel less self-confident! There're a lot of emotions that come with someone intentionally breaking your leg, just because they hate you for some reason. The act is sending a message that you're hated, and this could also be somewhat of an eye opening experience. You may start doubting whether or not you're a 'good' or 'decent' person. This may cause some more internal conflict.

What you do whenever someone tells you a type of story like this is you begin to empathize with the character, and start to become them in a sense mentally. This mental stimulation parallels the third step to inducing hypnosis; namely, stimulating the hypnotic subject's emotional mind (hypnotic mind). When we experience what the character of the story experiences, we're becoming empathetic, uncontrollably, and we enter into a state of mental perturbations, which lead us to narratively be transported into the story, and therefore be hypnotized. As we learned in the previous chapter, once we have been transported, empathizing with the protagonist, we come back changed. And, why is this? It is simple; when the protagonist has a problem, and becomes changed as a result, we too have a problem and become changed as a result. This is why sometimes people dream, and awaken unsure if they're still asleep, or awake. They become confused, wondering what is real, and what fantasy is. Keep in mind, and don't be shocked by this: Your hypnotic mind, doesn't distinguish between what is real and what is imagined. It is all the same to the emotional mind. This is why people are emotionally connected to their dreams and fantasies. The conscious mind is the differentiator between what is real and what is not. Which raises some interesting questions about reality, doesn't it. I'll let you have a think about that one. I don't want to be the one to change your persuasions about what is real and what is not. I'm sure you can draw your own conclusions.

So a transformation happens to the character in this type of story, as well as in us human beings. The next step is to solve the problem. This is important, because when a decision needs to be made to correct an imbalance, which is causing a mental disturbance, it is important to achieve a resolve, to regain consonance. Consonance is the harmony of our persuasions being in alignment with our actions. Dissonance is the disharmony caused when our persuasions are misaligned with our actions. This is important to understand when it comes to hypnotically persuading your hypnotic subject to take actions you want them to take. You first must succeed in changing their beliefs to take harmony with the actions you want them to take; otherwise, you run into cognitive dissonance issues. Cognitive dissonance is the same phenomenon that happens when you sell someone something, by using various sales tactics, but after the sale is made, the new customer comes to quickly regret the decision, believing they were manipulated, and thus trust is lost, and a refund may ensue—buyer's remorse. The key to long term persuasion, using this hypnotic story type, is to ensure the hypnotic subject, won't experience regret with their decision to take the actions you want them to take. In order to achieve this, you must change their persuasions, and you can do this using a simple transformational story, as we're covering here.

Once the problem is solved in the story, consonancy is achieved, and at the hypnotic level the hypnotic subject perceives reality differently, and takes action consistent with this new perception of reality. A cult leader, may influence new recruits telling this type of story, to the new recruit to think differently, thereby changing their perceptions and beliefs, and then shape behavior toward this newfound persuasion. This lets the leader hypnotically persuade the new convert without directly having to do so. When the leader is being overtly direct, too soon, during the conversion process, this can nurture dissonance, which can inhibit the conversion process, slowing it down.

After the problem is solved, the final step in telling this basic transformative story is to show the effect of solving the problem in the broader context. Actions have ripple effects, which can both directly and indirectly affect a character in the story, as well as influence certain outcomes. Sometimes winning is losing; while losing can be a win. There are things we don't always see on the surface of reality, because, again, we can only process seven plus or minus two bits of information at any given moment, and for this reason don't know what the result of our problem-solving initiative will be. We may gain some relief in the short term; however, we may gain more serious problems a little ways down the road.

> TIP: One way to make your stories even more hypnotic is to repurpose an earlier event in your stories, into later scenes. Many stories and Hollywood and Bollywood movies will have

something happen in the early stages of the book, which seem rather random, and later, toward the end, the occurrence will be repurposed back in, making sense of why it was there in the first place.

Hypnotic Hero's Journey

As I've mentioned this type of story is more complex, and requires more of an understanding of the work of the late Joseph Campbell's work. I will summarize the common thread that runs through most (if not all) great narratives, which will suffice for your general understanding. I do wholly recommend you read Campbell's book: *The Hero with a Thousand Faces*. It is an enjoyable read, and will take you more in depth with this material I'll be covering now. Once you understand the basic framework, I'll be teaching you how to make this story and the other two we cover, hypnotic.

The Departure

The departure is part 1, of Campbell's mono-myth (hero's journey retold in different forms). The departure begins the journey of the protagonist.

Every journey begins with a character that is called to take some adventure. The character is defined, originally at this point, as someone consistent with normalcy. Their lives reflect the essence of a normal existence. Then something happens.

Call To Adventure

The first stage of the departure part is a call to adventure. The call to adventure is where the hero, comes face to face with an opportunity to disembark his or her normal existence to travel afar to some great unknown territory, with a purpose in mind.

Refusal Of The Call

The second stage is a refusal of the call. In many myths and narratives the hero resists going, citing excuses for why the journey would be an impossibility. The refusal usually is a result of the protagonist's unwillingness to give up what is seemingly secured and certain. The journey is a metaphor for the unknown, the untimeliness of death, destruction, and loss. It would make more sense to stay in normalcy, than venture in a direction of uncertainty, having to give up what has already been established. It can be a frightening proposition. People naturally resist change, because they feel more secure knowing what tomorrow will look like, than being subjected to a great mystery, where nothing is guaranteed.

Supernatural Aid. The third stage is when the wise seer or sage provides some impetus for moving the character closer to the embarkation of the journey. In Paulo Coelho's *The Alchemist*, the young shepherd boy, meets this magical figure, who gives him two stones, which are meant to assist him at some point during his travels. The wise figure's stones, eventually inspire the young shepherd to rejoin his journey, after he has spent time working for a crystal merchant. The wise old man is a metaphor for the supernatural aid, Campbell mentions in his mono-myth. The guidance of the Supernatural Aid is found in many myths and narratives. The Supernatural Aid is a guru in one sense, though usually is dissociated from the journey/mission itself. We equate instinctively that this aid knows more than we do, and expect the aid to assist whenever the protagonist is in trouble, or moving away from the journey.

Crossing Of The First Threshold

At the starting point of any great journey is a guardian of the gate. This guardian usually serves the role of testing the protagonist to determine if the protagonist is worthy of entry or not. Defeating the guardian at the gate takes endurance and the will of a true hero. Once the First Threshold is crossed there's also no going back. The journey has begun, and the new world is entered into. Usually, the character has been put into a position where they cannot go back to normalcy, as they've been ostracized by their society, or some parental figure (usually a male, but not always). They cannot return, elsewise they face persecution, and judgment.

The Belly of the Whale. Campbell's implied metaphor, 'Belly of the Whale' is a symbolic death and resurrection, which happens just upon crossing the first threshold. The character undergoes some type of experience, where it is implied they have died, or at least been near enough to death to come to terms with the idea that they are predestined for the journey, or worthy enough to continue onward. This is a crucial element that has become a common thread through most myths and narratives. It is symbolic of baptism. When the hero emerges from the near death experience they are changed. They exhibit more an inner confidence and strength about themselves. In a sense, until they confront the fear of death, they remain transfixed as they are, but after confronting death's door, the hero isn't fearful anymore, at least not in the way they were before. This is a metamorphosis that propels the hero onward stronger than ever. I think it is the character owning the journey, and taking more a leadership responsibility for fulfilling the quest a head of them.

"It is worth dying; to find out what life is." —T.S. Elliot

The next part of the hero's journey is what Campbell has labeled: Initiation. This is the part of a narrative or myth where the hero undergoes test after test to prove his worth, but also to make him more prepared for the final confrontation that will happen later.

The Road Of Trials

We see it happen so often in stories where the protagonist is confronted with a series of tests. Sometimes these tests are an inroad, for the hypnotic subject, into the character and inner-strength the protagonist possesses, yet perhaps didn't know he/she possessed. For the hypnotic subject, this can stir-up inspiration and confidence about traveling to unknown destinations. This might, for a new cult member, be what is needed to transition into the great void or great mystery that is the cult's ideology and culture. It can help the hypnotic subject become more attached to the culture and expectations of the cult.

The Meeting With The Goddess

The goddess is an archetype that we see time and time again repeated in many myths, Hollywood movies, Disney Cartoons, and other narratives. The goddess figure is symbolic of higher spiritual precepts, understandings, and insights. The goddess in Campbell's words is: "...the final test of the *talent* of the hero to win the boon of love (charity: amor fati), which is life itself enjoyed as the encasement of eternity." The goddess represents immortality, and knowledge, and the hero who masters her, is the knower, who has taken his father's place, and become a man. This is stated to represent a male hero; however, this is the same metaphorical representation a female heroine would come to know as well. It is the coming of maturity.

Woman As The Temptress

The temptress figure is able to lure the hero by her feminine charms, and sexuality, yet also destroy the character by her very nature. A prime example of this takes place in the Garden of Eden, where Eve lures Adam into eating the forbidden fruit. Again, we see this hypnotic archetypal trigger, labeled 'Forbidden' played out here. We want what we cannot or should not have. This is encoded into our psyches. The temptress is significant in Campbell's mono-myth, as it represents in many ways a final test, before the hero comes frontally confronted with the final battle in which he/she will fight to achieve what is, 'the sought after boon'. Referring back to the Alchemist, the young shepherd boy eventually meets a Bedouin girl, where he nearly steps away from his quest to remain with her. As in most myths, he sacrifices the temptation of lust and love, to complete his mission—the goal of life is a higher spiritual purpose; not an attachment to something carnal, and misleading. Some Hindu sects believe that until a person succumbs to living a celibate life, without taking a house-holder position, then, the individual is destined to reincarnate, to live once more in this painful cycle of birth, death, and rebirth (samsara).

Atonement With The Father

Throughout history, the father archetype is known by his strength, uncompromising qualities, fierceness, masculinity, strictness, and dominance over the universe—he is the 'king' of his universe, everyone else, is secondary and competition; including his children. In order to rule as the father, and know him as an equal, the son must pass a series of tests, and prove himself worthy of ruling the kingdom. Until this happens, the son is thought of as weaker, and a mother's son—needing nursing, and support from his mother. Atonement comes when the son has become a man himself and is ready to confront and face the father, to challenge him for power. Once the son proves himself, that is, his capabilities, he is atoned to the father. The father is then proud of the son, and the son sees his father as an equal, and is no longer fearful, envious, or hateful of his father.

Apotheosis

To transcend human existence, to know the universe; not merely the world you exist in, is the plight of human imperfection—true nature being oneness with God, or godlike ourselves. Apotheosis is the act of becoming god, or the elevation to the highest station possible. In politics, it is the president's station. In religion, it's the relevant moksha, nirvana, heaven, or liberation sought after. At this leg in the journey, the protagonist discovers his inner and outer divinity and oneness with god. It is the sudden realization that you and god are one and the same, and no longer will you fear life, the unknown, evil, or anything at all. An inner peace and serenity prevail, and nothing can hinder your path, any longer. You are the master of your universe.

The Ultimate Boon

This is the leg of the journey in which the protagonist defeats the final evil demon, or the evil force(s) that stands in the way of him/her gaining the pursued after boon. This is the purpose of the journey. The battle that ensues is perhaps the most dangerous, and deadly, and many have come to claim the boon before, and have suffered punishment, or worst—perished in their efforts. However, this evil is usually not as severe for the hero, because of his/her experiences and because of all he/she has overcome thus far. This is also the last phase of Campbell's 'Initiation' part. Once the final obstacle is overcome, the ultimate boon is gained.

The final 'part' of Campbell's mono-myth is the 'Return' segment. There is nothing left to be accomplished. The hero has mastered the new world, declared victory over the journey, yet, still, there exists the return, in order to complete a full circle.

Refusal Of The Return

Not always does a hero return home—usually though they do. Campbell uses the example of the Hindu warrior, Muchukunda, who retreated away from his return, though opted not to stay in the land of his journey. There are many instances where the hero returns home, but usually there is something, that is, some reason, or impetus, that holds them back from wanting to return. You see they're changed and to return seems pointless. They've also mastered the new world, so why should they return to the old way of living, i.e. normalcy.

The Magic Flight

When you think of The Wizard of Oz, and Dorothy's clicking of the ruby-red slippers, to return home, you're presented with what Campbell referred to as "The Magic Flight." In many myths and narratives, the return home happens through some type of magic-like means. It could be the protagonist waking up from a dream. It could be the protagonist flying home on the back of a mythical character.

Rescue From Without

Sometimes the protagonist is harmed, and unable to return, and for this reason a rescue by some other means happens. Sometimes something external causes the protagonist to need to return, and brings the hero home. Other times, it's a helper who assists with ensuring the safe return of the hero.

The Crossing The Return Threshold

Campbell gives us this metaphor of the two worlds actually being one. The home turf is the world of mortals. The new world is the world of the gods. One is mortal, while the other immortal. The hero leaves the new world, and crosses the threshold back into the world he/she once knew, and returns a changed individual. The meanings the place of origin had, no longer carry the same weight. The hero has expanded his/her awareness. The 'otherness' does not seem foreign or strange anymore. Things are different upon return.

Master Of The Two Worlds

Campbell gives insight into what he means by "Master of the Two Worlds" when he tells us that the worlds cannot be bespoken of as one being more superior to the other. The true master recognizes the virtue in both worlds; thus, masters them equally. Campbell gives a passage, quoted from the Kena Upanishad: "To know is not to know; to not know is to know." A fitting paradox, one determines. As confusing and hard to grasp as this might seem, a master of two worlds knows he doesn't know everything, and in knowing this, knows everything.

Freedom To Live

After the journey is over, the hero is home, the hero has mastered both worlds, and then, it comes to pass the hero insightfully understands that nothing in nature is perishable. All sins are forgiven, because of the detachment of actions, which cannot be controlled through human means—but, except through god(s). With the newfound understanding of the universe, and a spiritual awakening, the hero goes on living, only in the future, knowing this is what's important—he/she is finally free to live life liberated from the agony of needing something more. The dissonance of having not lived is liberated, so that the hero can live in peace, freely.

> *For to be free is not merely to cast off one's chains, but to live in a way that respects and enhances the freedom of others.*
>
> —Nelson Mandela

The mono-myth is a metaphor for change and transformation. Cults can apply (and do apply) its principles, for indoctrinating and transforming new recruits into the fold. Take the road of trials for example: When the new recruit is put through a series of tests and obstacles, this helps to sell them on why joining and being a part of such a cult is their spiritual destiny. It becomes a transformation that is used as persuasion reinforcement. Fraternal organizations use tests, hazing, and so on to likewise deepen the new member's loyalty and belief that they are worthy enough to be a part of the organization. This also adds intrinsic value to the dimension of the cult or fraternal organization, where the cult or fraternity is less viewed from the perception of an outsider looking in, and more from a member attaching them to the organization. As I have mentioned earlier, cults may use mystery, and forbiddances as hypnotic archetypal triggers to attract new recruits, but when they have them, something like a test can be utilized to reinforce the mystery or intrinsic value that the cult creates ingeniously through indoctrination methods.

The mono-myth is a metaphor for how we humans live our lives. We all, in many instances, circle the mono-myth through our life experiences. It is a metaphor also for life. We're born into existence from nothingness, we embark on our own journeys, and in the end we return back to where the nothingness resides. We may resist the journey at first, crying as we enter, yet, as we leave we may refuse to go willingly back from whence we came from originally. That's life. The Hypnotic Hero's Journey parallels life experiences, which are relatable, as the journey is present in most stories told. This is a blueprint for life, in many ways. For this reason it is very hypnotic; yet, we'll still add in the hypnotic elements, drawn from this book, in a short while. First let's understand the last story type: Nested Loops.

Nested Loop Hypnotic Stories

I want you to think of a story or a program on television you recently heard or watched where something happened to cause you to miss the ending. Got it in your head? Good! A single story, as I've illustrated in the last two hypnotic story types, a typical story possesses a beginning, middle, and end. It is a cycle. After one story is told, another may happen—for example, you're watching one television program, it ends, and so you watch the next one. Each program, i.e. story, finishes and another begins. Inside of each program, are short interruptions or breaks. We call these commercials. Sometimes commercials are mini-stories in and of themselves. So they're what we call 'nested' inside of the program you happen to be watching at the time. Sometimes these commercials repeat during the same program several times. These are advertisements sponsored by companies, which help to pay for the program you're enjoying. Some commercials are irritating, some are laughable, some are interesting, and others are educational and informative. There are all types of different commercials, aren't there?

A nested loop hypnotic story is similar to the nested commercials that interrupt your program on television. The difference is they're stories within stories—sometimes within even other stories, and so on. Think of them as you having an interaction with a good friend, telling story after story, but never ending your stories. Just about the time you get to the climax, you begin telling another story. We do this naturally all the time. We'll hold a conversation with someone and start recounting something that happened to us or someone we know, and then remember something else that happened, because something in the first story jogged our memory about another incident that happened to us. We keep switching gears, starting one story, stopping it about two-thirds of the way through, and begin telling another story. Sometimes when we do this, we tell a story that is completely unrelated to the story we were telling before that story. Other times, we tell a story relevant to the one we were telling. Sometimes when we begin telling another story we smoothly transition into the next benignly, but other times we hard break and it is apparent that we're now telling a completely different story. Welcome to nested loop stories.

I'm going to give you an example of a nested loop story so you can better grasp what I mean:

> I was talking to my friend the other day who was telling me he was about to begin an MBA program. He was very excited. Susan, another friend mentioned yesterday how she liked spaghetti. I'm a vegetarian, so I only eat meatless spaghetti. Brandon, my brother moved to Bowling Green, Kentucky, and he is a forklift operator. His friend recently moved up there. Last year was quite busy for me. I was involved in a web of tasks, which kept me on my toes. Brandon's friend actually lives with him. He's about to get a job working for the same outfit as my brother. Brandon had previously lived in Murray, Kentucky, and worked as a forklift operator for a manufacturing company. He's driven forklift for about four years now, as I recall. I've been a vegetarian all my life. I grew up in a religious household, where vegetarianism was a part of the religious culture. Susan, my friend, she's from Italy, originally, so she grew up eating fine Italian food. She told me spaghetti never gets old. When my friend finished his undergraduate degree it was in business administration, so it really does make perfect sense that he would go on to do an MBA.

Notice in the story I told, how the break between the first story and the second story is a 'hard break'; whereas the break between the second and third story is a 'soft break'. The break between the third and fourth is again a 'hard break'. The break between the fourth and fifth is again, another 'soft break'. The break between the fifth and sixth is again, another 'hard break'. I then complete the sixth story (last year being a busy year for me). Then I loop back to the story just preceding it, and complete it. I then complete each prior story, until I finish the original story (my friend starting his MBA story). This is the form of a basic nested loop story. If I wanted to make this story more complex, I could embed stories within each one of these stories, and then go back and complete the loops, before telling some more new stories. You get the idea.

Hypnotic nested loop stories create what in hypnosis terminology is known as 'fractionation'. We're taking people into a hypnotic story, then taking them out of hypnosis by breaking the story, and then back in again, and this goes on back and forth. Fractionation is useful because each time you take someone out of trance, and drop them back in again, immediately, the hypnotic subjects falls that much deeper under the influence of hypnosis. Each time you break a story, an amnesia effect happens also to the hypnotic subject. After a while, telling many stories, total amnesia happens and the hypnotic subject begins forgetting the previous stories you've told. This is useful, because you can implant post-hypnotic suggestions into your stories, and quickly have them forgotten. This can be done using embedded commands which are covertly nested in your stories. By the time you're to the last story, you can give instructions to your hypnotic subject's hypnotic mind (unconscious/subconscious) and they will become imprinted in the subject's hypnotic mind, and later carried out, unconscious that they're being carried out because they've been suggested.

You have to be careful telling hypnotic nested loop stories. You see, sometimes, some people will block you out, and not pay attention, simply because they get annoyed you're not finishing any of your stories. To keep this from happening you need to tell stories that induce them to pay attention and which captivate their attention, and holds it. You also should know you have something going for you, which is, because you haven't finished your stories, it creates a die-hard need for them to wait until you finish, so they can find out what happens. Leaving a loop interrupted, without completing it is the Zeigarnik Effect. Simply put, human beings have a natural impetus to complete tasks. If something is left incomplete, while other things are started, the conscious mind experiences dissonance. Research has indicated that a story left unfinished, begs to be completed, and is rarely forgotten. Years can pass, and someone will come back into contact with the person who started a story and didn't finish, and they will out of the gates insist that the storyteller finish telling the story. Human beings need closure on tasks. It is part of our psychological constitution. For this reason, when you tell a hypnotic nested loop story, because you're leaving the story incomplete, the focus in on the story left incomplete, and not so much on the new story being told. You can utilize this to your advantage, and at the start of each new story, or shortly thereafter starting a new story, incorporate or repeat your embedded commands and they will simply become imprinted in the subject's hypnotic mind, later to be followed out automatically. This is a powerful means of persuading someone to change beliefs, take actions, adopt new behaviors, and so on.

Layering In Hypnotic Elements

The next step to take is layering in all of the hypnotic constituents, learned throughout this book, and nest them into our stories to make them even more hypnotic (as if they weren't already hypnotic enough).

One of my favorite ways to layer in hypnotic elements is to use the power of repetition. I'll often embed commands into mult-nested stories, and in each story, pronounce the command, using tonal marking. I'll also utilize several hypnotic language patterns throughout my stories, to insert the embedded commands properly.

A key thing to keep in mind is when you're telling a story, you're using your entire body, as well your emotions, and voice. With so much going on, it become very, very, difficult for the hypnotic subject to keep up with everything you're talking about, and so, for this reason, trance is inevitable.

Trance Signs

There are many ways to tell if someone is hypnotized. The easiest way, in my opinion, is to look at the hypnotic subject's eyes. When the pupils are dilated, the subject is narrowly focused, and in trance. I also look for slowed breathing. You want to look at the shoulders of the subject, and watch them lower and rise as the subject breathes. The slower they're breathing, the more relaxed they are, and the more probable they're hypnotized.

Other signs include, slowed speech patterns, a solid gaze that leads off into infinite space, an over agreement from the hypnotic subject, facial muscles softening, open mouth, slow pulse rate, still body movements, and yawning.

Once you have paid attention to enough to the people you hypnotize, or people who are experiencing natural ultradian rhythm cycles, you'll start to know instantly when someone is hypnotized and when they're not. Certainly, it helps to be hypnotized yourself, when you're hypnotizing others. You'll know how they feel, because you'll know how you feel. The only difference will be you'll have control over your hypnosis and theirs; they will not.

Final Purport

In this chapter, you learnt three unique hypnotic story models. The basic transformational story is simple to remember, and you'll use it often, whether aware you're using it or not. The Hypnotic Hero's Journey, is a standard screenwriters and novelists use when creating their storyboards and outlines. The story is a metaphor for human life, and the journey all people make, whether they want to or not. This journey was set in motion the minute we were born, and will stay in motion until the day we die. For this reason it is a powerful thread that runs through most myths, and narratives. The last story we covered was the nested loop story. This story is actually a multitude of stories told in a broken sequence, and eventually (though they don't have to be) are closed back up in reverse order.

The key takeaway from this chapter is that nothing is less innocent than a story. We use metaphors and stories all the time. Metaphors, too, are highly hypnotic, because they cause the hypnotic subject to make associations between something usually abstract, and associate it to a problem, or solution, which seems to bring forth a great insights from associating one to the other. When you use metaphors, and these other three story types I've covered, you get people inside their heads thinking things at the hypnotic level. Great things can happen. People will more likely follow your indirect covert instructions, because they'll truly believe that they're their own ideas coming to the surface of consciousness; however, you will know, all too well, that they're actually your instructions, which you imprinted on your hypnotic subject's hypnotic mind.

Take Action Now

In order to get any value whatsoever from this book you must take action now on the instructions I'm going to be laying out for you. Do not be like most people—buy a book, half read it, set it aside, forget about it, never take action, never gain the advantages and benefits it has to offer you.

There is a reason you purchased this book. Do not forget that reason. If you attended one of my live training workshops, you would have participated in doing many exercises at the end of each module I taught you. This is because you get considerably more value practicing the techniques in a safe environment, before going out and practicing them in the real-world. Many people do not feel comfortable testing techniques they've just learnt blindly on real-life contexts. Do not be afraid to do these exercises: They are for your own good and self-development. Your personal power will increase when you proactively apply this knowledge to your specific contexts. Part of learning this information (the largest part) is applying it hands-on. Suspend your doubts and disbeliefs that you can do these exercises, because your insights will elevate to a higher level once you do them. You will only learn a fraction of what I teach in this book from reading the book. The great majority of your learning comes when you apply this information in whatever contexts you have been intentioned on learning it.

To prove this point: Think about your first kiss. You may have talked to friends about their first kiss to get some insight. Maybe you read a book on adolescent sexuality, where kissing was covered. You may have watched movies of actors kissing on the big-screen. Until you actually kissed a girl or guy for the first time, you didn't realize all that was involved in kissing, as you hadn't practiced it, and learned from that experience. I bet after you kissed for the first time, regardless how good or bad the kiss was; you felt pretty amazing afterward, and felt much more confident in kissing other people. I'm right, and you know it, so do these exercises! In fact, make a promise to yourself; you will not move on to the next chapter until these action steps have been completed. You'll thank yourself. I promise.

I. Make yourself take out a piece of paper and a pen/pencil and write down exactly how you'll utilize the information found in this chapter to fit your particular persuasion context.

II. Find an opportunity to apply what you learned in this chapter and apply it. After you have taken this initial action, journal your discoveries and results.

III. Take a 3x5 index card and summarize the leading points from this chapter. Let this summary serve as a quick flash card to jog your memory once a day, as you continue reading this book, and doing future exercises. This is important, because this book has a lot of information, and a fast flash card to look at daily will help you not to forget what you have learned. Over time, this knowledge will become imprinted on your hypnotic mind, where you'll take action on this knowledge without thinking about it consciously.

IV. Teach what you have learned in this chapter to a trusted friend whom you think might benefit. Teaching information to others helps you gain greater clarity and insights you'd likely not have gained trying to keep it all in your own mind.

V. Discuss with the friend you've taught this information to and take notes on their thoughts and understanding of the material. This way, you'll gain another person's perspective and likely gain a deeper understanding of the material.

After you have successfully completed each of these exercises, only then, proceed in moving forward to the next chapter. Do not take shortcuts and tell yourself the lie you'll come back and do the exercises later. Statistically speaking the probability is improbable you ever will. Take a leap of faith and do the exercise, please! Trust me; it's worth it, if you want to gain true mastery in hypnotic persuasion.

====================XX==================

CHAPTER 17

HOW CULTS MANAGE TO RECRUIT, INDOCTRINATE, DECEIVE, MANIPULATE, CONTROL, HYPNOTIZE, AND BRAINWASH PEOPLE

You've learned a lot up to this point concerning hypnotic persuasion. In this chapter I'm going to teach you how cults in general recruit, indoctrinate, deceive, manipulate, control, hypnotize, and brainwash people. What I'm going to be sharing with you is common practice in many cults.

The reasoning for teaching you this is twofold: (a) I want you to be able to recognize cult behavior, so you can avoid being recruited (assuming you don't want to join a cult), and (b) because the basic techniques can be applied elsewhere in a more positive context. For example you may be an entrepreneur, wishing to apply some of these techniques to your organization, for the purpose of improving your corporate culture.

Many of the words used in the title of this chapter may instantly evoke some strong emotions. It may turn you away from this book. Perhaps, some of you reading this book have been in a cult. Others of you may be looking to advance your religious organization to improve the culture. When we hear words like 'manipulate' instantly the reaction is to avoid going there and learning more, or; for some, the natural reaction might be to pinback your ears and pull out your highlighter so you can immediately begin digging into this material. I'm not here to offend anyone. In fact, let me share, I was once a member of a religious cult, as well an organization who operated along these same guidelines. I'm no longer affiliated with either organization, but having been, I think it makes me qualified to write this chapter, and encourage you to avoid these practices if ever confronted with them.

Being recruited into a cult can happen very quickly—scarily quick, in fact. The actual religious cult I was recruited into happened when I was much younger, more naïve, and truth be told I didn't believe it was a cult, until years later, when I could reflect on the organizations practices and intent. The organizational cult I was recruited into scared me much more, believe it or not. I think you have to have a healthy respect for cults, and understand first and foremost anyone can be recruited into one. Cults, when most people think of them, are religious in nature, practice brainwashing techniques, and have a central purpose. I'm here to tell you that cults take many forms. The organizational cult I was recruited into was actually a restaurant. I was recruited exactly in the cults would recruit a new member. I was depraved of sleep, given a high-carbohydrate diet for free, love-bombed by other employees and managers, and depraved of sleep, and made to engage in chants, heavy reading assignment, tests, and extracted personal information from—which was later used against me—all in the span of three days. I was also isolated off to a training restaurant that was over a day's drive from my hometown. I escaped the first chance I got, and did not call the company, until I had reached home. It took me a couple weeks to come back to my usual self—my family was very concerned for my wellbeing. While I was being indoctrinated I was never more scared in my life. It was scary.

Why You Need To Know How Cults Recruit, Indoctrinate, Deceive, Manipulate, Control, Hypnotize, And Brainwash People

The first logical reason that comes to mind is to protect you from being recruited and indoctrinated into a cult. Knowing the practices, you'll be better prepared, should you ever find yourself recruited, to get out as soon as possible. Knowing how they indoctrinate and manipulate people will give you the necessary internal resources to know how to deal with the cult, so you can plan your escape, without suspicion from cult members surfacing. The key help for you will be, knowing what to say, how to act, and so forth, so you can buy yourself some time, to plan your immediate escape. Brainwashing happens more quickly when you fight the brainwashing sessions. If the cult leaders believe you're a 'good' recruit pick, and your initial behavior is congruent with how they think of you initially, they'll be less likely to use the more extreme measures to ensure you're fully indoctrinated. Even so, keep in mind, cult leaders are usually well knowledgeable when it comes to reading non-verbal communication, and spotting 'fakers'. A faker is someone who pretends to be indoctrinated and fully brainwashed, but who actually is not.

The second logical reason is to gain a better understanding of the information already presented in this book. You bought this book for a particular purpose, I have to assume. Maybe you want to be a better persuader? Perhaps you want to start a cult? Perchance you are just fascinated by hypnosis and persuasion? I don't know what your individual reason is for having purchased this book; like I told you before though, I'm not going to hold anything back from you. It could be that you simply want to harness the techniques to do 'good' and unite the members of your organization, and get them to eat, sleep, and breathe your organization. Again, I don't know. However, understanding this information will glue together the lessons in this book you've already learnt, and make it to where you can apply the parts you find advantageous, so you feel incredibly empowered as a manager or director of your company, or leader of your organization.

What You Need To Know Upfront Concerning How Cults Recruit, Indoctrinate, Deceive, Manipulate, Control, Hypnotize, And Brainwash People

First you need a lesson in what these terms mean. After this I'll present you with a holistic picture of the overall process a cult takes to recruit, indoctrinate, deceive, manipulate, control, hypnotize, and brainwash people. This big-picture perspective is like a map you look at, before planning out a trip you want to take. This is going to give you some clue as to what the sequential order of steps will be, and then in the next section I'll break those down and go more in depth in explaining to you're the psychology behind the steps.

Recruit

"Enlist new members"—UrbanDictionary.com Example: "We're going to recruit a new cult member every single day, from a different college campus."

Indoctrinate

"To convince others to see things your way no matter what you have to do to get them to agree. Often by using threatening and false accusations against someone, something, or any idea that does not fit into the concept of how you personally think or feel it should be, for whatever reason you have, at any given time or moment."—UrbanDictionary.com

Deceive

"Deliberately cause (someone) to believe something that is not true, especially for personal gain."—UrbanDictionary.com

Manipulate

"Making people do what you want."—UrbanDictionary.com

Control

"To exercise restraint or direction over; dominate; command."—Dictonary.com

Hypnotize

"The act of putting someone into the altered mindstate of hypnosis."—UrbanDictionary.com

Brainwash

"To effect a radical change in the ideas and beliefs of (a person), esp by methods based on isolation, sleeplessness, hunger, extreme discomfort, pain, and the alternation of kindness and cruelty."—Dictionary.com

General Overview

The first stage to recruitment is the use of deception. You don't, in other words, want to tell someone you're in a cult, and want them to join. Instead, lead them to believe, either through direct or indirect means, you're someone who really cares for them, and who is genuinely a good person, who can be trusted. This can be accomplished by lying, distorting information, or leaving out information. Think back to NLP where we discussed people generalize, distort, and delete information in everyday conversation with others.

Establish front-groups that mask the cult's true identity. These can be religious groups, personal development companies, and so on.

Make promises that fill a void in the person's life. This could be helping them 'fix' their life, etc. These promises are customized to each individual's sense of individuality; however, they are usually lies, and usually only told to recruit the person into the group—to fulfill the cult's agenda. Incidentally these types of promises can be vague and done using the hypnotic archetypal triggers—for example, you can say, "We can help you understand your secret nature." What exactly is 'secret nature'? People will infer the meaning for themselves, internally.

Offer something free. Many cults use a 'free meal' to attract new recruits. The meals can be as simple as a cheaply prepared, high in carbohydrates, 'pancake dinner'. Then, after giving something free, the law of reciprocity applies, and the individual is now indebted to you for something. So ask a favor in return, bringing them closer into the fold.

Use 'scarcity' tactics to get them to take immediate actions. This could be coming to a special weekend retreat, or meeting the founder of the company, etc. You might say something like, "This is your one and only chance; don't miss out!"

Don't give your recruit time to think. Keep them busy, and if you're recruiting friends, separate the friends, and surround them with 'devout followers' who are 'happy seeming'. Do this so the recruit believes this is normal behavior, caused as a result of being a part of the group (i.e., cult). The recruits will also tend to behave like everyone else is behaving; assuming it is normal, and expected of them. It won't seem weird or strange, that is to say. This period of warm, friendly, and love-bombing behavior should extend for a good period of time. Think back to hypnotic rapport techniques we've talked about in previous chapters. This is the time where you'll want to get information from them, learn what their weaknesses are, and develop close bonds with them.

Gradually you'll use this information to manipulate your new recruits, and use their weaknesses against them, to get them to do what you want them to. You'll also be 'shaping' their behavior by granting and withholding your kindness and interest in them. Think back to social conditioning too (classical conditioning/respondent conditioning). When they do what you want them to, you reward them with friendliness. When they don't you withhold your friendliness, and act in a way they cannot bare to deal with.

Once you have built rapport, make demands on the new recruit. These demands should be in alignment with the cult's mission. Perhaps you'll want them to believe the only thing that matters is their loyalty to the cult's agenda.

Control behavior. This is where you start telling the new recruit to dress like you, act like you, live in the compound, distribute and sell items produced by the cult, and other related activities. Keep in mind, the longer they are in the cult, the more dependent they become, thus the more willing they are to do what you want them to. This controlling of behavior is a stepping-up-process. It happens a little bit at a time, over time.

Make them adhere to an unbending schedule. Reduce their sleep to very little. Keep them busy each hour of the day, doing mundane repetitive tasks. This will help ensure they become more compliant, and more reliant on the cult to make their decisions for them. Sleep deprivation will make them automatically hypnotized and stop their thought patterns. They'll become puppets, and you'll be their puppet master; pulling their strings, making them do what you want them to.

Control their thoughts by showering them with repetitive ideological conveyances that indoctrinate them into the cult's ideology, mission, and purpose. With little sleep, and a low protein diet, they will stop thinking for themselves, and think, believe, and act in a way you desire for them to.

Control their emotions by inducing guilt and other hard to swallow emotions. Make them feel small and worthless, as this creates a childlike dependency on you to take care of them. You can also use what you originally gained from them, when you were building trust with them—gathering information you'd later use to induce emotions like guilt and fear. You'll also, by now, know their hot buttons and common words they tend to lean on for support. You'll be able to use these words against them to cause more dependency to happen.

Control information by only letting them read the cult's literature. Isolate them from outside news sources, reading, and other information sources. Make it impossible for them to see a different point of view, because this keeps them unable to critically think and defend their position, or able to dispute your claims.

Keep the mystery a mystery. Referring back to the hypnotic archetypal trigger 'mystery' make sure you don't reveal everything about the inner-workings of the cult. Only give them some information—only what is necessary. Keep them in the dark, at all times.

Encourage spying and reporting on one another. This way the group stays loyal, and fearful of going against the cult's mission and principles. It also lets you know when a recruit might need punishing or re-educating. Sometimes it is necessary to re-indoctrinate members who start having doubts and hesitations about their involvement with the cult.

Create mental breakdowns, which you disguise as spiritual awakenings or profound insights. This can be done by dissociating the new recruit from themselves, and declaring that they're old 'self' is worthless, and harmful. This makes them hate their old life, and despise the person they once were. This is known also as 'breaking down' the new recruit. This is done in military bootcamps. The new recruit is made to feel worthless, and not in power; rather, reliant and dependent on the cult for achieving a better state of mind—one in alignment with the cult's purpose and initiatives.

Create paranoia by making statements claiming they are in conflict and battle with their old 'bad' self. Whenever they start talking about how they feel, use Milton Erickson's Utilization Principle, to turn it around on them—for example, the recruit says, "I feel like I'm losing myself," you say, "You are losing that part of you that has been holding you back all these years."

Tell them they must turn off a part of their thinking holding them back, whenever they start to share ideas or thoughts incongruent with the cult's mission. You can use titles like, 'toxic mind' or 'ego' for accomplishing this. If the new recruit, for instance, says, "I think I should call my family, to let them know I'm alright," you say, "That's your ego speaking, which you must learn to rid yourself of if you want to achieve true happiness."

Manipulate them using lies and bogus expert data. This is done to persuade them to more believe what you want them to. Remember to reiterate; repetition is a great way to induce hypnosis, where you can plant ideas into their hypnotic mind.

Make-up stories about the cult, yourself, and whatever else will help advance the cult's mission. Refer back to the chapter on hypnotic storytelling to help you with this. These stories can be highly captivating and help create intrinsic value whereas the cult is concerned. Nothing is less innocent than a story; especially one that is hypnotic.

Induce hypnosis and trance states using thought-stopping rituals like chanting, singing, repetitive acts (e.g., dancing, spinning, making crafts, etc.), and so on. This reduces 'critical thinking'—something you don't want your recruits doing. Also, make your recruits engage in hours of non-stop meditation. This makes them more suggestible and receptive to your instructions.

Return them back to childhood reliance and mindless obedience. Treat them like children, and punish them whenever they act like disobedient children.

Encourage dependency always, as well as conformity. These are behaviors that you reward with your friendliness. Discourage autonomy and individuality—punish these behaviors with your disapproving ugly treatment of them. This is how you shape their behavior and make them more reliant on you.

Rewrite their past as terrible, regardless if it was great or not. Demonize their old self, and make them grateful you have helped them see past this past of theirs. At this stage also isolate them from everything else (e.g., family, other people, etc.). A cult compound that isolated from everything, out in the middle of nowhere, would be ideal. Also create scapegoats and imaginary evil outside forces that want nothing more than to infiltrate the cult and bring it down. This builds a stronger bond within your group. Whenever everyone in the group feels threatened by outside 'evil forces' they tend to become more reliant, loyal, and willing to remain in the cult; regardless of the conditions they're being subjected to. Basically what you're doing is creating an 'us' v. 'them' mentality within the cult.

Tell your members that their 'critical thoughts' are evidence they are being disloyal to the cult, taking the other side, i.e. 'evil forces'. Let them know they'll be punished for having these types of thoughts. All thoughts must be only the thoughts given them by the leader/cult. Other incongruent thoughts mean they're against the cult, i.e. an enemy that must be dealt with severely.

Use fear tactics to keep them from ever leaving the cult—for example, tell them, "If you ever leave, something bad will probably happen to them, and that they will no longer be protected by the group." You can even go so far as to infer that the cult itself might come after them for their disloyalty.

How-To Recruit, Indoctrinate, Deceive, Manipulate, Control, Hypnotize, And Brainwash People Into Joining And Actively Participating In Your Cult

I. Step one: determine the ideal recruit; then, go after them. Smart marketers understand their target market, and spend their time, money, and resources penetrating people who are most likely to want to buy their products. I once taught a marketing training course and asked someone what their market was, and their response was, "Everybody." Good thing they sat on my course, as I had to inform them otherwise. There is an 'ideal' customer, for every product—explicitly, niche markets. It's no different for cults. There are ideal recruits who are more likely to be a 'fit' over other entrants.

A lot of people think immediately that someone who is a likely candidate is someone who is weak minded, naive, or gullible. This isn't actually the case, though these factors do play a helpful part in recruiting people into cults. There are actually two primary reasons people get recruited: (a) they are going through some problems, i.e. low points in their life, and the cult is able to apparently able to rectify these problems, and (b) they are lonely, and want to belong to a group. When people are being recruited into a cult, they generally don't know they're being recruited, and usually didn't ask to join on their own freewill and accord. Take for example when I was recruited into the organizational cult (i.e. restaurant). I needed a job in the worst sort of way, and the cult organization seemed to pay better than any other restaurant job I had ever heard of paying. They solved problems of mine—I needed to work, I needed money, and I needed to get my girlfriend at the time off my back (she was my roommate and wanted me paying my share of the bills). There are also a lot of lonely people out there who have a difficult time being alone. Usually these are people who aren't married, transitioning from childhood into adulthood (they've flown the nest, so to speak). Sure, the world can be a scary place, and for this reason, being people tend to want to join tribes (groups/cultural organizations) as we're all hardwired that way.

Keep in mind I'm talking about generalities. Naivety definitely plays a role in recruitment, since many young people haven't had enough life experiences to properly discriminate a wolf-in-sheep's-clothing. Many young people, leaving home for the first time, may very well, also, experience separation depression, which causes them to be more susceptible to joining groups. All these factors contribute to the 'ideal' recruit for a cult. Once you have identified places where potential 'ideal' recruits may be hanging-out at, it's time to move onto the next step.

II. Step two: use your conversational hypnosis, NLP, and interpersonal communication skills to build instant hypnotic rapport with your potential recruit. Get them to open up to you. Then begin asking questions to uncover possible problems they may be experiencing. You can even use NLP anchoring techniques in order to trigger this same emotional state at a later time in the future, when it might be necessary.

III. Step three: take tiny steps to lead your new recruit to a front-group. Remember, these front-groups help to mask your cult's true identity. They are a publicly open location with other cult members, whose sole mission is to be friendly and help in the recruitment process. The idea is to immerse the new recruit around other friendly, upbeat, positive people.

IV. Step four: make deceptive promises to your new recruit, promising to fill the void in their life, and guaranteeing them you'll do whatever it takes to help them through their dilemma. This helps reinforce your intent to truly want to help them.

V. Step five: offer something free, so you can later ask them for a favor. This harnesses the law of reciprocity, which is takes advantage of the psychological principle people do not want to feel indebted to others. People do not want to appear greedy, and for this reason, most people will help others, who have helped them out.

VI. Step six: continue taking steps to encourage the person to spend more and more time with cult members. Offer to let them stay the night. Offer them food and make it fun and easy for them to participate in group activities. Take the pressure off from them. Keep your face lit with a smile and ensure other recruits do the same thing.

VII. Step seven: trick the new recruit by keeping them so busy, they don't want to leave, can't think, and begin participating to the extent they give up everything to associate with their newfound friends.

VIII. Step eight: at this stage you slowly start shaping behavior, turning on and off your friendliness toward the new recruit whenever they behave counterproductive to the cult's mission. You also start educating the new recruit, sharing the hypnotic story behind your cult's history. You will have by now changed up the diet of the new recruit to a high carbohydrate laden diet. The reason for carbohydrates is because of their instant energy, and sudden crash effect. You also don't want your recruit eating proteins, as you want them weakening. What's more you want to ensure your new recruit is staying busy around the clock, and kept with very little sleep. They're now doing what you and everybody else is doing; namely, living a regulated life. Every hour of the new recruit's day should be planned accordingly. You want to keep them so busy, burning calories they're not getting, because what happens is the recruit enters a deep hypnosis, where they're highly suggestible.

This susceptibility trance won't take long at all. Maybe only a couple days, tops, and then the new recruit will be mind-controlled with conversational hypnosis, manipulation, and brainwashing. This process of controlling the new recruit can be augmented with activities like chanting, singing repetitive songs, dancing, and other activities that are monotonous. What's more the group dynamic will encourage the new recruit to think this completely regulated lifestyle is normal, as everyone in the group is in total compliance with it.

IX. Step nine: Push the new recruit to a breakdown session. This will naturally come about as a result of everything up to this point (e.g., sleep deprivation, planned activities). However, you can augment this process by brainwashing; flipping back and forth from good to evil when you communicate to your new recruit. You'll be seemingly upset by them one moment, and a short while later flip back to being friendly and kind. They will be so much in their head, wondering about everything going on, they'll start to have a mental breakdown.

X. Step ten: now that your new recruit is broken-down, keep them isolated from the outside world, and start indoctrinating them with half-truths, where you take a little bit of truth, coupled with a whole lot of lies, to feed them information, until which time it becomes the gospel for them. They will believe you, and due to the isolation, deprivation, and so on, they'll now be a loyal recruit. Sometimes you may have to have a re-training session, to help with keeping them completely loyal to the cult. You'll know when this is needed when other, senior recruits, spy on them, and inform you whenever the new recruit starts to have doubts, second guesses being a part of the cult, etc.

This entire process is extremely hypnotic in nature, and very persuasive. The information you vet from your new recruit during the recruitment phase, will be used later on against them, when it becomes necessary to throw in their face the fact they were lonely, without friends, and sadly depressed. It's hard to argue with these arguments, because the new recruit is the person responsible for sharing these facts in the first place.

Over time, you'll certainly want to develop your new recruit into a loyal follower, who will likewise go out and recruit new people, carrying forth the mission of the cult. People are blind, most often, to these techniques, because these early steps are most welcome, considering the state of mind the new recruit is in when they're being recruited.

What If We Take This Knowledge And Apply It Positively To Other Contexts

The purpose of this chapter isn't to encourage you to start your own cult, necessarily; however, that's up to you if you want to or not (don't let me stand in your way if that's your intention). What I really wanted you to learn was the process cults use to hypnotically persuade people to become indoctrinated into the cult's message, environment, and culture. The reason for this to help you take what you've already learnt in this book, and be able to systematically apply it to whatever context you might have in mind.

This system can be adapted to organizations; namely, to create loyalty amongst employees. It can also be useful for motivating, inspiring, and pushing employees to be their absolute best, in which they constantly think their best isn't good enough, and so they try harder and harder to please you. When you are able to indirectly take away people's free will and choice you can pretty much get them to do whatever you want them to, and that's a pretty powerful position to be in.

Take a few minutes to think about how you can ethically adapt this blueprint to whatever context you may want to hypnotically persuade someone to take action. I realize there are tons of gold-nuggets in every chapter of this book, again though, without action, none of it really matters. My best advice to you is to take what I've taught you and take a few moments to work out a strategy where you can implement a plan of attack to get your desired outcome(s).

Final Purport

In this chapter, we took one application; namely, 'cults', and worked through an integration process where we analyzed how it is possible to incorporate this forbidden hypnotic persuasion tactics usefully. I shared with you how I personally had involvements with two cults. I shared with you how I was treated, in a round-about way, in terms of being recruited, indoctrinated, deceived, manipulated, controlled, hypnotized, and brainwashed (not an easy thing to others). I also gave you an exact blueprint that generalizes the overall process used to recruit, indoctrinate, deceive, manipulate, control, hypnotize, and brainwash people. Then I gave you the steps that sequentially followed this blueprint (steps successfully used on me in fact). I have also, just now, given you a call to action, encouraging you to put into practice what you've learned in this book.

Take Action Now

In order to get any value whatsoever from this book you must take action now on the instructions I'm going to be laying out for you. Do not be like most people—buy a book, half read it, set it aside, forget about it, never take action, never gain the advantages and benefits it has to offer you.

There is a reason you purchased this book. Do not forget that reason. If you attended one of my live training workshops, you would have participated in doing many exercises at the end of each module I taught you. This is because you get considerably more value practicing the techniques in a safe environment, before going out and practicing them in the real-world. Many people do not feel comfortable testing techniques they've just learnt blindly on real-life contexts. Do not be afraid to do these exercises: They are for your own good and self-development. Your personal power will increase when you proactively apply this knowledge to your specific contexts. Part of learning this information (the largest part) is applying it hands-on. Suspend your doubts and disbeliefs that you can do these exercises, because your insights will elevate to a higher level once you do them. You will only learn a fraction of what I teach in this book from reading the book. The great majority of your learning comes when you apply this information in whatever contexts you have been intentioned on learning it.

To prove this point: Think about your first kiss. You may have talked to friends about their first kiss to get some insight. Maybe you read a book on adolescent sexuality, where kissing was covered. You may have watched movies of actors kissing on the big-screen. Until you actually kissed a girl or guy for the first time, you didn't realize all that was involved in kissing, as you hadn't practiced it, and learned from that experience. I bet after you kissed for the first time, regardless how

good or bad the kiss was; you felt pretty amazing afterward, and felt much more confident in kissing other people. I'm right, and you know it, so do these exercises! In fact, make a promise to yourself; you will not move on to the next chapter until these action steps have been completed. You'll thank yourself. I promise.

I. Make yourself take out a piece of paper and a pen/pencil and write down exactly how you'll utilize the information found in this chapter to fit your particular persuasion context.

II. Find an opportunity to apply what you learned in this chapter and apply it. After you have taken this initial action, journal your discoveries and results.

III. Take a 3x5 index card and summarize the leading points from this chapter. Let this summary serve as a quick flash card to jog your memory once a day, as you continue reading this book, and doing future exercises. This is important, because this book has a lot of information, and a fast flash card to look at daily will help you not to forget what you have learned. Over time, this knowledge will become imprinted on your hypnotic mind, where you'll take action on this knowledge without thinking about it consciously.

IV. Teach what you have learned in this chapter to a trusted friend whom you think might benefit. Teaching information to others helps you gain greater clarity and insights you'd likely not have gained trying to keep it all in your own mind.

V. Discuss with the friend you've taught this information to and take notes on their thoughts and understanding of the material. This way, you'll gain another person's perspective and likely gain a deeper understanding of the material.

After you have successfully completed each of these exercises, only then, proceed in moving forward to the next chapter. Do not take shortcuts and tell yourself the lie you'll come back and do the exercises later. Statistically speaking the probability is improbable you ever will. Take a leap of faith and do the exercise, please! Trust me; it's worth it, if you want to gain true mastery in hypnotic persuasion.

====================xx=================

POSTLOGUE

I hope you've read this entire book before reading this page. I hope you've learned a lot. Some of this book was a personal walk down memory lane, in my mind. I've mastered the techniques and principles laid-out in this book. When you do also, you'll have spent many countless hours, as I have, practicing, refining, and doing the techniques and lessons in this book. I think the separation of greatness from mediocrity lays in the amount of action a person is willing to commit to doing. These lessons, I present you with, are actionable; meaning, you can adapt them to multiple contexts.

What's astonishing to me is you can be as subtle or as direct as you wish to be when implementing most of these techniques and strategies. Experience has taught me the more hypnotized someone it, the more direct you can be when controlling and instructing them. The same applies with controlled dependency: The more controlled and dependent someone is on you, the more compliant they will be—for example, some employees have more to lose, if they lose their jobs, than others would. A parent, working for a company, having four kids to support, in a small town, where there are few jobs, not owning an automobile or driver's license, making just enough to get by, and having not completed her/his high school education, and who is now in their thirties, has a lot more to lose than a single person, in their early twenties, still living with mum and dad. In your mind, do one last thought experiment, whom do you believe will be more compliant, willingly helpful, and sacrificing for the company's agenda? I think you know the answer by now. If you recruit people in the right way, you can recruit the right people, who are likely to do the most good for the organization. I'm not declaring you should run your company like a cult, but every company has a unique culture, and that can be improved upon to help with company gains.

Hypnotizing people while having what seem like 'normal' conversations can help you change minds, and influence people to believe your persuasions. Add in a hypnotic story, and this can enhance your success as a conversational hypnotist as well—making you more persuasive.

Some people reading this book will take a little of what I have shared and do a lot with it. Others will take more, and have massive results. The more you apply what you have learnt, the more success and self-confidence you will gain. Prosper yourself to the extent beyond what you think is possible; yet, more than that aside from that. The world is your hypnotic playground; now knowing this secret forbidden knowledge—take ownership of this truth—do great things with it!

THE BIBLIOGRAPHY

Appel, M., & Richter, T. (2007). Persuasive effects of fictional narratives increase over time. *Media Psychology, 10*(1), 113–134.

Bauer, T., & Erdogan, B. (2010). *Organizational behavior V1.1.* Nyack, NY: Flatworld Knowledge. (text).

Bohm, J., & Alison, L. (2001). An Exploratory Study in Methods of Distinguishing Destructive Cults. *Psychology, Crime amp; Law, 7*(2), 133–165.

Brock, T. C., Green, M. C., & Strange, J. J. (Eds.). (2002). *Narrative impact: Social and cognitive foundations* (pp. 157–181). Mahwah, NJ: Lawrence Erlbaum.

Cialdini, R. (1993). *Influence: The Psychology of Persuasion* (2nd ed.). New York: William Morrow.

Deighton, J., Romer, D., & McQueen, J. (1989). Using drama to persuade. *Journal of Consumer Research, 16*(3), 335–343.

Einstein, GO, McDaniel, M., Wilford, CL, Pagan, JL, & Dismukes, RK. (2013). Forgetting of intentions in demanding situations is rapid. *Journal of Experimental Psychology: Applied, 9*(3), 147–162.

Erickson, M. H., & Rossi, E. L. (1979). *Hypnotherapy, an exploratory casebook.* New York: Halsted Press.

Erickson, M. H., Rossi, E. L., & Rossi, S. I. (1976). *Hypnotic realities: The induction of clinical hypnosis and forms of indirect suggestion.* New York: Halsted Press.

Ernest Lawrence Rossi. (1991). *The 20-minute break: Reduce stress, maximize performance, and improve health and emotional well-being using the new science of ultradian rhythms.* New York: St. Martin's Press.

Gerrig, R. J. (1993). *Experiencing narrative worlds: On the psychological activities of reading.* New Haven, CT: Yale.

Green, M. C., & Brock, T. C. (2000). The role of transportation in the persuasiveness of public narratives. *Journal of Personality and Social Psychology, 79*(5), 701–721.

Green, M. C., Strange, J. J., & Brock, T. C. (2002). *Narrative impact: Social and cognitive foundations* (pp. 315–341). Mahwah, NJ: Lawrence Erlbaum.

Jones, D., & Company. (2012). Art of Persuasion becomes key. *The Wall Street Journal.*

Kotler, P, & Keller, K. (2011). *A Framework for Marketing Management.* Upper saddle River, New Jersey: Pearson Prentice Hall.

Ledochowski, I. (2003). *The deep trance training manual.* Carmarthen, Wales ; Williston, VT: Crown House Pub.

Mills, H. (2000). *Artful persuasion: How to command attention, change minds, and influence people.* New York: AMACOM.

Miltenberger, R. G. (2012). *Behavior modification: Principles and procedures* (5th ed.). Belmont, CA: Wadsworth Cengage Learning.

Nell, V. (1988). *Lost in a book: The psychology of reading for pleasure.* New Haven: Yale University Press.

Nell, V. (1988). *Lost in a book: The psychology of reading for pleasure.* New Haven, CT: Yale University.

Overdurf, J., & Silverthorn, J. (1995). *Training trances: Multi-level communication in therapy and training* (3rd ed.). Portland, OR: Metamorphous Press.

Petty, R.E., & Cacioppo, J.T. (1981). *Attitudes and persuasion:Classical and Contemporary Approaches.* Dubuque, Iowa: Wm. C. Brown Company.

Phillips, B. J., & McQuarrie, E. F. (2010). Narrative and persuasion in fashion advertising. *Journal of Consumer Research, 37*(3), 368–392.

Ramnerèo, J., & Tèorneke, N. (2008). *The ABCs of human behavior: Behavioral principles for the practicing clinician.* Oakland, CA: New Harbinger Publications.

Silverthorn, J., & Overdurf, J. (2004). *Dreaming realities: A spiritual system to create inner alignment through dreams.* Williston, VT: Crown House Pub.

Stacks, D. W., & Salwen, M. B. (Eds.). (2009). *An integrated approach to communication theory and research: Communication series* (2nd ed.). New York: Routledge.

Staf, M. R. (2005). *Advertising, promotion, and new media.* Armonk, NY: M.E. Sharpe.

Van Bergen, A. (1968). *Task interruption.* Amsterdam. Holland: North-Holland Publishing Company.

Van Laer, T., De Ruyter, K., Visconti, L.M., & Wetzels, M. (2014). The extended transportation-imagery model: a meta-analysis of teh antecedents and consequences of consumers' narrative transportation. *Journal of Consumer Research, 40*(5), 797–817.

THE INDEX

absorb, 293
accepting, 124, 256
actions, xxii, 2, 23, 31, 91, 92, 97, 136, 137, 143, 156, 201, 205, 234, 300, 326, 329, 341, 348, 362
advantage, 11, 31, 32, 94, 97, 106, 121, 172, 175, 190, 223, 275, 309, 316, 318, 348, 372
advertisement, 155, 190
affected, 165, 217, 244, 302
affinity to other, 43, 44, 47, 48, 49, 52
agreed, 150, 166
analogical marking, 222, 239
anchor, xxii, 27, 34, 52, 79, 178, 246, 247, 248, 249, 250, 251, 252, 253, 254, 255, 257, 259
Anchoring, 245, 247, 248, 255, 256

applications, 10, 64, 65, 82, 142, 151, 156, 181, 186, 192, 200, 208, 211, 240, 254, 260, 261, 297, 310
archetypes, 18, 19, 24, 35
arguments, 210, 294, 295, 375
art, 109, 124, 135, 197, 270, 315
associate, 7, 24, 30, 35, 51, 77, 95, 97, 110, 114, 154, 163, 170, 186, 191, 250, 325, 350, 372
attention, xxii, 1, 17, 57, 65, 87, 128, 177, 185, 187, 188, 190, 197, 199, 201, 202, 207, 211, 212, 237, 238, 241, 242, 244, 252, 268, 275, 277, 304, 316, 317, 325, 347, 349
attitude, 234, 256, 288, 294

391

authority, xix, 46, 90, 91, 92, 96, 122, 252
automatic, 1, 30, 34, 49, 201, 205, 251
autonomy, 368
awareness, 19, 29, 190, 199, 202, 210, 234, 320, 340
basic transformational story, 324
behavior, 23, 27, 48, 92, 104, 114, 139, 158, 164, 166, 201, 215, 230, 255, 256, 302, 330, 355, 358, 363, 364, 368, 373
believe, xxi, 3, 5, 10, 18, 21, 24, 28, 36, 44, 51, 62, 64, 71, 74, 81, 88, 93, 94, 97, 103, 108, 120, 122, 125, 153, 154, 164, 168, 171, 192, 200, 210, 216, 257, 267, 299, 307, 309, 310, 337, 351, 356, 358, 360, 361, 364, 365, 367, 374, 382
bell curve, 163, 164, 171
big-picture, 359

brains, 34, 204, 266
brainwash, 355, 359, 377
breakdowns, 366
business, 31, 44, 46, 49, 51, 82, 91, 93, 96, 120, 124, 128, 142, 165, 240, 245, 345
buy, 10, 11, 13, 23, 31, 37, 41, 44, 49, 53, 58, 64, 66, 72, 74, 78, 82, 87, 89, 96, 97, 104, 106, 110, 115, 119, 122, 125, 126, 130, 137, 139, 140, 144, 151, 153, 158, 170, 181, 186, 193, 217, 245, 250, 253, 258, 261, 270, 283, 310, 351, 358, 369, 377
buying, 4, 25, 32, 42, 72, 74, 78, 80, 93, 105, 110, 112, 152, 163, 173, 245, 250, 260
buying state, 72, 78, 80, 250
buzz, 155
capable, 32, 296

captivated, 58, 59, 186, 190, 201, 287, 291, 305
captivating, 60, 185, 192, 241, 303, 326, 367
cause & effect implied, 224
celebrity authority, 91, 92
change minds, xxi, 4, 139, 382
childhood, 17, 89, 105, 137, 203, 214, 367, 370
circumstances, i, 2, 21, 25, 27, 33, 81
classical conditioning, 363
command, 139, 227, 239, 240, 242, 243, 244, 245, 273, 275, 348, 361
communicating, 30, 122, 172, 210, 230, 242, 317
Complex Equivalence, 224
conceivable, 41, 221, 223

conditioned, 3, 20, 24, 27, 28, 30, 59, 107, 123, 164, 168, 172, 181, 203, 207, 256
conflicts, 164
conformity, 158, 368
conscious mind, 35, 202, 242, 319, 328
consequence, 113, 292
contrary, 163, 164, 165, 166, 167, 169, 177, 179, 181
contrast, 35, 152, 163, 165, 167, 170, 173, 177, 178, 181, 192
control, xxiv, 7, 8, 58, 63, 109, 171, 225, 249, 299, 350, 355, 359, 377
controlled, 341, 373, 377, 381
controlling, xxiii, 364, 373, 381
conversation, 3, 26, 31, 41, 45, 48, 102, 174, 188, 210, 240, 241, 242, 243, 253, 288, 344, 362
conversational hypnosis, xxii, 26, 170, 200, 221,

222, 223, 240, 244, 250, 260, 266, 371, 373
conversational hypnotism, 200
Conversational Postulate, 225
covered, i, 2, 14, 38, 52, 54, 65, 67, 80, 81, 82, 83, 96, 98, 116, 129, 131, 143, 145, 159, 181, 182, 192, 194, 197, 200, 216, 218, 251, 262, 265, 284, 311, 350, 351, 352, 378
cult, xxii, 11, 13, 61, 62, 82, 108, 156, 174, 178, 192, 240, 256, 257, 287, 289, 290, 307, 330, 335, 342, 355, 356, 358, 359, 360, 361, 362, 363, 364, 365, 366, 367, 368, 369, 370, 371, 372, 373, 374, 375, 382
Cults, 342, 357, 358, 359
culture, 151, 157, 256, 260, 335, 345, 356, 376, 382

cycles, 205, 207, 349
dangers, 151
deceive, 355, 359, 377
decide, 8, 31, 64, 79, 97, 141, 172, 241, 245, 254, 276
decision, 4, 11, 12, 21, 31, 34, 49, 73, 93, 139, 140, 143, 158, 171, 210, 225, 231, 300, 329
delete, 362
delved, 81
demonstration, 92
dependency, 365, 368, 381
dependent, 157, 364, 366, 381
depressed, 77, 175, 178, 375
deprivation, 364, 374
detachment, 293, 341
different, 17, 21, 27, 33, 51, 60, 64, 65, 76, 102, 106, 107, 112, 113, 120, 121, 128, 129, 150, 163, 166, 169, 175, 180, 185, 186, 188, 190, 192, 207, 211, 212, 213, 217,

248, 251, 260, 266, 300, 317, 320, 324, 331, 340, 344, 345, 360, 365, 369
differentiated, 191
difficult, xxiv, 3, 59, 190, 204, 302, 349, 370
disappoint, 176
disbelief, xxi, 2, 3, 4, 5, 7, 8, 10, 11, 12, 13
disbeliefs, xxi, 2, 6, 7, 8, 11, 12, 14, 37, 53, 66, 83, 98, 115, 131, 145, 159, 182, 193, 218, 262, 283, 311, 352, 378
discomfort, 74, 153, 156, 173, 257, 361
dissociating, 21, 366
dissonance, 31, 153, 173, 329, 330, 341, 347
distort, 319, 362
doubt, xxi, 1, 2, 4, 5, 7, 8, 10, 11, 13, 299
driven, 114, 198, 345
elevated, 32, 79
Embedded Commands, 226, 243
emotional benefit, 190

empathize, 9, 175, 287, 299, 301, 319, 327, 328
empathy, 292, 293, 298, 299, 302, 305
energy, 207, 373
erratic, 23, 29, 30, 174
excitement, 71, 72, 73, 74, 75, 76, 77, 78, 79, 80, 81, 82, 155, 258, 290
exclusive, 87, 88, 89, 91, 92, 94, 96
exclusivity, 87, 89, 94
exercises, 13, 14, 15, 16, 37, 38, 39, 53, 54, 55, 66, 67, 68, 83, 84, 85, 98, 99, 100, 115, 116, 117, 130, 131, 132, 133, 145, 146, 147, 158, 159, 160, 161, 182, 183, 184, 193, 194, 195, 218, 219, 220, 261, 262, 263, 264, 283, 284, 285, 310, 311, 312, 313, 351, 352, 353, 354, 378, 379, 380
exploit, 120, 151
express, 92, 321

Extended Quotes, 227
fail, 91, 179, 190, 259
faith, 6, 7, 8, 10, 11, 13, 16, 20, 39, 55, 68, 85, 100, 118, 133, 147, 161, 184, 195, 220, 244, 264, 285, 313, 354, 380
famous, 123, 256, 288, 290
feeling, 12, 74, 81, 87, 114, 191, 215, 228, 246, 248, 249, 251, 257, 258, 269, 292, 320
forbidden, xxiv, 21, 43, 59, 101, 103, 104, 106, 107, 109, 111, 112, 113, 114, 336, 377, 382
formula, 17, 114, 185, 200
free, 45, 111, 126, 155, 175, 178, 179, 341, 342, 357, 362, 372, 376
friendliness, 128, 363, 368, 373
friendship, 175, 256
front-groups, 362, 371

frustration, 214, 265
generalize, 319, 362
gesture, xxii, 79, 254
God, 7, 22, 23, 205, 338
heart, 5, 46, 73, 80
high-value, 91, 93, 94
holistic, 359
hypnosis, xxii, xxiii, 4, 28, 58, 79, 81, 108, 142, 168, 170, 172, 177, 190, 197, 199, 200, 202, 203, 208, 209, 211, 212, 213, 214, 216, 222, 223, 224, 225, 226, 228, 232, 238, 240, 246, 257, 267, 303, 316, 317, 320, 328, 346, 350, 359, 361, 367, 373
hypnotic, xxii, xxiii, xxiv, 2, 12, 15, 16, 18, 19, 22, 23, 25, 26, 30, 31, 32, 34, 35, 39, 40, 43, 44, 48, 50, 51, 52, 55, 56, 57, 58, 62, 63, 64, 65, 68, 69, 71, 75, 77, 78, 79, 80, 81, 84, 85, 87, 93, 94, 96, 99, 100, 103, 104, 106,

107, 110, 111, 112,
113, 114, 117, 118,
120, 121, 127, 129,
130, 132, 133, 136,
142, 144, 146, 147,
151, 152, 156, 160,
161, 164, 166, 167,
169, 170, 177, 179,
183, 184, 185, 186,
187, 188, 189, 192,
195, 196, 197, 200,
201, 202, 205, 209,
212, 213, 216, 219,
220, 222, 223, 227,
228, 229, 230, 232,
236, 238, 239, 240,
241, 243, 244, 245,
248, 249, 251, 252,
254, 257, 259, 260,
261, 263, 264, 265,
267, 282, 285, 286,
289, 291, 292, 295,
297, 298, 299, 301,
302, 303, 304, 305,
306, 308, 309, 310,
312, 313, 315, 316,
317, 318, 320, 321,
322, 323, 325, 326,
328, 329, 330, 331,
335, 336, 342, 343,
344, 346, 347, 348,
349, 350, 353, 354,
355, 362, 363, 365,
367, 371, 373, 375,
377, 379, 380, 382
hypnotic archetypal trigger, 18, 27, 33, 43, 44, 48, 50, 51, 52, 57, 62, 64, 65, 71, 80, 81, 87, 96, 103, 104, 106, 107, 110, 112, 113, 114, 120, 121, 127, 129, 130, 136, 142, 151, 152, 164, 166, 177, 180, 185, 188, 325, 336, 365
hypnotic hero's journey, 318
hypnotic stories, 291, 299, 303, 315, 318, 322
hypnotic subject, xxii, 62, 63, 65, 79, 80, 81, 93, 114, 177, 178, 189, 228, 231, 240, 241, 244, 250, 257, 298, 299, 300, 301, 305, 306, 318, 319, 320, 322, 326, 329, 330, 335, 346, 350

hypnotist, 58, 109, 172, 202, 210, 214, 226, 228, 240, 244, 245, 259, 290, 382

hypnotize, xxi, 26, 59, 62, 65, 71, 77, 82, 123, 171, 187, 192, 197, 201, 213, 214, 216, 240, 241, 243, 291, 306, 309, 318, 349, 355, 359, 377

hypnotizing, 57, 61, 62, 78, 80, 120, 181, 188, 189, 200, 211, 216, 290, 303, 305, 318, 326, 350

hypothesis, 181

ideas, 2, 5, 12, 17, 25, 29, 36, 62, 72, 76, 78, 106, 123, 124, 125, 127, 128, 137, 152, 154, 165, 166, 167, 168, 175, 179, 181, 186, 188, 189, 203, 216, 230, 245, 265, 301, 305, 318, 351, 361, 366, 367

imagine, xxii, 4, 23, 28, 41, 42, 76, 149, 171, 174, 268, 269, 276, 277, 281, 327

imprinted, 15, 39, 55, 68, 80, 84, 99, 103, 112, 117, 132, 146, 160, 183, 195, 203, 219, 242, 263, 285, 300, 312, 347, 348, 351, 353, 379

improved, 382

Inanimations, 234

individuality, 157, 362, 368

indoctrinate, 62, 168, 355, 358, 359, 364, 366, 377

indoctrinated, 20, 28, 168, 288, 357, 358, 376, 377

indoctrination, 240, 342

Induce, 367

induced, xix, 81, 202, 212

influence, 3, 19, 22, 26, 36, 43, 44, 48, 64, 96, 104, 110, 127, 136, 137, 142, 144, 153, 156, 181, 185, 192, 200, 210, 261, 265,

266, 290, 321, 330, 346, 382
influences, xxii, 77, 158, 203, 210
influencing, 6, 36, 76, 255, 308
information, i, xxiii, 2, 14, 15, 16, 28, 37, 38, 39, 44, 53, 54, 55, 66, 67, 68, 83, 84, 85, 87, 98, 99, 100, 109, 115, 116, 117, 119, 121, 131, 132, 145, 146, 147, 159, 160, 161, 168, 169, 172, 174, 182, 183, 184, 186, 188, 189, 193, 194, 195, 200, 204, 216, 218, 219, 220, 262, 263, 264, 266, 283, 284, 285, 288, 296, 298, 308, 310, 311, 312, 315, 319, 320, 330, 352, 353, 354, 357, 358, 362, 363, 365, 374, 375, 378, 379, 380
insights, 14, 15, 37, 39, 53, 55, 66, 68, 83, 85, 98, 100, 115, 117, 131, 132, 145, 147, 159, 160, 182, 184, 193, 195, 214, 218, 220, 234, 262, 263, 283, 285, 309, 311, 312, 315, 316, 325, 335, 351, 352, 353, 366, 378, 380
inspiring, 127, 376
intention, 45, 244, 288, 294, 375
interest, xxii, 46, 50, 51, 59, 63, 80, 105, 140, 171, 192, 197, 305, 363
interrupted, 187, 347
intrinsic value, xxii, 30, 87, 104, 120, 121, 124, 126, 127, 135, 137, 138, 185, 192, 200, 258, 289, 307, 342, 367
join, 11, 50, 61, 82, 104, 130, 151, 156, 174, 288, 356, 361, 370
Keyword, 253
kiss, 14, 38, 54, 67, 83, 98, 116, 131, 145, 159, 182, 194, 218, 262, 284, 311, 352, 378

kissed, 14, 38, 54, 67, 83, 98, 116, 131, 145, 159, 182, 194, 218, 262, 284, 311, 352, 378
knowledge, xxiv, 14, 15, 26, 37, 39, 53, 55, 66, 68, 83, 84, 98, 99, 109, 115, 117, 119, 131, 132, 145, 146, 159, 160, 182, 183, 193, 195, 218, 219, 234, 247, 262, 263, 283, 285, 288, 298, 310, 312, 336, 352, 353, 378, 379, 382
language pattern, 188, 229
leap of faith, 6, 8, 9
learnt, xxiii, 2, 14, 37, 53, 66, 83, 98, 115, 130, 145, 159, 182, 193, 218, 252, 261, 262, 283, 310, 350, 352, 359, 376, 378, 382
lesson, 12, 13, 238, 359
linked, 8, 34, 52, 191, 246, 289, 320
literature, 122, 294, 365

logical advantages, 81, 141, 172, 190, 326
Lost Performative, 228
love, 9, 23, 58, 179, 189, 197, 214, 215, 216, 224, 246, 252, 282, 318, 336, 357, 363
lower value, 91, 96, 97, 122
loyal, 61, 127, 129, 289, 365, 368, 374, 375
manipulate, 291, 355, 356, 358, 359, 363, 377
marketplace, 90, 91, 92, 96, 105, 126, 173, 317
Maslow, 178
mechanisms, 19
meditation, 367
meeting, 82, 124, 180, 273, 363
memories, 137, 246
memory, 15, 38, 54, 67, 84, 99, 103, 117, 132, 146, 160, 183, 194, 219, 230, 246, 249, 263, 284, 312, 344, 353, 379, 381
metaphorical, 316, 336

Milton Model, 221, 222, 223, 224, 228, 229, 230, 232, 233, 234, 235, 236, 237, 238, 239, 260, 265

mind, xxi, xxiii, 2, 3, 4, 5, 10, 15, 16, 21, 22, 24, 27, 29, 30, 32, 35, 39, 41, 51, 52, 55, 61, 64, 68, 76, 77, 80, 84, 85, 88, 99, 100, 106, 109, 111, 112, 114, 117, 122, 132, 135, 139, 141, 143, 146, 147, 160, 166, 172, 174, 177, 183, 184, 187, 195, 201, 203, 205, 207, 209, 212, 213, 216, 219, 220, 223, 227, 228, 229, 230, 232, 234, 236, 237, 238, 239, 241, 243, 245, 247, 249, 252, 263, 266, 285, 290, 291, 295, 298, 300, 301, 303, 305, 306, 308, 312, 318, 320, 325, 328, 332, 347, 349, 351, 353, 358, 361, 364, 366, 367, 371, 373, 375, 376, 379, 380, 381, 382

Mind Reading, 228

mnemonics, 292

Modal Operator, 229

mystery, 21, 33, 43, 57, 59, 60, 61, 62, 63, 64, 65, 109, 110, 114, 222, 227, 240, 288, 333, 335, 342, 365

narrative transportation, 287, 289, 292, 293, 294, 295, 296, 297, 298, 301, 303, 306, 309

Narrative transportation theory, 290, 292, 298

Narrative Transportation Theory, 298, 303, 307, 315

narratives, 322, 331, 332, 333, 334, 335, 340, 350

newspapers, 87

NLP, xxii, xxiii, 34, 44, 48, 52, 79, 80, 122, 221, 239, 245, 247,

248, 249, 250, 265, 362, 371, 411, 413
nominalizations, 231, 238
Non Sequitur conclusion, 232
obsessive, 197
opinions, 3, 167, 291
opportunity, 8, 11, 15, 38, 46, 49, 54, 67, 84, 87, 99, 116, 132, 136, 137, 140, 141, 142, 146, 160, 176, 179, 183, 191, 194, 209, 219, 263, 284, 312, 315, 324, 332, 353, 379
original, 120, 121, 123, 124, 125, 127, 128, 129, 300, 346
originality, 120, 121, 123, 124, 125, 126, 127, 128, 129, 130, 189
outcome, 1, 12, 30, 42, 93, 114, 158, 189, 241, 254, 255, 280, 304, 376
outcomes, 8, 65, 76, 81, 103, 108, 156, 170, 174, 221, 233, 255, 281, 295, 330
paradox, 157, 341
path, 11, 169, 338
perceive, xxi, 21, 60, 91, 92, 95, 97, 121, 124, 125, 127, 157, 168, 179, 229, 233, 243, 266, 300, 316
persuade, xxi, xxii, 4, 19, 44, 47, 48, 49, 52, 72, 81, 93, 94, 108, 114, 136, 173, 178, 181, 185, 192, 210, 216, 261, 265, 297, 299, 307, 330, 367, 376
persuasion, xxi, xxii, xxiv, 2, 12, 13, 15, 16, 26, 36, 38, 40, 52, 54, 56, 60, 67, 69, 80, 84, 85, 99, 100, 114, 116, 118, 132, 133, 146, 147, 160, 161, 166, 169, 183, 184, 186, 187, 191, 192, 194, 196, 219, 220, 251, 260, 263, 264, 265, 267, 284, 286, 287, 289, 290, 292, 293, 294, 296, 297, 300,

301, 303, 306, 308, 309, 310, 311, 313, 316, 329, 330, 342, 353, 354, 355, 359, 377, 379, 380
persuasions, xxi, xxii, 2, 4, 36, 44, 51, 52, 61, 65, 76, 81, 93, 108, 124, 136, 190, 192, 200, 203, 267, 299, 304, 309, 328, 329, 382
planning, 360
poor, 11, 21, 64, 79, 89, 210
popular, 126, 149, 151, 152, 153, 154, 155, 156, 157
popularity, 149, 151, 153, 154, 156, 157
Popularity, 149, 151, 152, 153, 155, 157
position, 3, 44, 62, 64, 74, 80, 88, 91, 92, 96, 97, 103, 106, 114, 120, 122, 124, 127, 129, 130, 135, 141, 143, 150, 151, 152, 153, 154, 174, 181, 187, 191, 192, 279, 317, 334, 337, 365, 376
positioning, 23, 58, 64, 65, 88, 90, 91, 92, 103, 121, 124, 128, 149, 154, 173, 186
positive, 8, 24, 77, 81, 164, 175, 215, 230, 234, 256, 356, 372
possibilities, 177, 323
predicting, 228
presentation, i, 126, 164, 191
presented, 23, 29, 42, 60, 87, 94, 141, 142, 143, 164, 166, 169, 171, 175, 178, 179, 180, 189, 199, 228, 248, 256, 340, 358
Presuppositions, 233
priming, 255
principle, 5, 8, 22, 44, 64, 72, 94, 101, 104, 106, 122, 129, 137, 153, 156, 171, 372
principles, 49, 57, 88, 90, 105, 297, 301, 342, 365, 381
product, 10, 23, 30, 45, 58, 60, 61, 64, 71, 72,

73, 74, 90, 92, 110, 112, 120, 121, 124, 125, 127, 137, 141, 149, 152, 153, 154, 155, 171, 173, 187, 190, 192, 258, 268, 270, 272, 369
promise, 14, 38, 54, 67, 84, 99, 116, 131, 146, 159, 176, 179, 183, 194, 219, 262, 284, 311, 352, 379
protagonist, 9, 10, 73, 287, 301, 319, 321, 322, 328, 331, 332, 333, 335, 338, 340
psychiatry, 290
psychological, 22, 57, 63, 89, 94, 101, 103, 104, 106, 157, 163, 180, 257, 287, 327, 348, 372
psychology, 63, 96, 114, 144, 179, 289, 293, 360
psychotherapist, 228
psychotherapists, 77
punishment, 256, 302, 338
Punishment, 255
puppet, 26, 299, 364
rank, 7
rapport, 44, 48, 52, 79, 80, 245, 363, 364, 371
rare, 17, 43, 95, 135, 137, 138, 139, 140, 141, 143, 294
reality, 8, 11, 17, 20, 28, 59, 73, 76, 168, 171, 202, 205, 212, 234, 237, 290, 293, 296, 297, 298, 300, 302, 306, 319, 328, 330
receptive, 5, 367
reciprocate, 105, 175
recommendation, 221, 228, 235, 237, 245
recruit, 49, 61, 156, 174, 256, 330, 342, 355, 357, 358, 359, 360, 362, 363, 364, 366, 369, 371, 372, 373, 374, 375, 377, 382
recruited, 355, 356, 358, 370, 375, 377
recruiting, 174, 363, 370
recruits, 330, 342, 362, 363, 367, 369, 371, 372, 375
reinforces, 177, 235

relationship, 30, 140, 197, 215, 231, 247
relaxation, 208
religious, 7, 61, 345, 356, 362
relive, 5
replication, 95, 157, 205
resources, 89, 104, 238, 260, 294, 358, 369
responded, 180, 189
respondent conditioning, 255, 363
reward, 256, 302, 363, 368
rhythms, 207
salespeople, 190
salesperson, 31, 74, 173
scapegoats, 368
scarcity, 64, 104, 137, 156, 362
secret, xxiv, 18, 88, 108, 124, 138, 300, 308, 362, 382
secrets, 108, 110, 289
sell, xxii, 2, 12, 41, 42, 45, 61, 72, 97, 105, 108, 121, 127, 140, 154, 156, 171, 186, 189, 250, 258, 267, 278, 329, 342, 364
senses, 29, 48
sequential, 81, 92, 130, 136, 192, 216, 303, 322, 360
shaping, 255, 256, 302, 363, 373
sleep, 202, 206, 207, 208, 357, 359, 364, 373, 374
Sleeper effect, 295
solution, 163, 174, 179, 186, 230, 351
spellbound, 65, 78
spin, 124, 187
state, 5, 21, 27, 29, 30, 32, 35, 36, 71, 72, 74, 76, 77, 79, 81, 82, 111, 142, 174, 197, 199, 202, 206, 207, 209, 216, 230, 244, 246, 247, 249, 250, 251, 254, 257, 270, 292, 295, 308, 317, 328, 361, 366, 371, 375
stimulated, 79
stories, 8, 20, 23, 26, 29, 34, 45, 95, 289, 291, 292, 293, 294, 295,

296, 297, 298, 299, 301, 302, 303, 307, 308, 309, 315, 316, 317, 318, 319, 321, 322, 323, 324, 330, 335, 343, 344, 346, 347, 348, 350, 367
story, xxiii, 8, 10, 11, 12, 24, 45, 50, 62, 73, 76, 96, 101, 114, 202, 217, 241, 243, 287, 290, 292, 293, 295, 296, 297, 298, 299, 300, 301, 304, 305, 306, 307, 308, 316, 318, 319, 320, 321, 322, 324, 325, 326, 327, 328, 329, 330, 331, 343, 344, 345, 346, 347, 348, 349, 350, 367, 373, 382
Storytelling, xxiii, 291, 315, 316, 318, 413
structures, 45, 247, 266
success, 255, 382
suggestible, 367, 373
suggesting, 127, 154, 156
Superman, 107
survival, 21, 95, 157

suspend, 2, 3, 4, 5, 7, 8, 9, 10, 11
Tag Questions, 234
taught, xxiv, 2, 13, 16, 33, 37, 39, 53, 55, 66, 68, 83, 85, 97, 98, 100, 114, 115, 117, 130, 132, 145, 147, 158, 161, 168, 182, 184, 193, 195, 218, 220, 244, 261, 264, 283, 285, 310, 312, 323, 351, 354, 369, 376, 378, 380, 381
teach, xxi, xxiii, 2, 3, 8, 14, 19, 25, 37, 53, 66, 71, 83, 98, 103, 115, 119, 131, 145, 159, 166, 168, 182, 185, 190, 193, 200, 218, 260, 262, 283, 297, 311, 352, 355, 378
techniques, xxiii, 14, 37, 52, 53, 66, 83, 98, 115, 130, 145, 158, 170, 182, 193, 218, 240, 241, 248, 250, 258, 260, 261, 283, 305, 310, 323, 351, 356,

357, 359, 363, 371, 375, 378, 381
testing, 14, 37, 53, 66, 78, 83, 98, 115, 130, 145, 159, 182, 193, 218, 232, 251, 262, 283, 310, 315, 333, 351, 378
therapy, 259, 260
think, 15, 17, 18, 19, 22, 28, 39, 42, 51, 55, 57, 58, 59, 60, 62, 64, 68, 71, 85, 90, 92, 94, 100, 105, 108, 117, 128, 132, 135, 137, 140, 141, 142, 143, 146, 150, 156, 158, 160, 163, 164, 167, 169, 170, 175, 178, 184, 195, 197, 199, 201, 202, 210, 214, 215, 220, 225, 226, 227, 230, 234, 238, 242, 252, 259, 263, 266, 269, 280, 285, 300, 302, 307, 309, 312, 316, 319, 327, 328, 330, 334, 339, 343, 353, 356, 357, 358, 360, 363, 365, 366, 370, 372, 374, 376, 380, 381, 382
thinking, xxii, 6, 15, 20, 27, 29, 33, 39, 44, 45, 55, 68, 75, 84, 100, 104, 110, 117, 123, 128, 132, 143, 144, 146, 157, 160, 164, 169, 172, 174, 178, 179, 183, 195, 198, 201, 207, 219, 228, 232, 242, 248, 256, 263, 285, 297, 298, 300, 303, 310, 312, 315, 327, 351, 353, 364, 366, 367, 379
thought experiment, 23, 28, 35, 204, 382
Tonal Marking, 222, 241
trance, 26, 77, 80, 123, 142, 197, 201, 202, 209, 212, 215, 222, 229, 230, 242, 322, 346, 349, 367, 373
transderivational search, 223
transferring, 78
Transitioning, 3
tribe, 95, 97, 151, 157

tribes, 95, 151, 370
trick, 372
tricks, 3, 170, 232
triggers, xxi, 17, 18, 19, 22, 23, 25, 26, 28, 30, 31, 32, 34, 43, 58, 109, 156, 173, 197, 200, 248, 289, 306, 342, 362
true, xxiii, 3, 5, 9, 16, 18, 20, 28, 40, 49, 56, 69, 85, 88, 100, 109, 118, 133, 137, 139, 143, 147, 152, 153, 161, 169, 177, 184, 192, 196, 197, 200, 210, 214, 220, 228, 232, 233, 235, 236, 264, 267, 272, 286, 287, 300, 309, 313, 333, 338, 341, 354, 360, 362, 367, 371, 380
true self, 140
Truism sets, 235
truth, 28, 59, 62, 63, 76, 110, 121, 166, 235, 257, 301, 316, 356, 374, 382
ultradian rhythm, 349
uncomfortable, 171, 179
unconscious, 30, 35, 104, 156, 198, 199, 201, 203, 204, 209, 210, 231, 234, 238, 246, 248, 267, 306, 320, 322, 347
unconvinced, 2
understand, 2, 4, 5, 9, 12, 19, 23, 25, 26, 30, 34, 35, 51, 52, 61, 65, 71, 72, 74, 75, 76, 81, 88, 90, 91, 94, 107, 112, 120, 122, 123, 124, 129, 141, 151, 152, 153, 154, 156, 157, 163, 166, 167, 170, 173, 185, 186, 188, 190, 192, 200, 206, 209, 211, 215, 216, 242, 288, 289, 293, 297, 299, 301, 309, 323, 325, 329, 331, 343, 357, 362, 369
understanding, 2, 16, 21, 39, 51, 55, 68, 79, 81, 85, 100, 104, 117, 133, 147, 161, 164, 169, 184, 188, 195, 202, 214, 220, 239, 255,

264, 265, 285, 312, 331, 341, 354, 358, 380
unforgotten, 154
Universal Quantifier, 236
Unspecific Comparison, 237
Unspecific Object, 237
Unspecific Verb, 238
utilizing, 112, 121, 155, 156, 177, 178, 181, 185, 188, 207, 212, 214, 217, 227, 230, 238, 239, 241, 323
values, 23, 49, 124, 139, 152, 157, 164, 203, 245
viewpoints, 158
Voice Tone, 243, 252
weaknesses, 363
win-win, 120
Yellow Pages, 72, 170, 190

ABOUT THE AUTHOR

Bryan Westra is a prominent lecturer and trainer. His background is in Hypnosis and NLP. He holds advanced degrees in Organizational Behavior, Sales, Marketing, Management, and Counseling. He is also the founder of Indirect Knowledge Limited.

www.indirectknowledge.com

MORE BOOKS BY THE AUTHOR

Hypnotic Storytelling by Bryan Westra
Link: http://amzn.com/B00KMWR7DO

Indirect Knowledge by Bryan Westra
Link: http://amzn.com/B009EAWSTI

NLP & Hypnosis Influence and Persuasion Patterns by Bryan James Westra
Link: http://amzn.com/B00F1I8WC4

A Manual for Creating Conversational Hypnotists: The Answers You Want by Bryan James Westra
Link: http://amzn.com/0989946487

Learn & Remember 25 Secret Hypnotic Language Patterns Now to Help You Become Rich: Change Minds, Earn More, Win by Bryan Westra
Link: http://amzn.com/0990513211

Secret Sales Hypnosis: Work Less, Be Number 1, Explode Your Bank Account by Bryan Westra
Link: http://amzn.com/0615782191

NOTES

NOTES

NOTES

www.ingramcontent.com/pod-product-compliance
Lightning Source LLC
Chambersburg PA
CBHW030103010526
44116CB00005B/83